# RELATING AND INTERACTING

## An Introduction to Interpersonal Communication

### SECOND EDITION

**Raymond S. Ross, Ph.D.**

*Wayne State University*

**Mark G. Ross, Ph.D.**

*Northwestern Michigan College*

**Heather L. Seipke, Ph.D.**

*University of Michigan – Flint*

BVT
PUBLISHING

COPYEDITOR: Joyce Bianchini

TEXT DESIGN AND COMPOSITION: Suzanne Morse

COVER DESIGN: Horizon Textbook Publishing, LLC

ILLUSTRATIONS: Suzanne Morse

PHOTOS AND PERMISSIONS: Robert Rappeport

COVER AND INTERIOR PRINTER: Lightning Source

ISBN: 978-1-60229-985-6

Copyright © 2009 by BVT Publishing, LLC

# Contents

# Preface

This text seeks a pragmatic yet sensitive perspective to the study of Interpersonal Communication. As practical communicologists, we have been predominantly behaviorally oriented with a touch of humanism (a "behavioral humanism," 1974) thrown in. We provide a realistic pedagogical view that draws the best from both the scientific and the humanistic approaches. A unique feature and strength of this text is its addition of a rhetorical orientation to studying interpersonal topics.

The major questions guiding our research and writing of this text have focused on how people are able to coordinate their language, thought, and actions. Our pedagogical aim in the text is to discuss these how questions without being overly prescriptive. The book is designed to equip students with an adaptive/reflexive sensitivity to the ways that communicative behaviors can "mesh." Successful interpersonal communication in our view lies in the successful negotiation and "meshing" of rules that both govern and constitute communicative action within contexts. Interpersonal communication, in this sense, is not all "fun and games." In many cases it involves conflict. Our book is not designed to detach the student from communicative life but rather to place him or her squarely in the middle of it. In this way we feel one better learns the skills and sensitivities necessary for the coordination and management of complex interpersonal behaviors.

This text does not attempt to answer all of the why questions of interpersonal communication because interpersonal communication is too context-specific for that. We have tried to focus on how questions: how interpersonal communicative behaviors covary. In our view, students need rules, skills, and a set of communication concepts that will help them be more responsive to others, more rhetorically sensitive to others, and more efficient and cooperative in their "relating and interacting" with others.

Your authors represent mostly similar orientations, but our experiences bring you the best of the "now" (Heather Seipke, PhD., Wayne State University 2002), the short-range past (Mark Ross, PhD., The Ohio State University, 1978), as well as the long-range, "historic" perspective (Ray Ross, PhD., Purdue University, 1954).

We have learned much in the writing; we hope you may learn much in the reading.

RSR

HLS

MGR

## ABOUT THE AUTHORS

**Raymond S. Ross, Ph.D.,** is Professor Emeritus, Department of Communication, Wayne State University, Detroit, MI.  Born in Milwaukee, Wisconsin, Professor Ross received his Bachelor of Philosophy and Master of Arts degrees from Marquette University.  He earned an interdisciplinary Ph.D. in communication and psychology from Purdue University in 1954.

Dr. Ross is best known for his several popular college textbooks: *Speech Communication,* now in its 12th edition; *Small Groups in Organizational Settings; Understanding Persuasion,* 4th ed.; *Essentials of Speech Communication,* 2nd ed.; *Communication and Interpersonal Relations;* and *Relating and Interacting: an Introduction to Interpersonal Communication.* His latest trade book, *When Your Number's Up, 2005,* is a nonfiction novel about his combat experiences in World War II. *Brother Incarnate,* a WWII novel, is now in the editing stage.

Dr. Ross is listed in American Men of Science, Directory of American Scholars, National Register of Scientific Personnel, Who's Who in the Midwest, Contemporary Authors, and Outstanding Educators of America. He is the recipient of a Distinguished Alumni Award from Marquette University and was a Distinguished Visiting Professor at Pepperdine University.  He is also a member of many academic and professional organizations including the National Communication Association and the American Psychological Association.

While at Ohio State University he was appointed Mershon Professor Air Science (AFROTC).  For many years Professor Ross was an educational advisor to ROTC programs and the 10th Air Force Reserve.  At WSU he was a staff member of the Institute of Industrial Relations, Wayne State University/University of Michigan, where he served as director of executive development programs. He has served as a research, training and communication consultant to numerous government, military, business and industrial firms.

Dr. Ross and his wife, Ricky, live in Traverse City, Michigan. They have two sons, Mark and Scott, and a golden retriever named Buddy.

**Heather Seipke, Ph.D.,** is a professor of Communication at the University of Michigan—Flint where she also serves as the Director of Communication in the Department of Communication and Visual Art. She earned her Ph.D. in Interpersonal Communication at Wayne State University where she also became a certified Gerontologist. Dr. Seipke studied Communication and Aging as a Postdoctoral fellow at the Institute of Gerontology at Wayne State University. The majority of her published research focuses on issues of Interpersonal Communication among the elderly population.

**Mark Ross, Ph.D.,** holds undergraduate and graduate degrees from Michigan State and Ohio State Universities and has held teaching positions at Kent State and Purdue Universities. He is currently a senior professor at Northwestern Michigan College in Traverse City, Michigan, where he teaches speech, interpersonal communication and mass media studies.

# CHAPTER 1

# INTRODUCTION TO HUMAN COMMUNICATION

On a daily basis human beings, regardless of who they are or where they come from, all take part in interpersonal communication. Often we are unaware of our participation in an interpersonal communication interaction because these actions have become such an ingrained part of our daily lives that we go about them mindlessly and automatically—in the same fashion our bodies go about automatically keeping our hearts beating.

We argue with our roommates and family members over who ate the last of the favorite cereal in the morning. We make comments about the weather with the individuals on the bus, in the elevator or at the coffee shop. We email professors for clarification on assignments and text friends to find out what's going on later that night. These are things that may seem ordinary and mundane, but are all acts of interpersonal communication.

At this point you may be asking, "If I am already an expert on interpersonal communication due to my life time of experiences, why then should I spend time learning more about it from a textbook?" The simple answer is that though we may "do" interpersonal communication on a daily basis, the majority of us aren't actually that good at it. Interpersonal communication creates the foundations for the majority of the things in life that bring us the greatest of happiness and the worst of sorrow. Therefore, we should all take time to get good at it.

This textbook will help you to understand what interpersonal communication is and how it works. Once we have a greater understanding of the processes of interpersonal communication, we can apply that knowledge to our personal situations. We can work towards a level of interpersonal communication competence that limits the times of sorrow and increases the times of happiness.

In order to understand the concept of interpersonal communication we must first have an understanding of communication in general.

## DEFINITIONS OF COMMUNICATION

Definitions of human communication range from "speech is the great medium through which human cooperation is brought about"[1] to the more specific definition of the American College Dictionary, "the imparting or interchange of thoughts, opinions, or information by speech, writing, or signs."

Though there are many definitions of communication, they all seem to agree that ideas must be shared before communication can exist. Communication should be thought of as a process, not simply as a transfer of meaning from one mind to another. There is something necessarily *mutual* about human communication; each party influences the other. Communication is a truly dynamic process.

Communication involves common experience and mutual influence. Real communication is very difficult if there is not at least some small opportunity for two-way influence. Whether we know it or not, we communicate hoping to influence others to respond as we want them to respond. This process has no beginning or end and is ever changing, dynamic, and mutual. The vast numbers of definitions of communication are very similar. For the purposes of this book, **communication** will be broadly defined as the use of verbal and nonverbal messages to create ongoing mutual influence.

## COMMUNICATION MODELS

It is often best to look at a visual simplification of the complex relationships involved in communication through models of communication. We will discuss three prevailing models of communication and introduce you to a fourth to help gain insight into our definition of communication and to work towards a better understanding of how interpersonal communication fits into this definition.

We will start with the oldest and most simple model of communication: the linear communication model. This model is based on the idea of one-way communication in which a message is simply sent from one person and received by another. This model appears to be quite simple, yet it captures a large part of what is going on in communication.

### Linear Model of Communication

The **linear model of communication** includes several concepts used in later, more complex models. (See Figure 1.1.) The **sender** is the source or originator of the **message**. The *message* is a verbal (spoken) or nonverbal (behavior or gesture) transmission of ideas. The sender goes through a process of *encoding* to translate ideas and emotions into a code (in our case verbal or nonverbal symbols). The message

**FIGURE 1.1**    LINEAR MODEL OF COMMUNICATION

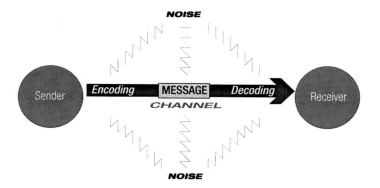

is then passed to the ***receiver*** or the intended target of the message. The receiver goes through a process of ***decoding*** to interpret the translated ideas of the sender. The passing of the message travels through a ***channel*** or pathway of communication. The channel can be anything from a text message to a face-to-face discussion to sky writing. Anything that interferes with the transmission of the message is considered ***noise***. Noise consists of anything that physically or psychologically gets in the way of the message being received and understood. ***Physical noise*** is any outside or external stimulus that makes the message difficult to understand by the receiver. An example of physical noise could be a police siren that drowns out the voice of the sender. ***Psychological noise*** is any internal stimulus that makes the message difficult to understand by the receiver. An example of psychological noise could be not understanding a message because you are too busy wondering if you remembered to turn off your stove.

To apply this model to your life, think about being out to dinner with a friend. You taste your potatoes and realize they are a bit bland and could use a dash of salt. You notice that the salt is on the other side of the table next to your friend. You ask, "Would you please pass the salt?" You have acted as the *sender/encoder* of a message (verbal transmission of your need for the salt) through the *channel* of your voice to the *receiver/decoder* (your friend next to the salt). As long as the server doesn't drop a tray next to your table (physical noise), and your friend is not daydreaming or not paying attention (psychological noise), this should be a fairly linear exchange of communication.

As we discussed while defining communication, we communicate hoping to influence others to respond as we want them to. Given the dinner table example, you are hoping to influence your friend to pass the salt. The success of your influence would be determined by the act of your friend actually passing the salt. Based on the one-way linear model of communication you really don't have any way of knowing the success of your influence. You don't even know if your message ever reached your friend based on this model because it is essentially linear; that is, it goes from a source to a destination. There is no clear representation of a circular response, and no clear explanation of the ongoing mutual influence involved in our definition of communication. The need for a way to measure if communication actually took place (if the influence even happened) leads to a more complete model of communication called the interactional model of communication.

## Interactional Model of Communication

The **interactional model of communication** contains all of the concepts of the linear model and adds the concept of **feedback**. Feedback is a response from the receiver to the sender about the message. The addition of the concept of feedback makes the linear model become more circular (See figure 1.2).

**FIGURE 1.2    INTERACTIONAL MODEL OF COMMUNICATION**

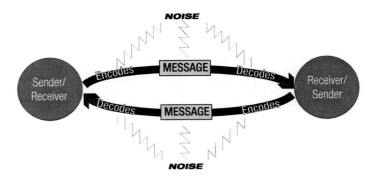

Wilbur Schramm is one of the early theorists to demonstrate the model of communication as circular (see Figure 1.2).[2] The decoding of a message by the receiver starts that person's process of encoding—hence, the complete circle.

The roles of encoder and decoder are interchangeable. Thus, each person in the communication process is encoder and decoder. This circular model also suggests the interesting notion that these functions can go on simultaneously. While you are talking, your listener is not only breaking your code and trying to make sense of it (decoding), but he or she is also considering his or her next transmission (encoding). In the case of nonverbals, messages may already be encoded and on their way. For example, when someone is saying something with which you disagree, but you don't want to interrupt him/her, you continue listening silently (decoding) while shaking your head back and forth in a "no" motion (encoding).

Schramm also suggests that the sender and receiver can perform their functions only in terms of their own fields of experiences. Thus, both the receiver and sender are limited by their experience. Nevertheless, there must be some experience common to both in order for the communication to be useful and for the intended message to be conveyed. For example, if you were asking someone that did not speak the language you speak to pass the salt you would most likely make a shaking motion over your plate of food, point to them, and then point to yourself hoping the other individual has had some common experience of shaking salt on food. If the receiver comes from a culture where salt is

*Both the sender and receiver must share a field of experience, such as language, to communicate effectively.*

not used for shaking on food and you don't share any common words that express your desire for salt, you may be communicatively out of luck, leaving you with bland potatoes.

We may sometimes have to build bridges or overlaps before we can have communication. Furthermore, for your messages to be most effective, they must somehow fall in the area of overlap. Two people from completely different cultures with different languages and no common experiences may find that communication becomes nearly impossible without help from a third party such as a translator. Even then, barriers are everywhere. The first priority would be to identify common ground. Common ground or mutual understanding is important in communication and essential for interpersonal communication.

## Transactional Model of Communication

The **transactional model of communication** more accurately reflects a real-world model of interpersonal communication by illustrating that people communicating act simultaneously as the sender and receiver in a cooperative fashion. This cooperation makes the sender and the receiver responsible for the effectiveness of the communication. The transactional model displays communication interactions as ongoing negotiations of meaning. As mentioned earlier, it is very difficult for two people coming from completely different cultures with different languages and no common experiences to take part in this negotiation of meaning. Individuals come to a communication interaction with their own **field of experience**. This includes things like personal culture, history, gender, social influences and past impacting experiences. Your field of experience is the frame of reference you bring to each situation you experience. At times, individuals' fields of experiences overlap and they share things in common. Other times, individuals' fields of experiences do not overlap; and because they share no common past experiences, it is difficult to negotiate meaning. (See Figure 1.3)

## An Instructional Model: The Ross Model

The Ross Model focuses on the *human* organism and particularly human sign-symbol behavior. In interpreting this model remember that we are capable of being both sender and receiver at the same time; we are *transceivers*.[3] The frame of the

**FIGURE 1.3    TRANSACTIONAL MODEL OF COMMUNICATION**

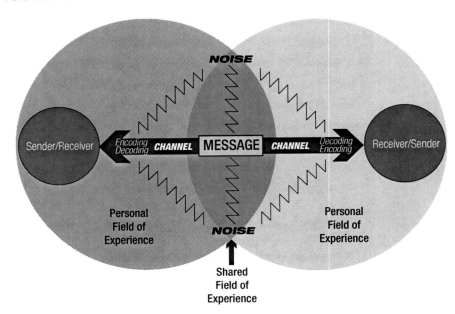

Ross Model attempts to show everything, including the world in which this communication takes place. The picture frame suggests the importance of situation, mood, context, and psychological climate.

The **situation** is the reason the interaction is taking place and could range from a date to a simple exchange of homework information. Situation could then make a real difference. **Mood** refers to feelings of the moment. At different times our mood might be happy, angry, tense, and so on. Our mood can greatly affect what we say or hear and how we say or hear something. **Context** is the framework into which your situation fits. Note how the word *paper* changes in the following contexts: The paper was late today (newspaper); the paper is crooked (wallpaper); it is an A paper (homework). If we used the phrase "the paper is crooked" in the context of a newspaper we may perceive some sort of corrupt management by the editor. Different contexts bring out different meanings. **Psychological climate** is a lot like weather or physical climate. Just as our weather might be bitterly cold, so too might the psychological climate of

**FIGURE 1.4** THE ROSS COMMUNICATION MODEL (1982)

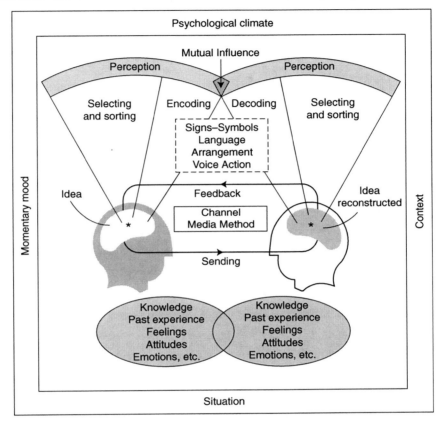

a classroom, a meeting, or a date. An unhappy, impersonal (cold) psychological climate would hinder rather than help communication. Sometimes climate is the most important part of a message.

Let's assume that the person on the left side of the model in Figure 1.4 is a woman who wishes to communicate a message (a concept or an idea) to the other person. The idea is represented by the star inside her brain. Let's suppose the concept is an abstract one, such as *love*. The fan projecting from each brain represents our twelve billion brain cells. In this woman's brain are stored her knowledge and past experience, her feelings, attitudes, emotions, and many more things (her frame of reference) that make her the person she is.

The brain, composed of 12 billion working parts, has enough storage capacity to accept 10 new facts every second. It is conservatively estimated that the human brain can store an amount of information equivalent to 100 trillion different words (which would mean acquiring one word per second continuously for 1,000,000 years). In a lifetime of 70 years, a human being may store information roughly equivalent to a mere trillion words.[4]

Our sender now sorts through and selects from her storehouse of knowledge and past experience, choosing items that help her define and refine what she is trying to say. She has to have a basis upon which to perform this operation—a program, if you will. We can think of the brain in some ways as a computer. The forebrain, for example, becomes a kind of input regulator into which we feed the program. This woman's program had better include at least three questions, or she is already in trouble! These are: (1) What do I have stored under *love?* (2) What do I know about the other person? (3) What do I have filed for this particular situation and context? You can almost visualize the program in action—assessing, accepting, rejecting, cross-referencing, and synthesizing the information in the storehouse—in short, selecting and sorting the appropriate knowledge, past experience, and so on.

Although there is some confusion among scholars as to exactly how and, in particular, *when* the encoding takes place, it is useful, if only for instructional purpose, to think of it as a sequence. Our sender must now choose her codes, and she should apply at least the same program or questions discussed previously. More will be said of this critical process of managing meaning in Chapter 3. The sender now transmits the message that, let's assume, is mainly oral (along with some critical nonverbals). Let's also assume that there is no unusual distraction or noise and that the sensory abilities of each person are adequate. Since our message concerns *love,* the situation itself may be fairly critical, to say nothing of the characteristics of the other person.

Finally (and this whole operation may last but seconds), the message is received by the other person. The resulting *sensations* experienced by the receiver are the first part of human perception; the second part, as discussed previously, is the *interpretation* of those sensations in this particular situation.

The model suggests that our receiver now *decodes* the signs, symbols, and language of the sender, sorting through his or her storehouse of knowledge and experience and selecting those meanings that will allow him or her to create a message concerning love. To the extent that this re-creation is similar to the sender's intended

*In the Ross Communication Model, the sender chooses items from her storehouse of knowledge and experience to help her communicate her intended message to the receiver. The receiver, in turn, decodes the message using his storehouse of knowledge and exerience.*

message, we have communication. This reconstructed idea is then dependent upon a person's prior knowledge and experience.

An understanding of how people receive, decode, and assign meaning to messages is critical to our understanding of communication. The receiver, or perceiver, makes hypotheses regarding the meaning of the message. He or she then accepts or rejects the hypotheses on the basis of personal constructs based on prior learning and experience. More will also be said about this in Chapter 3.

The term *feedback* in the model requires a moment of important consideration. In engineering, feedback refers to some of the transmitted energy being returned to the source. The automatic pilot used in airplanes is an example of self-correcting machinery that uses feedback. For speech purposes we may think of feedback as useful in a self-correcting or adaptive sense. As our transmitted signal is "bounced off" our receiver, it feeds back information that allows us to correct and refine our signal. A quizzical look, a frown, a yawn, the sound of our own voice—any of these may cause us to reevaluate and recode our signals. For now, let's think of feedback as something that we should make work for us.

As stated earlier, the model shows that communication assigns meaning and that it *works well* when the person receiving a message interprets it in the *same* way that the sender intends. It is clear that human communication is not simply a transfer of meaning at all. Earlier in this chapter we broadly define communication as the use of verbal and nonverbal messages to create ongoing mutual influence. Based on the four communication models presented we can more accurately define **communication** as a *process of sorting, selecting, and sending symbols in such a way as to help a receiver find in his or her own mind a meaning similar to that intended by the sender.* We communicate hoping to influence others to respond as we want them to. That we seldom have perfectly clear communication, and probably should not expect it, now seems obvious. This more concrete definition of communication, in general, lays the foundation for understanding the most common type of communication used on a daily basis, **interpersonal communication.** **Interpersonal communication** is *a distinctive, ongoing, ever changing transactional form of human communication that involves mutual influence—usually for the purposes of relationship management.* This definition will be discussed in more detail later in the chapter when we talk about the principals of interpersonal communication.

## CONTEXT INTERRELATIONSHIPS

Interpersonal communication is mostly a **dyadic** or a one person-to-one person interaction. The context of the interaction can range from face-to-face, to telephone, to text messaging, to email. This kind of basic relating and interacting goes on in many different types of organizations, groups, settings, and even in the media.

### Hierarchy of Contexts

According to Stephen Littlejohn these various contexts all overlap, and they should be viewed "… as a hierarchy of nested contexts in which the higher level includes the lower but adds some additional constraints and qualities."[5] His diagram illustrates how interpersonal communication cuts through, or is a diminishing part of, the larger contexts. (See Figure 1.5.)

Interpersonal communication is clearly a large part of what goes on in small-group interactions. The diagram that follows (Figure 1.6) suggests that 80 percent of such contexts may be interpersonal communication. Most small groups are face-to-face, interactive, oral exchanges.

Organizational contexts are thought to be largely involved with small-group communication. The pyramidal structure of most organizations is thought to be one of overlapping or "linking" group memberships. The superior in one group is a participating subordinate in the next. The structure has been referred to as a "linking pin" arrangement as diagrammed in Figure 1.7.[6]

Since interpersonal communication is a large part of group communication, it is clearly a major part of all organizational contexts. We suggest that it is 50 percent of organizational contexts with some trepidation since organizations vary widely in their goals, size, importance, and the like. A large part of organizational communication is quite obviously dependent upon special knowledge in areas such as planning, organizing, accounting, contracting, and so on. Nevertheless, managing is basically a process of getting work done through people, and that takes interpersonal communication.

The last context shown in Figure 1.6 is public communication or "relating to audiences." A public speech to a large audience is obviously quite different from an

**FIGURE 1.5    THE HIERARCHY OF COMMUNICATION CONTEXTS**

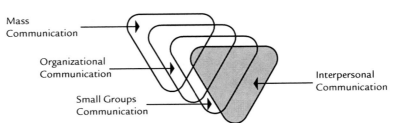

**FIGURE 1.6**    **INTERPERSONAL COMMUNICATION CONTEXTS**

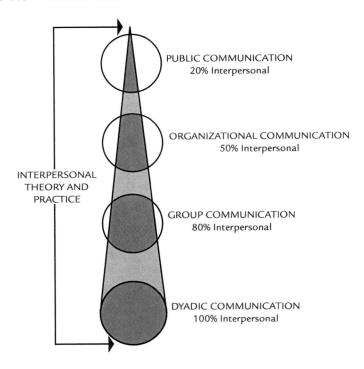

INTERPERSONAL THEORY AND PRACTICE

PUBLIC COMMUNICATION
20% Interpersonal

ORGANIZATIONAL COMMUNICATION
50% Interpersonal

GROUP COMMUNICATION
80% Interpersonal

DYADIC COMMUNICATION
100% Interpersonal

**FIGURE 1.7**

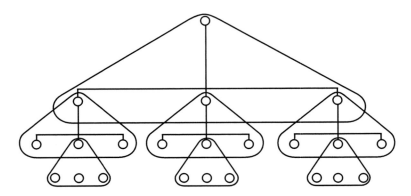

intimate, dyadic interaction. However, most of the basic speech communication processes are involved. Language is still critical (sometimes more critical). Voice is special; so are all of your nonverbals. Listening (especially if you're in the audience) is involved; so are all the problems of messages, attitudes, perception, attraction, and so on. Audience participation contexts may call for applications of interpersonal practice as well as integrations of interpersonal theories and processes. Public-speaking texts find dyadic communication models valuable instruction devices for the same kinds of reasons just discussed.

## SETTINGS AS CONTEXT

Reacting and interacting must occur within some place, at some level, and in some context or setting. The place in which a communication, and its *ritual,* occurs is important for it affects both the senders and receivers of messages. We may not always like or approve of certain settings, but sensitive human interaction demands that we take them into account. We should take the setting into special account when we evaluate a person's social adjustment. A "nut" may not be a "nut" when he or she is out of the special setting you are observing. A berserk football fan may be calm and collected when we find him or her in church.

### Place and Ritual

Communication at any level is often limited by *where* we are. Some settings may restrict communication, whereas others may aid it. In addition, settings may have a ritualistic aspect. Much of our communication is dictated by the place and ritual alone. Observe the impact of a place of worship, an elevator, a commuter bus, a 400-seat Boeing 747 on communication; study their rituals to see how people communicatively behave with in each place.

Now let's illustrate the often awesome impact of place. Visualize an impressive place of worship complete with stained-glass windows, exquisite statues, and a high arched ceiling. In it we may feel close to our creator. There is a temptation to whisper. People seem to alter their voices, their language, and their dress to meet the communication requirements of this powerful setting. The ritual associated with this setting also dictates much of the verbal as well as the nonverbal

*Some communication settings, such as a wedding, are an important influence on interpersonal communication.*

communication. Even an empty place of worship is a powerful communication setting, and we adjust our signals accordingly.

Ceremonial settings such as weddings, funerals, initiations, and graduations are important influences on interpersonal communication wherever they are held. Weddings are held in gardens, living rooms, and woods, as well as in places of worship. Graduations may take place inside, outside, in a gym, in an auditorium, and so on. Part of the influence of such an occasion comes from its obvious purpose, but much of the influence is also tradition and ritual, which seem to go beyond the obvious. Human communication in such settings is somehow different.

Think about the last wedding you attended and consider your total verbal exchange. It probably concerned the bride and groom, their families, their apparel, and the wedding arrangements. Being present at the wedding had a strong impact on what you said. The same holds true to an even greater extent at funerals. However, once you are out of the setting, the controlling aspect of place and ritual disappears.

Even the dinner hour is a rather formal setting for some families. It is a time for prayer and thanksgiving and not a time for deep conversation or heated argument. You can test this idea of setting when you are a dinner guest where you can very easily break the ritual; and, therefore, much of the communication that that would have normally taken place might no longer be possible.

Visualize yourself at a football game. We live in a spectator world, often finding ourselves jammed into a stadium watching our favorite team. In this interaction context we may find ourselves talking to total strangers, but not about dress styles, war, or elections. Our communication usually takes the form of amazement at an impressive play, disgust at the end of a rally, or second-guessing the management on some trade or maneuver. Our nonverbal communication is often affected by the press of the crowd, our empathy with a goal-line stand, or our ecstasy over a circus catch. Once we leave the setting, however, the effect of the place and ritual ends. We may no longer even exchange pleasantries and observations; the influences of the sports arena setting are removed, and we usually adjust our interpersonal communication with strangers accordingly.

The lesson is clear. Time, place, and ritual have a tremendous influence upon human communication; and we are well advised to take them into account.

## Purpose

In some settings the *purpose* or the agenda is so important that it has a greater impact on interpersonal communication than the place. If the purpose is strictly social, the political advocate may be poorly received. If a person's communication purpose is to obtain reassuring messages from you, all the jokes in the world are not apt to be received very well. A few of the many general purposes of communication interactions are discussed below.

**SOCIAL**   Many times we get together for sheer joy, fellowship, and fun. Perhaps the setting is a party. In this instance we get together primarily to have a good time (however, a party could be a disguise for another purpose). After the party we usually evaluate the time spent in terms of fun. "Did you enjoy yourself?" "Was it fun?" "Why don't we get together more often?" "That was a dull party." "Those two loud men were arguing about politics." Party topics are predictably uncontroversial, such as sports, weather, or current gossip. The communication pattern is without clear direction or agenda; many discussions may occur at the same time. If we tire of one subject, person, or group, we may not have as many communication options or as many people with whom to talk. However, watch for some ritual even in principally social communication settings.

**VENTILATION**    Another reason we interact is to unload grievances and generally express pent-up feelings—to unwind. In this situation we are usually looking for a sympathetic ear. We are not interested in having our statements and viewpoints challenged, at least not critically.

Have you ever been misunderstood by family or friends when your purpose was really simple ventilation? You're trying to blow off some steam, but your listener misinterprets the situation and proceeds to give you some point-by-point arguments on all the gross generalizations you've blurted out. All you really wanted was a quiet, sympathetic listener, and now you've committed yourself to an emotional argument you really didn't need or want. Responsibilities run both ways in these ventilation situations. Take care when ventilating; hear your friend out to discover his or her *real* purpose.

**SEEKING HELP AND INFORMATION**    In the previous category, we were seeking a listener who did not interfere continually as we complained, vented our emotions, and otherwise used him or her as a release for accumulated strong feelings. This category leads us to a more specific call for help—a call for a response, for information, support, and reinforcement. There are many such situations, ranging from the simple request for time, date, or directions to asking a person to assume a more emotionally complex, supportive role. Once again, the *why* is the influencing factor. Some call these types of purposes therapeutic in that we are seeking a cure or answer for a difficulty. It is quite important and sometimes difficult for a receiver to really know when someone wishes help and support or when he or she prefers only a sympathetic ear.

Have you ever asked one of your classmates a simple question, only to receive a lecture on transcendental hermeneutics? Your classmate may honestly have misunderstood the intent and scope of your question or may have simply found a victim on which to try out some new learning! That's not all bad either; communication is often a compromise of purposes and intentions.

Sometimes the real help we seek is a nonverbal presence, not talk at all. When the play is awful, the team has fumbled near the goal line, or you've flunked the exam, you may just prefer silent, miserable company—unless you're ventilating. Misery does love company, especially people with the same problem.

**BARGAINING**    Still another purpose that greatly affects interpersonal communication is bargaining—working out differences together. This purpose is sometimes evident, as with known, honest differences of opinion. However, it may also operate quite subtly, sometimes by design and sometimes quite by accident. In bargaining, the response to a statement often determines the next response. A statement may contain a specific intent unknown to the receiver. This intent may be concealed in some code or message intended to have a persuasive effect on the receiver. Notice the bargaining influence in the communication when you are buying a used car or a motorcycle. The seller may suggest $5,000 as an asking price. You are interested in determining just how low in price the seller is really willing to go. In this special kind of setting there is often a hidden motive and a payoff (which we expect as part of the game). The setting is sometimes called a game because of this payoff aspect. Unless you recognize this purpose and adjust accordingly, you may come off second best in the negotiation without really having played the game.

Bargaining among unions and employers is a similar communication interchange, except that it is much more formal. Most of these bargaining situations are worked out cooperatively. We usually hear about the few that are deadlocked as if they were typical.

Sometimes we bargain without knowing it. Asking to use big brother's car may really be more bargaining than a simple request for help. If this is so, your initial purpose may be to seek information. You may then shift to an expression of feelings as you attempt to establish common ground. You may next prepare to move into the bargaining stance. Whatever your line may be, you must be aware that in this type of context the receiver may not always give you the specific answer you want (that's part of the game, too). If after several exchanges you sense that your goal is not likely to be achieved, you may decide to offer more in exchange, modify your time requirement, or do whatever is possible to work out the bargaining together. That bargaining is often unsuccessful is another fact of life. Most bargaining would probably be more successful if the participants knew more about the process and recognized a bargaining situation when they were in one. We will have more to say about interpersonal persuasion later.

**EVALUATION**   Even in giving feedback about something relatively trivial, such as spelling errors (which would not be trivial in the setting of an English class) or minor arithmetic mistakes, you may be surprised at how threatening this purpose and setting is to some people. If you are in a position of giving negative feedback—such as an umpire, referee, traffic officer, or teacher—and everyone expects this kind of discipline or feedback from you, it is one thing. When you offer such advice freely in a different setting and with a less specific purpose, it is quite another thing!

The evaluative or negative-feedback setting is never easy, even for professional counselors and skilled teachers. When our purpose is to direct negative feedback at someone else, we must work especially hard at being our best self, our most sensitive self. When you *ask* for evaluation or feedback, prepare yourself for some blunt remarks. Most people will be quite honest, but not always objective, and rarely as kind as you think they should be.

Do not be too eager to evaluate others. The great counselor and psychologist Carl Rogers was known to say, "The older and wiser I get, the less eager I am to rush in to fix things."[7] Objectivity is critical to sensitive feedback situations, and so is tact.

## THE PSYCHO-ENVIRONMENT AS CONTEXT

A near poverty-stricken family finds happiness, high morale, and a certain amount of self-realization. How can this be in view of their physical environment? Because a poverty-stricken *physical* environment need not be a poverty-stricken psycho-environment, any more than a rich physical environment necessarily leads to a rich and happy psycho-environment. This is not to deprecate the importance of creature comforts and the physical environment, but rather it is to make clear that the psychological climate is, in most things, a more critical context than the physical climate.

Psychological climate refers to *all* of the influences that affect any of the purposes and settings discussed above. It includes all of the *environmental dimensions,* both physical and psychological, and particularly those human aspects of climate variously described as *accepting, understanding, facilitating,* and so on. These aspects could also be negative—that is, strongly *judgmental, evaluative, defensive, dogmatic,* and the like.

All human communication and interaction take place in some kind of psychological climate. Our surroundings and our involvement with them may or may not lead to motivation and better human relations. The attitudes people hold about their organizations and the style of leadership they encounter (or express) are critical to the communication climate. The subtlety and importance of appropriate human interactions and transactions are often lost in a sea of organizational or environmental requirements.

Elton Mayo and F. J. Roethlisberger taught the lessons of the psycho-environment and human relations years ago. Too few of our organizational leaders, they argued, were alert to the fact that it is a human social, and not an economic, problem which they face.[8]

*The attitudes people hold about their organizations are critical to the communication culture.*

It took the Hawthorne studies of the 1930s, starting out in quest of knowledge about physical environment, to make very clear that it was the *human* environment that offered most in terms of motivated effort and moral conscience. The widely growing industrial unions of the thirties made quick note and quick demand for not only wage adjustments, but also for human considerations. Today the fringes are truly misnamed psychologically as well as economically.

Horrendous amounts of pseudosophisticated, naive, and sometimes opportunistic manipulating of human relations and the work environment have undoubtedly slowed the emergence of a unified theory of human relations and the psycho-environment. In any event, it is now clear that a person's motivation depends to a large extent upon how he or she relates to his or her organizational environment and the important people in it—those people and arrangements that affect a person's life, attitudes, and perception of the psychological climate.

## Human Relations Theory

It is doubtful that any efforts parallel in human relations impact the studies done from 1924 to 1932 at the Chicago Hawthorne plant of the Western Electric Company. Mayo and his Harvard associates did not join the Western Electric team until 1927. In 1924, Hawthorne, in collaboration with the National Research Council, initiated a study with the purpose of determining the relationship between illumination intensity, or lighting, and worker efficiency as measured by production or output. The results were to confound the engineers, delight the social psychologists, and usher in a new age of human relations and involvement.[9]

The assumption of this early study was that the better the lighting, the better the production of induction coils. With one group of workers the light intensity was held constant. With the experimental group the light intensity was varied, first made higher and then made lower than with the control group. When the lights went up production went *up;* when the lights went down production went *up!* To confound things even more, in the control group with which the lights remained constant the production also went *up!* In near desperation the lights were brought down even more. It was not until near moonlight that production slipped even a modicum. Obviously, something more than lighting was operating here. The researchers did not rule out a relationship between work and light, of course, but they did become dimly aware of another variable running wild in their experiment. They labeled it *psychological.* They then devised an expectation study with light in which they replaced bulbs of equal, rather than more, wattage. The workers, living up to expectations, commented favorably on the increased illumination. These early researchers were disturbed by the extraneous psychological variables and attempted to design a way of eliminating them. They thought they might isolate and control some of them, such as fatigue, rest periods, equipment, and the like. It was decided that if a small group of workers could be isolated in a specially partitioned-off room and asked to be their normal selves, then some of these psychological variables would be suppressed. Output could finally be correlated to physical conditions. At this point, Mayo and others from the Department of Industrial Research of the Harvard Graduate School of Business Administration became involved. Earlier studies by Mayo in a Philadelphia textile mill had prepared him for assessing the psychological and human variables. He had found that it was not so much rest periods that helped production, morale, and turnover as it was the workers' *involvement* and attention in *scheduling* the rest periods.

In this special room partially described above, the now famous "Relay Assembly Room" experiment was started. In the spring of 1927 six women were chosen as average representative workers of the 100 persons who assembled telephone relays. Moving these six workers into the test room made it possible to accurately tabulate the number of relays produced literally from one moment to another. Records were kept from 1927 to 1932. The plan was to get a normal output number and then vary payment, rest breaks, days off, and. company lunch and quitting times to see the effect of each under these controlled conditions. To keep things scientific, a very attentive observer was also present to maintain records and counsel with the women.

The results made the dimly emerging lesson of the lighting experiment much brighter. In brief review of a mountain of data, the following general findings can be reported: when wages were varied production went up; when breaks were varied production went up; free snacks, production went up; variations in quitting time, production went up. After eighteen months of this the researchers decided to take away all of these special conditions and go back to the first day in the special test room—let output return to normal, as it were. No one was quite prepared for the result! Production set an all-time high! It was also found that the usual fatigue curve did not pertain, nor did the one for absenteeism. Everything was better. Perhaps this is what Thomas Wolfe meant when he wrote, "You can't go home again," or what Heroclites meant when he said, "You can't step in the same river twice." No one could ever go back to day one; "Nothing, nothing is the same."

The research staff saw the light. People had begun to feel important. Stuart Chase's interpretation of what happened, first written in 1941, goes a long way toward defining human relations in its very best sense.

> What was this X? The research staff pulled themselves together and began looking at it. They conferred, argued, studied, and presently they found it. It wasn't in the physical production end of the factory at all. It was in the girls and their group. By segregating them into a little world of their own, by asking their help and co-operation, the investigators had given the young women a new sense of their own value. Their whole attitude changed from that of separate cogs in a machine to that of a congenial team helping the company solve a significant problem.

They had found stability, a place where they belonged, and work whose purpose they could clearly see. And so they worked faster and better than they ever had in their lives. The two functions of a factory had joined into one harmonious whole.[10]

## Psychological Safety

A healthy communication climate might be described as a *cohesive* context and environment in which the discussants, through *interaction,* achieve a mental state of relative psychological safety and freedom. According to Shepherd, **cohesion** refers to the forces that bind members of a group—the degree of closeness and warmth they feel for one another, their pride as members, their willingness to be frank and honest in their expressions of ideas and feelings, and their ability to meet the emergencies and crises that may confront them.[11]

**Interaction**, in this context, is communication behavior directed toward another person or persons when their reactions or mutual behavior are taken into account. It pertains directly to our interpersonal responsibilities in communication.

*What* is being discussed is obviously a large part of the psychological climate. If we are faced with bad news, deserved criticism, necessary evaluation, or generally unhappy feedback, some cold or even defensive psychological climate is perhaps unavoidable. This is precisely the time when we must be our very best communicative selves, or we may make an already difficult psychological climate really impossible.

"Left lane, Jane. Left lane! *Left lane, Jane!!* Damn, we make left turns from the left lane. That's three bad mistakes." If you remember your driver training, you probably recall at least a few bad days during which criticism of your driving behavior seemed harsh (to you) or threatening, however necessary it may have been in the name of highway safety and your own driving skill. The way in which such criticism is given, as well as taken, is what is known as psychological climate.

If an English professor objectively criticizes a bad essay of yours line by line (as he or she is paid to do), it is easy to become defensive in a subsequent one-to-one encounter. Human interaction is, of course, a knife that cuts both ways. Someone may lack *sensitivity* as a message sender, but be too sensitive as a receiver. If on a given day someone is feeling super defensive about race, national origin, or some other large dimension of personality, his or her communication partner may find communication very difficult indeed. At this point the receiver has a considerable communication obligation to avoid being overly sensitive in his or her role as a receiver and to strive to reestablish a healthier communication climate. It is as if we must have both thick and thin skins at exactly the same time. We need to develop a tolerance for conflicting information, beliefs, and perceptions, as well as a general tolerance for doubt and uncertainty.

The climate and both persons' assessments of and contribution to it are truly essential to how each learns, communicates, and grows. A flippant, sexist, or cute remark is sometimes all it takes to put your foot in your mouth (or worse).

We probably feel less safe psychologically in communication settings pertaining to evaluation than in social conversations or loving relationships. Where there is good rapport and basic respect for one another, a person may achieve a kind of *psychological freedom,* a happy climate in which the person's status is not unreasonably threatened, in which he or she feels accepted as a person, and in which he or she has the freedom to be wrong and to become involved. Both psychological safety and freedom involve being accepted as an individual of some worth in a climate in which the individual is not persistently evaluated as a person.

When the setting is tense and angry, emotional voices are heard and we are put to a real communication test. When our feelings are out of sync or out of balance with our beliefs, we are apt to ruin the psychological climate. Our emotions may affect the way we think in a given situation or communication episode, but the reverse is also true—the way we think affects the way we feel. If we *think* someone is going to ridicule or insult us, we are probably going to *feel* angry or defensive. If we *think* our relational partners really intend to threaten the relationship, wouldn't we feel fear and apprehension?

## COMMUNICATING INTERPERSONALLY

### Importance of Interpersonal Communication

We define **interpersonal communicatio**n as a distinctive, on going, ever changing transactional form of human communication that involves mutual influence usually for the purposes of relationship management. The key word here is relationship. Most humans have a desire for long-term, satisfying relationships. You can't build and manage relationships without interpersonal communication. As we all know, communicating in close relationships can be challenging. Just imagine how much more peaceful and productive your life would be if you could improve your listening skills, learn to use sensitive and nondefensive language, and learn to accurately place responsibility for feelings in your interactions. Understanding interpersonal communication can actually enhance our emotional, psychological, and physical well-being.

Studies show that communication skills, particularly interpersonal communication skills, are paramount for employability.[12] Without solid interpersonal communication skills you will not only have a hard finding a job in today's market, you may also have trouble keeping it. Communication skills are closely linked with ability to be productive.[13]

Interpersonal communication skills are also linked with high academic performance. Studies show that students that have the ability to interact with peers and instructors productively are able to increase their learning experience, are more motivated, and find class much more satisfying. All of these things lead to increased academic performance.[14]

Another benefit of studying interpersonal communication is that it can help us become the best person we can be. The process of being the best we can be is called **self-actualization**. This idea comes from psychologist Abraham Maslow.[15] In order to become self-actualized we must be able to gain information about ourselves. Once we come to know our assets and weaknesses we can work on enhancing the assets and eliminating the weaknesses. One of the ways we are able to gain this vital information about ourselves is through interaction with others.

Regardless of which benefit of interpersonal communication seems most appropriate to your individual situation, it is safe to say that interpersonal communication is a necessary tool for building a happy and successful life.

## ETHICS: RESPONSIBLE RELATIONSHIPS

### Lies and Mental Reservations

A communicator is morally responsible for telling the truth and for the social consequences that result if the truth is not told. This critical statement is meant to include not only our words but all the nonverbals as well. "He tells a lie who has one thing in his mind and says something else by words or by any signs whatsoever." (St. Augustine) To some moral philosophers the natural end of speech is to communicate our thoughts, and a lie is evil because it frustrates the very end and purpose of speech.

Being honest and fair to the facts are obvious moral obligations. We must play by the game rules and obey the law. Using outright lies, manufactured facts, and "dirty tricks" are clearly unethical. Even here we encounter some problems.[16] Prudence is a virtue. Can the ethical person be honest without being unkind? Can he or she be both tactful and forthright?

Are some broad mental reservations allowed? Yes, say the ethitians, in the same way that a defendant pleads not guilty, or a doctor, questioned about professional secrets, replies "I don't know." Yes, they say, because there were fair and sufficient *clues* within the special contexts and situations. A courtroom would not allow for any kind of mental reservation (a very special context). According to moralists, the common good is at stake here superceding the private good of the individual.

A strict mental reservation without any clue is a lie in any context. So, too, are all communications that are grossly unfair to the facts, or so subtle that they give the receiver no clue about possible alternatives.[17] The clue is important, as is the context.

Honest clues protect the receiver's fundamental right of choice. Even in social compliance situations there is usually some choice. When choice is minimal, at least there are some alternatives (the courts when necessary). The ultimate decision of how to behave, act, interpret, or believe must in some way, however small, be left to the receiver. That choice must be a viable one.

## Special Situations

If moral law permits some concealing of the truth, to what situations does this pertain? What are some guidelines? First, some generalizations with wide ethical acceptance in a democracy are the following:

We have a right to do what is necessary or helpful to preserve our own personal dignity and independence.

We have a right to keep our private affairs secret.

We should do that which promotes mutual trust among men. (Doctors, lawyers, and others should not reveal secrets except in extraordinary circumstances in which the common good demands it.)

All of these generalizations deal with situations in which trust and some kind of secret put us in a double bind.

Joseph Sullivan, S.J. deals forthrightly with the ethical principles that should govern the keeping or revealing of secrets.[18] We offer them for your consideration.

## Definitions

*Secret*—is a truth which the possessor may (right) or ought (duty) to conceal.

*Natural Secret*—is a truth, which *from its own nature* gives the possessor said right or duty.

*For example:* One's own or one's neighbor's private affairs, the revelations of which, at least in ordinary circumstances, would cause reasonable offense or injury.

**Secret of Promise**—is a truth, which *because of a promise made,* the possessor has a duty and, therefore, a right to conceal.

**Secret of Trust**—is a truth, which, because of the fact that it was confided to one by another on the express or tacit agreement that having been communicated for a serious purpose it be held in trust, the possessor has a duty and right to conceal.

*For example:* Knowledge communicated to a lawyer or doctor, or even in some circumstances to a mere friend can be kept secret.

**At times permits**—*i.e.,* man sometimes has the *right* to keep a secret.

**At times command**—*i.*e., man sometimes has *more than a right,* he has a *duty.*

*Question:* When are these times?

*Answer:* a) *Man has a duty* to keep:
1) A *natural* secret—as long as
    a) the truth is not made common property by some one else;
    b) he cannot reasonably presume the leave of those concerned, to reveal it;
    c) concealing the truth works no serious harm to a community;
    d) he is not questioned about the matter by legitimate authority;
    e) it can be kept without serious inconvenience to himself or another.
2) A secret of *promise* as long as a, b, c, d, as above.
    a) It can be kept without serious inconvenience to himself or another and, even at the cost of such inconvenience, if he *has expressly promised* to do so.
3) A secret of *trust*—as long as
    a) *revelation is not necessary* to avert serious and impending harm from
        1) the community,
        2) the holder of the secret,

    3) a third and innocent party who is endangered by the person who has confided the secret in another.

  4) the one who confided the secret.

The reason why the obligation of keeping a secret, even of promise, ceases in the circumstances mentioned above is because even when assuming obligations of a strict contract, no man can reasonably be thought to intend to bind himself in such circumstances. Cf. approved authors in Moral Theology.

    b) *Man has a right* to keep all secrets

        1) in all the above-named cases where he has a duty;

        2) in some of the cases mentioned where he has no duty.

Nilsen challenges interpersonal communicators to take into account the special circumstances, the intent, the feelings behind questions, and to combine honesty with respect for sensitivities. He goes on to say,

> Morally good communications are those which best preserve the integrity of the ego, contribute to personal growth, and harmonize relationships. These ends are served by communications, which, in addition to providing the information needed in a given situation, permit and encourage the expression of thought and feeling, and reveal respect for the person as a person.[19]

## Culpable Ignorance

The intent of the sender is, of course, critical to an evaluation of the morality of his or her message. Equally important is the *role*, or *status*, of the sender. A person qualified to serve and serving in a leadership role has special ethical obligations. We expect our political and religious leaders and our professional people to be responsible, regardless of intent. A doctor convicted of malpractice rarely *intended* to do harm. An incompetent teacher may have *good intentions*. We judge such people harshly and hold them ethically responsible, even though their intent may have been good. Our laws accommodate this notion not just for professionals but for political leaders, as well. Senators, congressmen, and other public figures have less protection from libel and slander than does the average citizen. (They, of course, do have their protective immunities, however.)

All of us have some ethical obligations beyond intent. Many people have been hurt by those who "meant well." All of us have some obligation to get our facts straight before sending messages that might capriciously misinform or injure the receiver. Moralists call this *culpable ignorance*—that is, ignorance usually from carelessness deserving blame.[20]

Most often we have an ethical responsibility to rhetorically analyze our receivers. For one not to care how people are apt to decode a message borders on immorality. A child may decode a message quite differently from a mature adult. How a particular person will interpret a particular message is an ethical consideration.

Let us not forget our ethical responsibilities as receivers.[21] As receivers we have a moral obligation to give *fair hearing* once we have committed ourselves to some legitimate interest in the issue. We must make an effort to understand the sender's biases and intent. We should show *tolerance* and work at understanding intent. Fair hearing replaces force in a free society.

To give fair hearing we must also analyze our own *range of acceptance*. Are we really stuck with a "hard" attitude? Is there some latitude in our position? To give a fair hearing also means allowing the other person some chance to talk. Ethical interpersonal communication doesn't outlaw aggressive arguing, but it does outlaw excessive monologue; it does necessitate giving the sender some chance to make and explain his or her point. Fair hearing also calls for fair fighting. Sandbagging or setting people up for an obvious embarrassment borders on unethical entrapment. Dragging in every superfluous issue to deliberately confuse is another question of ethics. These unfair interpersonal conflict techniques will be discussed in later chapters. We have a moral obligation to ourselves and the society we represent to stubbornly protect our own independence and dignity.

## SUMMING UP

Interpersonal communication is largely a face-to-face or voice-to-voice thing. It goes on in all kinds of organizations, groups, and settings. Reacting and interacting always occur somewhere, at some level, in some context or setting. Some settings restrict communication while others aid it. Interpersonal communication cuts through all of the larger contexts. Some of these are mass, organizational, group, and public communication. Various levels of communication in ascending order are described by some as intrapersonal, interpersonal, group, and cultural. A model is shown.

The instructional model we have used (Figure 1.4) includes an idea or concept, selecting and sorting, encoding, transmitting, receiving and decoding, selecting and sorting, and a reconstructed idea or concept. Feedback is information being returned from receivers, and it is vital to the correction and refining of the signals we send. Communication is a process of sorting, selecting, and sending symbols in such a way as to help a receiver find in his or her own mind a meaning intended by the sender. Current definitions seem to agree that ideas must, in some way, be shared before communication can exist and that communication should be thought of as a process—not simply as a transfer of meaning from one mind to another. Communication involves common experience and mutual influence. Real communication is very difficult if there is not at least some small opportunity for two-way influence. Whether we know it or not, we communicate hoping to influence others to respond as we want them to. This process has no beginning and no end; it is ever changing, dynamic, and mutual.

Much of our communication is dictated by the setting. Time, place, ritual, and purpose have great influence on communication. Some general purposes for communicating are: social, ventilation, seeking help, bargaining, and evaluation.

Motivation depends, in large part, upon how we relate to our psycho-environment, our organizations, and the important people in them. Human relations theory teaches us that a would-be leader is poorly trained if he or she is unaware of the informal communications and social units that develop within the environment of any formal organization. The spirit of such groups should be a communication and leadership objective.

A healthy communication climate is a cohesive context in which interactants achieve a state of psychological safety and freedom. The climate and the interactants' assessment of and contributions to it are essential to how they each learn, grow, and communicate. Psychological freedom is a climate in which our status is not unreasonably threatened, in which we feel accepted, and in which we have the freedom to be wrong and to become involved.

Interpersonal communication has great importance. Good interpersonal communication can heighten our emotional, psychological and physical well being. It can increase our chances of getting and keeping a job, help individuals to become better students, and allow us to reach a state of self-actualization or being the best we can be.

Ethics involves moral responsibility in our interactions with others. A communicator is morally responsible for telling the truth and for the social consequences that result if the truth is not told. If mental restrictions are involved, fair and sufficient clues must be present regardless of context. Honest clues protect the receiver's fundamental right of choice. "Morally good communications are those which best preserve the integrity of the ego, contribute to personal growth, and harmonize relationships." [22] The intent of the sender is critical to the morality of his or her message. Equally important is the role or status of the sender. A person qualified to serve and serving in a leadership role has special ethical obligations. We expect such people to be responsible regardless of intent. We should show tolerance and an effort at understanding intent. If we are involved at all, we have a moral obligation to give fair hearing. As senders all of us have some obligation to get our facts straight before encoding messages that might capriciously misinform or injure the receiver. Moralists call this culpable ignorance—that is, ignorance from carelessness deserving blame.

## NOTES

1 Grace A. de Laguna, *Speech: Its Function and Development* (New Haven: Yale University Press, 1927), p. 19.

2 Schramm, Wilbur. "How Communication Works" in *The Process and Effects of Mass Communication,* ed. W. Schramm (Urbana, Ill.: University of Illinois Press 1955), pp. 4-8

3 Harold P. Zelko and Frank E. X. *Dance, Business and Professional Speech Communication* (New York: Holt, Rinehart & Winston, 1965, 1978), pp. 6-7.

4 D. C. Barnlund, *Interpersonal Communication: Survey and Studies* (Boston: Houghton Mifflin Co., 1968), p. 10.

5 Stephen W. Littlejohn, *Theories of Human Communication* 11 ed. (Columbus, Ohio: Charles E. Merrill Publishing Company, 2006), p. 204.

6 Rensis Likert, *New Patterns of Management* (New York: McGraw-Hill Book Company, 1961), p. 104.

7 Carl Rogers, *On Becoming a Person* (Boston: Houghton Mifflin, 1961), p. 21.

8 Elton Mayo, *The Human Problems of an Industrial Civilization* (New York: Macmillan, Inc., 1933).

9 Excellent accounts of these studies may be found in Elton Mayo, *The Human Problems of an Industrial Civilization* (New York: The Viking Press, 1960); F. J. Roethlisberger and W. J. Dickson, *Management and the Worker* (Cambridge, Mass.: Harvard University Press, 1939); George C. Homans, "The Western Electric Researches," chap. 4 in *Fatigue of Workers: Its Relation to Industrial Production,* by the Committee on Work in Industry of the National Research Council (New York: Reinhold Publishing Corp., 1941); Stuart Chase, *Men at Work* (New York: Harcourt Brace Jovanovich, 1945).

10 Chase, *Men at Work,* p. 19. For a scientific analysis see T. N. Whitehead, *The Industrial Worker* (Cambridge, Mass.: Harvard University Press, 1938).

11 Clovis R. Shepherd, *Small Groups: Some Sociological Perspectives* (San Francisco: Chandler Publishing Co., 1964) p. 26.

12 National Association of Colleges and Employers (2002). *Do employers and colleges see eye to eye? College student development and assessment.* http://www.econedlink.org.

13 Coplin, W. (2004). *10 things employers want you to learn in college.* Berkley, CA: Ten Speed Press.

14 Myers, S.A., & Bryant, L.E. (2002). Perceived understanding, interaction involvement, and college student outcomes. *Communication Research Reports,* 19, 146-155.

15 Maslow, A.H. (1954/1970). *Motivation and personality.* New York: Harper and Row.

16 M. Knapp and M. Comadena, "Telling It Like It Isn't: A Review of Theory and Research on Deceptive Communications," *Human Communication Research,* 5, no. 3 (Spring 1979), 270-85.

17 See J. Jaksa and S. Rhodes, "A 'Content-ethic' for Interpersonal Communication," *Michigan Speech Association Journal,* 14, 1979,80-88.

18 J. F. Sullivan, S.J., *Special Ethics* (Worcester, Mass.: Holy Cross College Press, 1948), pp. 26-27.

19 T. R. Nilsen, *Ethics of Speech Communication* (Indianapolis: The Bobbs-Merrill Company, Inc., 1966), p.78.

20 See L. Flynn, "The Aristotelian Basis for the Ethics of Speaking," *The Speech Teacher,* VI, no. 3 (September 1957), 179-87. See also R. Johannesen, *Ethics and Persuasion* (New York: Random House, 1967), p. 117.

21 See F. Haiman, "Democratic Ethics and the Hidden Persuaders," *Quarterly Journal of Speech,* XLN, no. 4 (December 1958), 385-92. See also Johannesen, *Ethics and Persuasion,* p. 70.

22 Nilsen, *Ethics of Speech Communication,* p. 78.

# CHAPTER 2

# INTERPERSONAL AFFAIR:
# OTHERS, SELF AND PERCEPTION

## OUR NEED FOR OTHERS

We are social animals and have a need to relate to others. That is not to say that after a hectic interpersonal day we don't sometimes enjoy some time alone, but sooner or later it helps to talk about it. We need healthy relationships with others if we are to achieve a sense of well-being and happiness.

## On Being Alone

**REAL ISOLATION**   Real isolation and sensory deprivation have been studied in the laboratory and reported from real experiences. In one study students were paid to remain alone in a locked room. Of five students individually tested, one lasted two hours. Three, one of which said, "Never again", made it for two days. One student did make it for the course of the eight-day experiment.[1]

In a survival study a Dr. Bombard attempted a solitary Atlantic crossing in a life raft. His log records this chilling entry on real isolation:

> I had begun to understand the difference between solitude and isolation. Moments of isolation in ordinary life can soon be ended; it is just a question of going out of the door into the street or dialing a number on the phone to hear the voice of a friend. Isolation is merely a matter of isolating oneself, but total solitude is an oppressive thing and slowly wears down its lonely victim. It seemed sometimes as if the immense and absolute solitude of the ocean's expanse was concentrated right on top of me, as if my beating heart was the center of gravity of a mass which was at the same time nothingness. ... It was a vast presence which engulfed me. Its spell could not be broken, any more than the horizon could be brought nearer. And if from time to time I talked aloud in order to hear my own voice, I only felt more alone, a hostage to silence.[2]

Physical isolation can be a terrible thing. Solitary confinement in prison may indeed be the most sadistic of all punishments. We do know from experimental research and real-life episodes that real isolation makes us more anxious, less cogent, more suggestible, and prone to hallucinations.

WISHING FOR A WRONG NUMBER

Call me, anonymous drunkard, tell me
that you are God and can create in seven
hours a much better world. And call me, sell me
anything, everything, even
the rusty wheels of the sun, whoever you are—
merchant or minister, harlot or child,
but let the sound of a human voice compel me
to be reminded suddenly of life going on
for man and mountain and tree
for valley and wing and ocean
for all except me.
Yes, I have heard of flights from dawn to sunset,
of Europe meeting Asia in an hour,
of man and moon becoming
closer and closer, as close as a stem to a flower.
Why should it be so hard, then,
for man to remember man,
for you to let me hear the sound of your voice?
Call me, whoever you are, and tell me
whatever you please. Speak even
of wind and heaven
to a wounded eagle in the grass, of bread and fire
to a famished beggar in the snow.
Be cruel and be rude.
But talk to me and let me know
that I am not alone
in this my human solitude.

—Joseph Tuisani

**SOCIAL ISOLATION**    Some of the same results occur to people who are not on life rafts or stranded like Robinson Crusoe. A form of social isolation may afflict all of us as we feel "left out" or, in one way or another, separated from others. These are serious matters, especially for some of our senior citizens who experience the very real pain of isolation from a lack of interpersonal communication.[3]

It is clear that life is no good alone; we need others. We need people for love, reassurance, approval, a sense of reality, and, most critically, communication, even if it is simply a nonverbal presence.

## On Needing and Helping Others

Our previous discussions make quite clear that we need others at least some of the time. In this section we will talk about some of the specific interpersonal needs thought to affect all of us. Our relationships with others are not always helpful, but ideally they should be. We will also discuss the characteristics of helping relationships. The large numbers of **interdependent** relationships that are a part of everyday life call for a great amount of coordination. Relationships that are *interdependent* are those in which the individuals involved are dependent on each other. This means that the actions of one person in the relationship will result in an affect on the other person and vice versa. We'll start with a brief look at coordinating relationships.

*Humans are so- cial animals and can be negatively affected by isola- tion. We need to communicate and interact with others.*

**COORDINATING RELATIONSHIPS**   "I think I'd like to buy that car." The salesperson responds, "We're ready to sell it at a bargain price." The buyer's family asks, "Are you sure it's large enough for the family?" "Will it pull our trailer?" The salesperson then asks, "How big is the trailer?" After this preliminary coordinating of *interdependent* opinions and preferences we're ready for still more communication. "I'll have the used car manager assess your trade-in." After this is done, "I'll have to take your offer to my sales manager." Assuming this works out, "Now what about financing?" We now have involved the family, the salesperson, the used-car manager, the sales manager, a banker, and, if title is a problem, the state licensing bureau. A paint scratch—add the paint shop manager; a loose tail pipe—add the repair shop manager.

Try an organizational bureaucracy. A young professor applies for promotion. First she must coordinate with the departmental personnel committee, then the college committee, then the university committee, and finally the president, who relays and relates it to the board of trustees. If there are informal lines of influence between these various committees, the example takes on even larger coordination dimensions.

One may or may not always be aware of this *interdependence* or of the specific type of coordination involved. One type is *cooperative;* another *competitive.* Most situations, like those above, are of the "mixed-motive" type since both cooperation and competition have to be dealt with. Sometimes we can agree with others about goals but not about means or vice versa. Americans were in agreement (cooperative) about the goal of protecting American citizens from terrorism; there was a difference of opinion (competition) about the means such as an invasion of Iraq.

Life is full of these interdependent relationships. It is through coordination, patience, and communication that we may achieve action.

**INTERPERSONAL NEEDS: INCLUSION, CONTROL, AFFECTION**   If you were attracted to a new group, a new organization, or just some new friends, it has been theorized that you would ask yourself three specific kinds of questions— those of inclusion, control, and affection. Suppose you are attracted to a much needed part-time job in the college bookstore. The kinds of interpersonal questions with which you probably would struggle are diagrammed in Figure 2.1.

Assuming that all mankind has some need for affiliation and association, it seems reasonable to contemplate questions of **inclusion** in the group that operates and works at the bookstore. Your need to both give and receive direction (and this varies with the

**FIGURE 2.1**

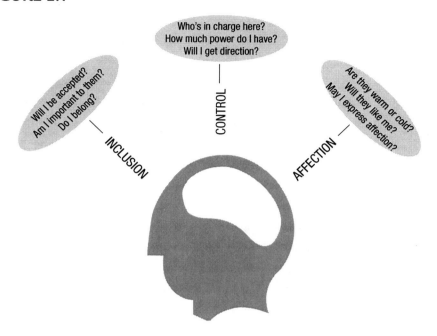

person and the circumstances) prompts you to contemplate questions of **control**. Your interpersonal need to belong and to be liked generates questions of **affection**.

William Schutz has postulated that inclusion, control, and affection are our primary social needs; and they go a long way toward determining how we behave and relate to others.[4]

These three interpersonal needs are thought to operate on their own continua. For example, inclusion might have the following continua:

| High affiliation————Low affiliation |
|---|
| High interaction————Low interaction |
| Much association————Little association |
| INCLUSION |

According to Schutz, *inclusion* deals with things such as attention, acknowledgment, recognition, prominence, identity, and participation.[5] Other terms thought to evoke positive or negative feelings of inclusion are associate, together, involved (positive), outcast, detached, and ignored (negative).

Control might have the following continua:

```
        Strong authority————Weak authority
        Much direction————Little direction
High achievement needs————Low achievement needs
                   CONTROL
```

According to Schutz *control* is communicated by behaviors expressing leadership, power, accomplishment, and intellectual superiority (among others). When control is perceived as repressive, oppressive, or unfair—"The bookstore managers are slave drivers"—then this side of the control need is typified by behaviors expressing rebellion, resistance, and—in some cases- submission.[6]

If the bookstore managers give you appropriate direction but still let you exercise decision making over your small part of the organization, you approach a kind of optimal fulfillment of this powerful interpersonal need. This state of affairs is thought to enhance, or at least preserve, feelings of self-respect.

Affection might have the following continua:

```
        Close (to others)————Distant
            Intimate————Hostile
            Acceptant————Rejectant
               AFFECTION
```

According to Schutz, the flavor of *affection* is embodied in "situations of love, emotional closeness, personal confidences, intimacy. Negative affection is characterized by hate, hostility, and emotional rejection."[7]

If you perceive the bookstore group as a clique that couldn't care less about you or is downright discriminatory, your affection need is not going to be met in the bookstore. On the other hand, if the bookstore job turns out to be a real joy (you're part of the group, you meet genuine friends), you may have achieved an ideal or at least optimal state of affection (at least for the bookstore part of your life). In any event, this happy episode at the bookstore should promote the feeling of being loved.

It is possible, of course, to be high on affection and inclusion and low on control, such as if you like the people you work and interact with, but hate the boss. Ideally we will find some optimal fulfillment not only within each need, but also across all the needs.

Our success and comfort with this balancing act is thought to have much to do with our relating and interacting, so much so that Schutz provides a still stronger lens for observing these behaviors and feelings. The lens has four parts or "states": desired, ideal, anxious, and pathological. It looks at such things as being under-social or over-social, submissive or dominant, under-personal or over-personal, and also some of the pathological continua (e.g., obsessive and compulsive). This lens or system became so ponderous that Schutz called it an "elephant."[8] The "elephant" is an attempt to relate all interpersonal behavior into all of the categories discussed above. It is worth reading if you are seriously interested in how and, perhaps, why you relate and interact the way you do. (See Table 2.1.)

**HELPING RELATIONSHIPS**    When we find ourselves in the role of facilitator, counselor, or just in the position of "big brother" or "big sister," we are in a rather special interpersonal relationship. Knowing when we are *in* that role is no small part of successful human relations. Professional therapists, counselors, and teachers usually have their roles fairly well defined. However client- or student-centered they might be, it is quite clear that they are the helpers. Carl Rogers, a professional therapist, feels that the same helping characteristics of a good counselor also pertain to interpersonal communication in general. In many ways we agree. However, everyone is not a therapist or a clinician, and people should take care not to play psychiatrist in their everyday encounters. We do, of course, meet genuine requests for help, often in subtle ways, from friends, teammates, brothers, and sisters. We also find ourselves in the role of procedural, task, or social leader on occasion. In a study in which students functioned as peer group teachers, those who were judged most successful interpersonally were perceived as being empathic, caring, understanding, and respectful of the learners.[9] For the students, these interpersonal skills were more important than instruction-related behavior and, interestingly, more important than the amount of self-disclosure engaged in.

**TABLE 2.1     NATURE OF RELEVANT INTERPERSONAL DATA, "THE SCHUTZ ELEPHANT"**

| | | INCLUSION | | | CONTROL | | | AFFECTION | | |
|---|---|---|---|---|---|---|---|---|---|---|
| | | Self to Other (Actions) | Other to Self (Reactions) | Self to Self | Self to Other (Actions) | Other to Self (Reactions) | Self to Self | Self to Other (Actions) | Other to Self (Reactions) | Self to Self |
| DESIRED INTERPERSONAL RELATIONS (NEEDS) | Act | Satisfactory relation re: interaction and inclusion behavior 1 | | Feeling that I am significant 15 | Satisfactory relation re: power and control behavior 19 | | Feeling that I am responsible 33 | Satisfactory relation re: love and affection behavior 37 | | Feeling that I am lovable 51 |
| | Feel | Satisfactory relation re: feelings of mutual interest 2 | | | Satisfactory relation re: feelings of mutual respect 20 | | | Satisfactory relation re: feelings of mutual affection 38 | | |
| IDEAL INTERPERSONAL RELATIONS | Act | Social 3 | People include me 4 | | Democrat 21 | People respect me 22 | | Personal 39 | People are friendly to me 40 | |
| | Feel | I am interested in people 5 | People are interested in me 6 | | I respect people 23 | People respect me 24 | | I like people 41 | People like me 42 | |
| ANXIOUS INTERPERSONAL RELATIONS (ANXIETIES) | Too much activity — Act | Over-social 7 | Social-compliant 8 | I am insignificant (I don't know who I am; I am nobody) 16 | Autocrat 25 | Rebel 26 | I am incompetent (I am stupid, irresponsible) 34 | Over-personal 43 | Personal compliant 44 | I am unlovable (I am no good, rotten bastard) 52 |
| | Too much activity — Feel | I am not *really* interested in people 9 | People aren't *really* interested in me 10 | | I don't trust people 27 | People don't trust me 28 | | *Really* I don't like people 45 | People don't *really* like me 46 | |
| | Too little activity — Act | Under-social 11 | Counter-social 12 | | Abdicrat 29 | Submissive 30 | | Under-personal 47 | Counter-personal 48 | |
| | Too little activity — Feel | I am not interested in people 13 | People are not interested in me 14 | | I don't *really* respect people 31 | People don't *really* respect me 32 | | I don't like people 49 | People don't like me 50 | |
| PATHOLOGICAL INTERPERSONAL RELATIONS | Too Much | | | 17 | Obsessive-compulsive 35 | | | Neurotic 53 | | |
| | Too Little | Psychotic (Schizophrenia) 18 | | | Psychopath 36 | | | Neurotic 54 | | |

The Interpersonal Underworld, *reprint edition. Palo Alto, California Science and Behavior Books, 1966. p. 19.*

Research on the helping function for therapists, counselors, and teachers clearly suggests that those most likely to be helpful in producing positive change for learners are proficient at skills such as listening, empathic understanding, expressing positive regard, genuineness, and giving feedback.[10]

The Rogerian characteristics are in general agreement with those discussed above. They are, however, expressed in a dyadic format (Rogers to a client). Their application to general interpersonal communication needs sensitive adaptation. Rogers' definition of a helping relationship clarifies the clinical orientation: "… one (a helping relationship) in which one of the participants intends that there should come about, in one or both parties, more appreciation, more expression of, more functional use of the latent inner resources of the individual."[11]

The more pertinent of his helping relationship characteristics are described and adapted below[12]:

1. A perception of *trustworthiness,* "… dependable or consistent in some deep sense"; "… not that I be rigidly consistent but that I be dependently real"; "… whatever attitude I am experiencing would be matched by my awareness of that attitude."

2. *Openness* and a consistency between my attitudes and communication behavior, "… it is safe to be transparently real"; "… aware of and acceptant toward my own feelings …"

3. A genuine *regard* and *respect* for the dignity of others.

4. A *concern* that I do not promote an unhealthy emotional dependency

5. *Acceptant* of others as they are, "Can I permit him to be what he is—honest or deceitful, infantile or adult, despairing or overconfident?"

6. An *empathic* understanding of others

7. *Nonthreatening* communication behavior

8. *Nonevaluative* (nonjudgmental) language and relational behavior

9. Acceptant of the notion that people are capable of change, growth, and development—"Can I meet this other individual as a person who is in the process of becoming?"

## INTERPERSONAL PERCEPTION

Whether we are helping, coordinating or meeting interpersonal needs, two common denominators exist: us and another person. The notion of others is an important one in the study of communication.  Others make up a big part of our daily experiences. Perception is the process of experiencing things in our lives and then making sense out of those experiences. We form perceptions about others, ourselves, and the world that surrounds us. Perception takes place in three stages. We first notice a particular thing, person, place, or event. Second, we attempt to organize, or make sense of, the thing that we have noticed. Lastly, we interpret the thing that we have noticed and organized and use those interpretations to help make decisions.

## Stages of Perception

**STAGE ONE: NOTICING**   One of the authors of this textbook studies communication and aging. Any time she watches a movie, looks at an ad in the paper or passes a group of people at a bus stop, she notices specific things about the elderly individuals she sees.  Usually the person she is with doesn't even notice that there was an elderly person present. Because your author notices things that others do not, her perception of events is quite unique. We experience several sensations at any time.  We see, hear, feel, smell and taste all the time; but we can't attend to everything we see, hear, feel, smell and taste. For this reason we notice particular things but not everything. What we select to notice is influenced by things like past experiences, areas of study, likes and dislikes.

**STAGE TWO: ORGANIZING**   Once we have noticed something we try to make sense of it. We make sense of things by organizing them in our mind. Think of your brain as a giant storage facility. Storage units may include doors labeled with words such as happy, important or offensive. When we notice something, it goes running through our storage facility until it finds a door that has a label familiar to it and then tucks itself into the unit. When your author that studies communication and aging is watching a television show with a friend about elderly people that overcome adversity, her friend may notice things that fit themselves into the happy storage unit while your author may notice things that fit into the important storage unit.

**STAGE THREE: INTERPRETING**    Even after we have noticed something and it has been organized in some way in our mind, we still have to go through the process of creating meaning for this already noticed and organized experience. The process of explaining perceptions in a way that makes the most sense is called **interpretation**. Continue with our example of your author. The interpretation of the important thing that she noticed may be that she has been looking for an idea for a new research project. The interpretation of the happy thing that her friend noticed may be that she has been worried about an aging mother. We provide an explanation for our reactions. When we interpret or make meaning of another's actions or reactions, we create explanations for them and form an impression of them.

## Impressions

In a busy, complex world of superficial acquaintances and strangers we are forced to create explanations *(interpretations)* or form impressions (sometimes very quickly, sometimes very inaccurately) about the mass of information being thrown our way. It is through these impressions that we organize our perceptions of others, that we get a "handle" on them. This leads us to make decisions about liking and possible future interaction.

We may sometimes form global impressions of a person on the basis of a single attribute such as height, weight, pipe smoker, and so forth. Some attributes are not trivial but may still lead our impressions astray. Status, position, title and even name are all important in impression formation, yet numerous researchers tell us that any of these, especially in isolation, can mislead us.[13] Even the most subtle of cues figure in our awareness and impressions of others—a perfume, grooming, a tie. The most important point is that these impressions have behavioral consequences.[14]

First impressions are then very important interpersonally. Even when aware of the risks we really have little choice in many interactions if we are to meet our overwhelming need to make sense (often nonsense) of the very complex social world in which we live. We are biased by first impressions. **First impression bias** means that

*First impressions are important as they have behavioral consequences.*

our first impression of others creates a lens through which later information about a person is viewed, processed and remembered. [15]

This need leads us to speculating about people's traits and attributes. These constructions help us decide all kinds of appropriate behaviors. The tendency to organize and synthesize cues is explained by **implicit personality theory**.[16] This theory suggests that we make inferences about people based on one or a few personality traits. This speculating is often fraught with oversimplifications and distortions, which may lead to stereotypic actions and unhappy communications. To **stereotype** is to attribute a set of qualities to another person simply based on their membership in some category. This happens due to preconceived expectations we place on a person, thing or event. We concentrate so hard on what we expect to experience that often we miss the reality of the experience. For example, as the instructor of a service-learning course I required students to work with individuals that were labeled "homeless". My students met with me in the parking lot of a particular homeless facility in our community. As the students began exiting their cars to go into the facility, I noticed that several of them were emptying their pockets of belongings such as wallets and cell phones. Some students even removed jewelry before exiting their cars. When I asked them about their behavior, they responded by saying, "These people are homeless, which means they don't have any money and they will be tempted to take our belongings." This is a *stereotype!* My students attributed a set of qualities (poor and prone to theft) to individuals just because they fall under the category of "homeless".

Expectations such as the ones discussed above create what is called a **self-fulfilling prophecy**. This occurs when we make assumptions about others or ourselves and then behave as if these assumptions are true. Have you ever not wanted to go somewhere? You know those family functions that you can't wait to leave before you have even gotten there? You sit in the corner with a fake, plastered smile and play count down until the "appropriate" amount of time has been spent at the function. You are so busy being frustrated by the passage of time that you force yourself to have an unpleasant experience. This is an example of *self-fulfilling prophecy.*

## Attributions

This tendency to apply *implicit personality theory* leads us to draw conclusions about a person's motives, traits, and personality characteristics often after only a minimal observation. **Attribution theory** creates a framework through which we determine the motives underlying the behaviors of others.[17] We attribute *causes,* as it were. Attribution theorists suggest several ways in which we can improve this process. We should, for example, spend less time on inferred dispositions (he or she is lazy, sadistic, etc.) and more time on actual observation of specific actions or attribute qualities only after taking the context and consequences of a person's behavior into account. Also, consider differences between conscious, direct observations and those based on feelings and indirect observations. Are you overlooking or misreading subtle nonverbals? Also important are the following factors: Is the person under pressure? Does the person have free choice? What do others, better informed than you, say about the person observed?

If a new, briefly met neighbor passes you by while you're stuck on the freeway, it is very easy to assume that this stupid, hostile, selfish person did so because he is stupid, hostile, and selfish. You assume that the person had the opportunity to help and chose not to do so. Later you may learn certain facts that will alter this first impression. His own car may have been operating on three cylinders and to have stopped would have put him in the same predicament as you. He may have been a doctor on an emergency call. It is so easy to be wrong.

## Perceiving Events and Things

Have you ever been on a train that was stopped next to other trains in a railroad terminal? Have you then felt, seen, and heard all the signs indicating movement, only to find that it was the other trains that were moving? Perhaps you discovered this by noticing that the other trains were gone or by fixing your gaze on something you knew was not moving, such as the ceiling of the station, a roof support, or the ground.

The point of this is that perception is essentially two things: (1) the *sensation* caused by the stimulation of a sense organ and (2) the *interpretation* of that sensation. We are concerned mainly with the interpretation. It is through our knowledge and experience that we interpret or attach meaning to events and things.

The complexity of human communication is indicated, also, by the various levels of perception now thought to exist. *Subliminal* or *subthreshold* perception, for example, is the reception of impressions below the level of conscious awareness. This is not to be confused with so-called extrasensory perception. Many experiments have been conducted in this field, most of them with images projected so fast that although we are subconsciously aware of them we cannot recognize them. Such experiments are complicated by the fact that people vary in their perceptual abilities and that a person perceives better at some levels of perception than at others.[18]

Your mood (or set) or your readiness to perceive in a certain way affects your ability to perceive and accept a stimulus. This set, or mood, causes you to select for attention or notice those things that agree with such a set. Look for a *vase* in Figure 2.2. You should find it very quickly because that is, after all, what you were looking for.

Now look at the *vase* again, only this time, it's not a *vase;* it's two *faces!* One face is on the left, the other on the right, looking directly at each other. Do you get the message? Some messages conjure up quite different meanings for different people.

The consciousness may even defend itself by refusing to accept certain messages. On the other hand, we may wish so much to hear something that, regardless of the actual message, we hear, interpret, and attach meaning to it according to what we wish to hear. One of the great barriers to good communication is the

**FIGURE 2.2**

tendency to hear what we wish to hear, see what we wish to see, and believe what we wish to believe—all examples of *self-fulfilling prophecy*.

A closely related perceptual and communication problem arises from our normal tendency toward sensible completeness. In communications that appear to be only partially complete, we often fill in the unsaid part or complete the pattern. If we do not have a sense of completeness about something, we often feel upset, ill at ease, confused, or unhappy about it. This tendency can be an important way to motivate people. Perhaps you had a teacher who communicated just enough knowledge in a stimulating way to motivate you to do further reading and research so that you could complete or close the pattern. A problem arises when we close incomplete communication patterns in ways not intended or when we become frustrated by confusion or a lack of details. Is it easier to see the left-hand part of Figure 2.3 as several strange marks, or can you fill in the missing information and find the wrench? Some patterns of reality make no sense at all in terms of what we know as reality. Engineers experience special frustration with the right-hand part of Figure 2.3.

**FIGURE 2.3**

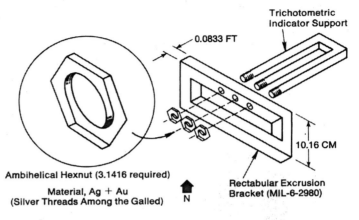

Trichotometric
Indicator Support

0.0833 FT

10.16 CM

Ambihelical Hexnut (3.1416 required)

Material, Ag + Au
(Silver Threads Among the Galled)

N

Rectabular Excrusion
Bracket (MIL-6-2980)

The "Trichotometric Indicator" courtesy NAA "Operations & Service News."

Even the way we perceive colors depends on our immediate physical field. Are the grays in Figure 2.4A the same? Our experience with distance and assumptions of consistency distort our perceptions of reality. But then what is reality? Are the poles in Figure 2.4B the same size?

**FIGURE 2.4A**          **FIGURE 2.4B**

**FIGURE 2.5**

Test your perceptual ability in Figure 2.5. Do you see anything familiar or identifiable? Do you see a message?

You should see a word in white on a partial black field. Your experience is usually just the opposite of this pattern in which the area between the letters is black instead of the letters themselves being black.[19] Even after you see the message it may escape you momentarily as your long-standing habits and previous patterns of experience assert themselves.

Experience should help you the next time. Let's see. Can you decode Figure 2.6? You've had practice! Stretch your experience a little.

Let's try another example of manipulating our set in order to affect what we see. Can you all see the young woman in Figure 2.7A?

Now study Figure 2.7B. You should find the young woman quickly because you've been *preset*. But do you also see the old hag? Your prior set didn't include her, and she should thus prove more difficult to find.

**FIGURE 2.6**

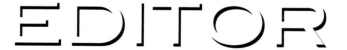

**FIGURE 2.7A**          **FIGURE 2.7B**          **FIGURE 2.7C**

R. W. Leeper, "A Study of a Neglected Portion of the Field of Learning: The Development of Sensory Organization," *Journal of Genetic Psychology*, 46, (1935), 41-75; see also Julian E. Hochberg, Perception (Englewood Cliffs, N.J.: Prentice-Hall, Inc., 1964), p. 70.

You should find the old hag easily in Figure 2.7C. Now perhaps it's easier to find her in Figure 2.7B, the composite picture. This picture is what E. G. Boring referred to as an *ambiguous stimulus*. R. W. Leeper performed this experiment with groups of subjects and confirmed the effect of *prior set:* Previous exposure to either version resulted in its being found first in the composite picture.

As we know from *self-fulfilling prophecy* your expectations obviously control a large part of what you see and understand. Figure 2.8 may have little meaning for you; but if you turn to the end of this chapter and look at Figure 2.14, you will be shown what you are "expected" to see. Then, theoretically at least, you will "see." If you haven't seen it by now, you may actually become annoyed, particularly if you've asked for help and your friends see something immediately. Communication is like that. We don't do our best when we begin to

**FIGURE 2.8**

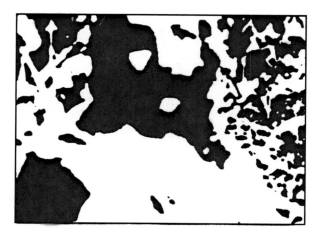

feel awkward, stupid, or left out. How are you doing with EDITOR? Have you lost it? When experiences are new to us, we may understand or "see" one moment and "not see" the next.

## Perceiving People

For Carl Rogers every individual exists in a continually changing world of experience in which he or she is the center. Whether this world is called the phenomenal field or the experiential field, humans exist in a sea of experiences, both conscious and unconscious. For Rogers, this is a private world that can really be known only by the individual. The way each person perceives his or her private world is reality for that person. We do not react to absolute reality but rather to our perception of reality. "We live by a perceptual 'map,' which is never reality itself."[20]

All people's perceptions are concerned with what might be called relationship communication since the meanings grow, to a large extent, from the notions we form about others while actively interacting with them.[21] There is also, of course, a content aspect; and both are ever present. Watzlawick and Beavin capture this distinction in the following:

If woman A points to woman B's necklace and asks, "Are those real pearls?", the content of her question is a request for information about an object. But at the same time she also gives—indeed, cannot not give—her definition of their relationship. How she asks (especially, in this case, the tone and stress of voice, facial expression, and context) would indicate comfortable friendliness, competitiveness, formal business relations, etc. B can accept, reject, or redefine, but cannot under any circumstances—even by silence—not respond to A's message. A's definition may, for instance, be a catty, condescending one; B, on the other hand, may react to it with aplomb or defensiveness. It should be noticed that this part of their interaction has nothing to do with the definitions of the nature of their relationship, although they may continue to talk about pearls.[22]

Oliver Wendell Holmes explained the problems of people perception as the impressions and notions two individuals might have of each other's, and their own, personalities.[23] He labeled the personalities John and Thomas and suggested that there are *three* Johns: (1) the real John, known only to his maker; (2) John's ideal John, never the real one and often very unlike him; and (3) Thomas's ideal John, never the real John, nor John's John, but often very unlike either. There are, of course, three equivalent Toms. To Holmes's three categories we can add a *fourth,* "John's Tom's John"—that is, John's notion of what Tom's notion is of him (see Figure 2.9).

Let's analyze the explanation in more detail. The real John (or real Tom) becomes an important philosophical concept if John feels that John's John is his own reality. If John's John is John's notion of himself, his self-concept, and if self-concepts can be incorrect, then John's John can also be incorrect. The model is useful in making this point clear: the real John and John's John do not overlap completely. That the circles overlap at all indicates that John's notion of himself is, at least in part, fair to the facts. We could argue about how much the two circles should overlap for the average person. If the circles did not overlap at all, the model would suggest that John's self-concept was in no way related to reality, and psychologists would probably label John schizoid. This is not to say that all of us do not lose touch at some time or another with some topic or with some person. That brings us to John's Tom (or Tom's John), which is John's notion of Tom (or vice versa). John's notion may or may not be accurate, depending upon how well he knows Tom and how objective he is. If he does not know Tom very well, he had better pay close attention to him and seek feedback to improve his evaluation. If John did not

**FIGURE 2.9**

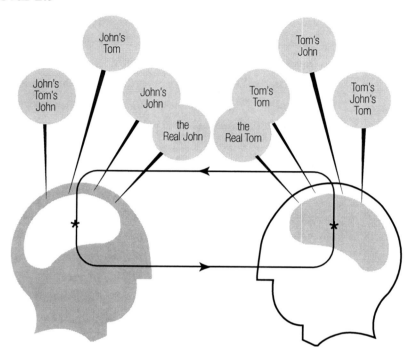

know Tom at all, he would normally proceed with a very tentative, general, or stereotyped notion. The danger of stereotypes is now obvious! Our notions of each other certainly affect our interaction with each other.

Now let's consider what the participants *think* the other person thinks of them. As will be discussed shortly, that is an important part of how one's self-concept develops. John's Tom's John is John's notion of what Tom's notion is of him—what John thinks Tom thinks of him. From Tom's point of view it is what Tom thinks John thinks of him (Tom's notion of what John's notion is of him). If either of these notions is much in error, Tom and John may have some very unusual, confusing, perhaps even unfortunate interaction ahead of them. With this much complexity is it any wonder that we have misunderstandings with one another?

Feedback, both verbal and nonverbal, is very important to John's and to Tom's attempts to communicate and interact in an objective, prudent, and non-threatening way. It is important that we be our best *self*, yet an honest and realistic best self, or we may quickly offend people. If a phony self is momentarily successful, it will almost always catch up with us in future interactions. We can also see in the model that John's John is also affected by Tom's John—or at least by John's Tom's John (John's notion of what Tom's notion is of him)—and vice versa.

It is obvious that our communication with others is heavily biased and shaped by the relationships we have with others—more specifically, how we *perceive* or experience the relationships. For R. D. Laing the *experiencing* is the critical part of communication. *Experience* is the feeling that accompanies the perception of another's behavior. It is personal and involves past experiences, perceptual ability, and imagination. It is inferred and, as we discovered with John and Tom, difficult and complicated. Laing puts it bluntly: "I see you, and you see me. I experience you, and you experience me. I see your behavior. You see my behavior. But I do not and never have and never will see your *experience* of me."[24]

Laing sharpens the Holmes' example (he uses Jack and Jill) by operationally defining the three related concepts of *understanding, being understood,* and *feeling understood.*

*Understanding* involves one's direct perspective with the metaperspective of another. If Tom sees himself as liked by John (a direct perspective), and John's perception of Tom is one of a person who knows he is liked (by John), then we have *understanding* (see Figure 2.10, Perceptions of Understanding).

*Being understood* involves the metaperspective of one person and the meta-metaperspective of the other. If Tom thinks John thinks Tom likes him, and if John thinks Tom thinks that he (John) thinks that Tom thinks he (John) likes him, we have Laing's notion of "being understood."

*Feeling understood* as opposed to being understood involves an individual's direct perspective and his own meta-metaperspective. If Tom thinks he is liked by John and also thinks John knows that fact—then Tom is *feeling understood*. How good we are at *people* perception clearly has a lot to do with our relationships with

**FIGURE 2.10    PERCEPTIONS OF UNDERSTANDING**

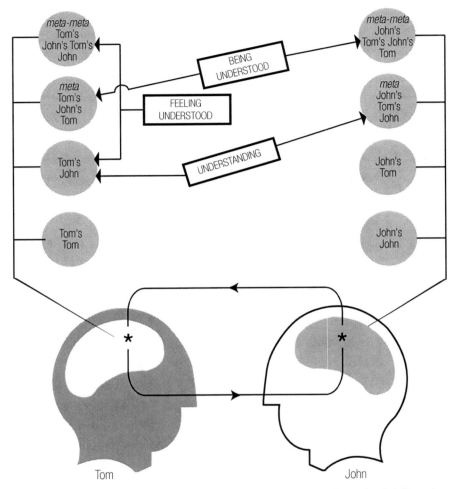

For explication see R. O. Laing, H. Phillipson, and A. R. Lee, *Interpersonal Perception: A Theory and Method of Research*, (London: Tavistock Publications, 1966; New York: Springer Publishing Company, Inc. 1966, 1972), Chap. III, "The Spiral of Reciprocale Perspectives."

others. Being good at perception of others has a lot to do with how we perceive ourselves.

# KNOWING OURSELVES

We have learned of our need for others; now we shall learn that we need others to discover and know who we are. Some social psychologists tell us that the process of inferring attributes about ourselves is much the same as the process of inferring attributes about others.[25]

We have also learned about the tricky business of perceiving events, things, and others. Now we look specifically at how we go about perceiving ourselves and how this knowledge can help us make better perceptions of and better inferences about others. Getting to know ourselves and determining our personal attributes is what self-perception and self-concept are about. *Attribution theory* involves not only our personal attributes, but also how we infer the personal attributes of others.

## Self-perception and Self-concept

How we perceive ourselves is important because it helps control our actions. It partially determines how an individual will behave and then perceive and evaluate that behavior. The principles of *self-fulfilling prophecy* apply to self-perceptions as well as perceptions of others. For example, if an individual perceives himself or herself to be uncoordinated, then that individual's behavior will reflect that belief. The individual will shun or at least avoid athletics and may even resent physical education. In contrast, an individual with similar physical coordination capabilities who perceives himself or herself to be adequately coordinated will be more likely to enjoy athletics and display a greater athletic prowess. Thus, self-concept can affect performance; and although the persons possess equal ability, the second individual may appear more coordinated. Self-concept can affect not only one's attitude, but also one's achievement and performance.[26] In a sense, self-concept directs the outcomes of our lives.

**Self-concept** has been defined as "the sum total of the view which an individual has of himself. Self-concept is a unique set of perceptions, ideas, and attitudes that an individual has of himself."[27] It is both conscious and unconscious, and it changes with our most recent experiences and self-perceptions. We use words such as *self-perception, self-concept,* and *self-identity* to talk about one's notion of oneself.[28] However, words such as *self-esteem, self-valuation,* and *self-regard* are of a slightly different order. We tend to think of these as positive or negative traits. A related term is *self-acceptance*. A person with high self-acceptance exhibits a willingness to accept both positive and negative notions as a part of his or her total self-concept. A discussion of some of the major influences of self-perception and self-concept follows.

**SIGNIFICANT AND GENERALIZED OTHERS**    A large portion of our self-concept is shaped by interactions and social comparisons with others, competence, judgments, and feelings from the clues we observe or infer from others—a word or look of approval, an honest criticism, even the appearance of another.[29] We thus develop concepts of our physical, emotional, and social selves; and we tend to perceive, respond, act, and communicate to a considerable extent using this complex self-image. Our self-perceptions are most affected by **significant others** or the individuals that play a significant role in our lives such as parents and teachers. We are also affected by **generalized others** or the social group or community as a whole that surrounds us. Generalized others are the individuals and groups of individuals that your mother refers to when she says, "What will *people* think?" For the most part we try to be consistent in our self-concept. However, when we are extremely frustrated, perhaps by too positive or too negative a self-concept, we may resort to various unrelated behaviors to compensate for our frustration. (For example, we may become over-talkative when insecure.) A realistic self-image can be a critical part of communication and perception as well as of motivation in general. Every person is the center of his or her own field of experience, and the way one perceives and responds to that field is one's own reality.

Research suggests that an unreasonable or unrealistic self-concept, particularly one low in self-esteem, may contribute to failure, thereby acting as a kind of self-fulfilling prophecy. A student who will not even discuss a math course because his or her self-concept says that he or she is mathematically illiterate is not apt to do well in a math course. This is tragic when *only* a student's poor opinion of himself or herself stands in the way of success. However, suppose a student really has little or no math aptitude. Were this person to develop an unrealistically positive conception of his or her mathematical ability, then he or she would obviously be headed for frustration and ultimately an even poorer self-concept than the original one.

The point is that your self-concept, whether good or bad, high or low, should be within the realm of physical or social reality. Knowing what is *realistic* as well as what is unique is, of course, the eternal problem.

**Self-Efficacy** or your sense of *competence* is also related to your self-concept. [30] "Competence means capacity, fitness, or ability. The competence of a living organism means its fitness or ability to carry on those transactions with the environment which result in its maintaining itself, growing and flourishing."[31] A self-concept that includes a feeling of incompetence or lacking sufficient *self-efficacy* may leave you in a state of helplessness and inertia and promote a sense of inferiority. You must build realistic confidence, as well as competence, leading into enhanced *self-efficacy* into your self-concept. A persistent challenge to your sense of personal and social competence is a prime contributor toward frustration and, not infrequently, aggression. Your self-efficacy is important to your interaction and communication with others.

## Communication and Self-Concept

The *situational* influences upon our self-concept and our total personality include those exceptional, unpredictable, and often accidental events that happen to all of us. These are events that can alter our lives, casting us into *roles* that may profoundly affect our self-concept—a jail sentence, a lost love, a scholarship, a riot, an insight or perspective suddenly and never before achieved. A really good teacher probably alters the lives and careers of many unsuspecting students. An unexpected failing grade or a hard-won A from such a teacher can either shake or make our self-concept.

**Role** pertains, in part, to a more specific aspect of group membership and is also thought to have a strong influence on self-concept. Some roles are cast upon us by society because of our age, our sex, our size, and unfortunately, sometimes our race. Some roles we assign ourselves on the basis of our life goals; and some are really disguises of our private personalities, disguises that we create in order to be accepted by certain groups. In its most important sense a role is that part we cast for ourselves on the stage of life. We may portray many roles to the world, but each of us determines, with the aid of society and its subgroups, what our particular role will be. Our self-concept is influenced by decisions we make in regard to how we present ourselves to others.

How others feel about us, or at least how we think they feel about us—particularly if they are *significant others,* whether reference groups, respected friends, or even those whose roles are ill defined—is probably the most important part of self-concept. What these others expect of us, how they react to us, and how socially realistic we are in evaluating these expectations and reactions form a large part of our self-concept.

Self-concept is a major part of one's **personality**. We may consider *personality* to be the sum of a person's knowledge, motives, values, beliefs, and goal-seeking patterns.

Human communication is affected by self-concept in several interesting ways. In general, we can expect others to perceive and react to us, and the rest of the world, in ways that are as consistent with their self-concepts as possible. Trying to "see" and understand others by understanding what their self-concepts are thus becomes a characteristic of sensitive human communication. We all should occasionally reevaluate our *own* self-concepts in terms of physical and social reality. Sometimes we either downgrade ourselves or take ourselves too seriously.

If the *self-regard* part of our self-concept is unusually negative, we might very well become difficult, negative, or even sullen communicators. An unrealistically positive *self-valuation* can, of course, make us different but equally painful communicators. A healthy, reality-centered, positive self-concept should, other things being equal, make us better and more confident communicators. Most important, it should include some willingness to accommodate change.

In review, a good self-concept is objective, realistic, positive, and yet self-accepting; it can live with negative notions, too. A healthy self-concept should include some willingness to change, a tolerance for confusion, patience with disagreement, and empathy for other self-concepts. If you are a "significant other" for someone, if only for a moment, you have a special communication responsibility, for we are reasonably sure that such individuals are a key to the development of one's self-concept.

## Self-presentation

> All the world's a stage, and all the men and women merely players.
> —Shakespeare, *As You Like It*

The creative sociologist Erving Goffman puts it more bluntly than Shakespeare.

> Indeed, it seems that we spend most of our time not engaged in giving information but in giving shows. And observe, this theatricality is not based on mere displays of feelings or faked exhibitions of spontaneity or anything else by way of the huffing and puffing we might derogate by calling theatrical. The parallel between stage and conversations is much, much deeper than that. The point is that ordinarily when an individual says something, he is not saying it as a bold statement of fact on his own behalf. He is recounting. He is running through a strip of already determined events for the engagement of his listeners.[32]

**IMPRESSION MANAGEMENT**    There are three parts to one's performance: an appropriate front, dramatic realization, and a sense of mystification.[33]

*An Appropriate Front*    Hollywood worked hard on defining John Wayne through his appearance, manner, and, of course, the roles he played. It was a powerful front. Some think that John Wayne, the actor, ultimately became John Wayne, the man.

*Front,* then, is your general behavior, which is designed (or is natural) to better define (persuasively we hope) who you are. Parts of your personal front include factors such as appearance and manner. Your front also includes things over which you have only limited control, such as sex, age, and size. Your clothes, posture, gestures, facial expressions, and language patterns are more modifiable dimensions of your front.

Should John Wayne appear as an un-American spy or a real "bad guy," we'd probably have some very confused admirers.

Closer to home, consider a college senior preparing for an employment interview. This student may attempt an impression of maturity, self-confidence, dependability, and being knowledgeable. Should this person appear for the interview wearing dirty clothes and profanely using the English language, quite a different front would be created.

*Dramatic Realization*    According to Goffman we must clearly realize the role expected of us and work it into the performance.[34] We may have to be talented actors to hide our lack of confidence.

If the role calls for attentiveness, we had better give such an impression. We may be paying attention; but if we are not perceived that way, however, it is unfortunate impression management. A patient may view a flippant physician who writes a fast prescription, however accurate the quick diagnosis, suspiciously.

***Mystification***   This notion of impression management refers to perceptions of social distances between the actor and the audience. The physician in the above example is more apt to be concerned with this kind of impression than the interviewee mentioned in the previous section. That is, the physician must not become too familiar lest he lose some of the mystery of the medical role. The college student, however, must accommodate the real or fancied social distance factors in the theater in which he finds himself.

## Self-disclosure

Politicians, advertisers, and students of persuasion know full well that their strategies are only as good as their information about the receivers. All interpersonal communication starts (or should start) with at least some *guesstimate* of where the other person is coming from. It would be convenient if everyone we were interested in simply disclosed everything about themselves—or would it? A first or second date might be a little less exciting without any surprises. It has been suggested that too much self-disclosure, even among married couples, causes some difficulty.[35] Social Penetration Theory allows us to understand how much and what type of disclosure we share with others at different stages of relationships.[40] *Social Penetration* is the process of increasing disclosure as a relationship develops.

The professional listeners—therapists, counselors, and clinicians—surely want all the disclosure they can get often from people truly threatened by even the thought of self-disclosure. Some therapists define an unwillingness to disclose as a "sickness" and suggest a transparent openness to achieve adjustment and health.[36-39] This is, of course, a very special context. A healthy openness from healthy people is one thing, but playing therapist and expecting or demanding self-disclosure (as in some encounters) does not facilitate interpersonal communication. These demanding interpersonal encounters have been described as a "tyranny of openness" by some social psychologists.[40]

***Openness***    What is a healthy openness? So very much depends upon the relationship you have with the other person. Some types of relationships may be described as **necessary,** others as **discretionary.** If you have a job, it is *necessary* to relate to your boss in at least some pragmatic, job-related way. It is not necessary that you relate in matters of a more personal nature, such as your politics and your feelings toward others. You have, of course, some *discretion* here (as does your boss). Knowing when to exercise that discretion, on what topics, how much disclosure, and so forth, is a cornerstone of interpersonal relations.

Since relating and interacting is a mutual transaction, listening is part of the decision. How much should I listen to non-necessary topics? Will I build a false intimacy? Will I encourage a dependency? Will I communicate a misleading sympathy for an idea or feeling? Perhaps there are times when I should not listen ...

Discretionary relationships involve mostly beliefs, attitudes, and emotions. Good marriages have necessary topics over which there is less discretion possible—the rent, the children, the dinner schedule, and so forth. These relationships should have a much higher degree of openness and self-disclosure than the more superficial but necessary relationships on the job.

These types of relationships might also be described as levels. The *necessary* would include a level described as practical, pragmatic, biographic—an information exchange. The *discretionary* would be at a higher level, involving beliefs and the more affective feelings and attitudes. As an example, the work line stops at the box factory:

*Superintendent:* What goes on here?

*Foreman:* Number three glue machine wasn't reloaded properly. (A necessary information exchange.)

*Superintendent:* It's the union attitude toward productivity! (A belief disclosure.)

*Foreman:* It's those damn affirmative action hires. (Disclosure of feelings.)

*Big boss:* Will you stop the yacking and build some boxes! (All types and levels?)

**FIGURE 2.11**     THE DISCLOSURE CURVE

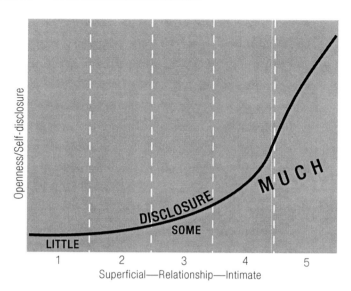

Given the situational and context qualifications illustrated above, let's attempt to get a perspective on an appropriate amount of openness and disclosure for relationships ranging from superficial to intimate, whether they be viewed as necessary or discretionary (see Figure 2.11).

There is also a short- and long-range dimension to self-disclosure. Manipulation of this knowledge by charlatans, even to intimacy, has led to short-term gains or advantages but usually long-term relationship disasters. Unintended or weak-moment disclosures can make or break relationships in both the short and/or the long term. How then should one proceed? Suggestions and systems follow in the next section.

## Interactive Understanding: The Johari Window

We need some level of disclosure to have any kind of relationship, even a pragmatic *necessary* one. For a long term, intimate relationship we obviously need mutual (reciprocal) open communication and self-disclosure. How much openness is appropriate? What type of openness is appropriate for the majority of our relationships (which are not intimate)? Much depends on whether we are building a relationship, just maintaining one, or perhaps easing out of one.

One model of interactive understanding that allows you to examine your relationship with another is the Johari Window (see Figure 2.12). It is named after its creators, Joseph Luft and Harrington Ingham.[41] It gives you an intrapersonal as well as an interpersonal perspective on what may be going on. The window has four panes: one clear glass, one opaque, one mirrored on the inside (one-way glass), and one mirrored on the outside. The model panes refer to the knowledge, beliefs, attitudes, and feelings that are part of your personality. Most importantly, the model refers to the extent you desire to share or are able to share such information. A better view through the window might appear as shown in Figure 2.12.

The panes are dependent upon one another. When one changes, the others change. As you disclose more **open self,** you have fewer secrets—**hidden self**—and the panes change accordingly. Healthy relating and reacting should primarily be related to the people, the situation, and the context. Your relationship analysis should direct the appropriate interactional openness and self-disclosure.[42] Nevertheless, some people seem to be more open across a great many situations and contexts. Others are more secretive. Personality attributions without a great many observations

**FIGURE 2.12    THE FOUR SELFS**

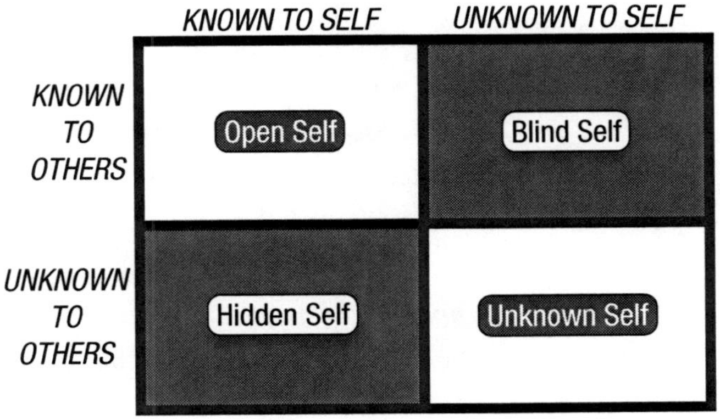

can be false. However, the model creators imply that all of us have "model"-size panes (perhaps constructs) that direct our behavior.

The **blind self** is that part of yourself that you don't know about or perhaps don't want to know about. A lazy person may not perceive himself or herself as lazy and may even tune out communication that suggests he or she is. A person not aware of body odor might shrink this blind spot very quickly when given a bar of soap. The **unknown self** or *nobody knows* area is a little more unusual. An undiscovered prodigy may pick up a musical instrument and surprise everyone with his or her talent. You may learn in your statistics class that you have a propensity for numbers. This works both ways; you may not know that you don't know. You may think you have the patience, manipulative dexterity, and so forth to become a great surgeon; but a life experience, a dexterity test, or perhaps an organic chemistry class may help you and others know your real self.

The window panes change in size as the relationship varies or changes. A long-term, intimate relationship of the type discussed earlier would probably be characterized by openness and self-disclosure by both parties. The open-self pane would be large, and the hidden or secret-self pane small. If your true friend offers feedback on what you don't know, your "blind self" might also be smaller. The unknown area may or may not change. It is probably smaller among people who know themselves and are sensitive to the world around them. A person involved in the relationship above might be windowed as shown in Figure 2.13.

## Dimensions of Self-Disclosure

*Is it a "necessary" or a "discretionary" disclosure?*    This is not always an easy question to answer because of the content or situation. An intimate disclosure about your estranged wife is surely discretionary unless you are involved in therapy or counseling, in which case it may be necessary. Disclosing your income, investments, and bills is necessary disclosure when dealing with the IRS, but discretionary for most other contexts. The important thing is to sense the difference.

*Is it a long- or short-term relationship?*    In some new encounters you may not really know. Some short-term relationships become long-term ones. Some of

**FIGURE 2.13    AN OPEN RELATIONSHIP**

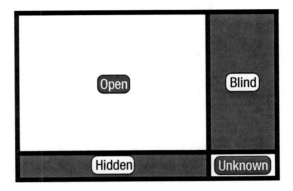

my students were one-course relationships that are long gone except for homecoming and other nostalgic moments. A smaller number have become lifelong friends. The short-term relationships are usually more superficial; the longer-term relationships may be more intimate, but not necessarily. Some long-time neighbors may enjoy a relationship that is pretty much superficial or somewhere between superficial and intimate. The guideline is that the amount of openness and disclosure usually increases as the relationship becomes more intimate. A good way to keep a short-term relationship short term is to disclose nothing; another way is to disclose too much intimate information too soon.

***What are the risks?*** The risks are not only to yourself and the relationship, but also to the other person or persons. Is there trust? Does the disclosure end here or have you told the world? Does it matter? Are you being pressured? "I've disclosed to you, now you've got to disclose." Is your disclosure compensatory? Are you apt to be sorry later? Have you disclosed enough? One may injure a relationship by appearing difficult to understand.

***What is the message/relationship importance?*** Do you value the message disclosed in the same way as the relationship involved, or in some cases is the relationship more important than the message? Perhaps we sometimes disclose more to the bartender or a stranger on an airplane because the relationship is short term and not all that important. A close and respected priest may not hear much social disclosure about your changing opinions on birth control because the relationship is all that important. Forthright discussions of necessary differences of opinions are to be applauded. However, if they preclude further discussions by destroying a relationship, you have a need to pause. Perhaps the relationship isn't worth the effort or the constraint. Perhaps the message pertains to only a small discretionary part of the relationship and you are well-advised not to disclose all.

## SUMMING UP

Isolation is a terrible thing. Life is no good alone; we need others. We need people for love, reassurance, approval, a sense of reality, and, most critically, communication, even if it is simply a nonverbal presence.

First impression decisions are very important. Even when aware of the risks, we really have little choice in many interactions if we are to meet our overwhelming need to make sense of the very complex social world in which we live. This need leads us to speculate about people's traits and attributes. These constructions help us decide all kinds of appropriate behaviors. This tendency to organize and synthesize cues has been described as *implicit theories of personality.* This tendency leads us to draw conclusions about people, often after only a minimal observation. Attribution theorists suggest that we should spend less time on inferred dispositions and more time on specific observation of actions, contexts, and consequences. Life is full of interdependent relationships. It is through coordination, patience, and communication that we may achieve action.

*Inclusion, control,* and *affection* are our primary social needs; they go a long way toward determining how we behave and relate to others. Inclusion deals with such things as attention, acknowledgement, recognition, prominence, identity, and participation. Control is communicated by behaviors expressing leadership, power, ac-

**FIGURE 2.14**

complishment, and intellectual superiority. The flavor of affection is embodied in "situations of love, emotional closeness, personal confidences, and intimacy."[43]

Research on the helping function for therapists, counselors, and teachers suggests that those most likely to be helpful are proficient at skills such as listening, empathic understanding, expressing positive regard, genuineness, and giving feedback.

Perception is sensation and interpretation. Subliminal perception is the reception of impressions below the level of awareness. Our mood (or set) affects what we perceive. One of the great barriers to communication is our tendency to hear, see, and believe what we wish to hear, see, and believe. All people's perceptions are concerned with relationship communication since the meanings grow, to a large extent, from the notions we form about others while actively interacting with them. There is also a content aspect; both are ever present. Our communication is heavily biased and shaped by the relationship we have with others—that is, how we perceive or experience the relationship. Experience is the feeling that accompanies the perception of another's behavior. Three critical states are *understanding, being understood,* and *feeling understood.*

The process of inferring attributes about ourselves is much the same as inferring attributes about others. Self-concept is the sum total of the view that we have of ourselves. It affects not only our attitude, but also our achievement and performance. Competence means capacity, fitness, or ability. Sense of competence is related to self-concept. Also related are significant others, group memberships, social roles we play, and the situations in which we find ourselves.

The three parts to one's impression management are an appropriate front, dramatic realization, and a sense of mystification.

Openness is related to relationships, some of which are necessary while others are discretionary. We need some disclosure to have any kind of relationship, even the necessary ones. How much openness depends on whether we are building a relationship, just maintaining one, or perhaps easing out of one. The Johari Window gives an interpersonal perspective on what may be happening. The four panes refer to the knowledge, beliefs, attitudes, and feelings that are part of an individual's personality—open, blind, hidden, and unknown. The window panes change in size as a relationship varies; they are interdependent, too. A "when to disclose" inventory includes: Is it a necessary or a discretionary one? Is it a long or short term relationship? What are the risks? What is the message/relationship importance?

## NOTES

1 Stanley Schachter, *The Psychology of Affiliation* (Stanford, Calif.: Stanford University Press, 1959), pp.9-10.

2 Alain Bombard, *The Bombard Story,* trans. Brian Connell (London: Andre Deutsch, 1953), p. 144.

3 Seipke, H. (2008) Assisted Living, elderly Women and Sense of Self: Communicating the Impact of Reduction of Long-Standing Activities. *Journal of Women and Aging,* Vol. 20, 1/2 , p. 131-148.

4 William Schutz, Firo: *A Three Dimensional Theory of Interpersonal Behavior* (New York: Holt, Rinehart & Winston, 1958), p. 13.

5 Ibid. p. 22.

6 Ibid. p. 23.

7 Ibid. p. 24.

8 From the fable of the blind men and the elephant.

9 A. P. Bochner and Janet Yerby, "Focus on Teaching Interpersonal Skills," *Communication Education,* 26, no. 2 (March 1977), 91-103.

10 Charles B. Truax and Kevin M. Mitchell, "Research on Certain Therapist Interpersonal Skills in Relation to Process and Outcome," in *Handbook of Psychotherapy and Behavior Change,* eds. A. E. Bergin and S. L. Garfield (New York: John Wiley and Sons, Inc., 1971), pp. 299-344. Robert R. Carkhuff, *The Development of Human Resources* (New York: Holt, Rinehart and Winston, 1971), pp. 284-307, David Berenson, "The Effects of Systematic Human Relations Training Upon the Classroom Performance of Elementary School Student Teachers," *Journal of Research and Development in Education,* 4 (1971), 70-85.

11 Carl R. Rogers, *On Becoming a Person* (Boston: Houghton Mifflin Co" 1961), p. 40.

12 Ibid. pp. 50-56.

13 Solomon E. Asch, "Forming Impressions of Personality," *Journal of Abnormal and Social Psychology,* 41 (1946), 258-90.

14 Harold H. Kelley, "The Warm-Cold Variable in First Impressions of Persons," *Journal of Personality,* 18 (1950), 431-39.

15 Wegner, D.M., & Vallacher, R.R. (1977). *Implicit psychology: An introduction to social cognition.* New York: Oxford University Press.

16 Ibid.

17 Spitzberg, B.H. (2001). The status of attribution theory qua theory in personal relationships. In B. Manusov & J.H. Harvey (Eds.) *Attribution, communication behavior, and close relationships* (pp. 353-371). Cambridge, UK: Cambridge University Press.

18 R. S. Lazarus and R. A. McCleary, "Automatic Discrimination without Awareness: A Study in Subception," *Psychological Review,* 58 (1951), 113-22.

19 This is referred to as a *figure-ground transformation.* The word is EDITOR.

20 Carl R. Rogers, *Client-Centered Therapy* (Boston: Houghton Mifflin Company, 1951), p. 485.

21 John Stewart, "An Interpersonal Approach to the Basic Course," *The Speech Teacher,* 21, no. 1 (1972), 7-14. See also, John Stewart, *Bridges Not Walls,* 2nd ed. (Reading, Mass.: Addison-Wesley Publishing Co., Inc. 1977), chap. 1.

22 Paul Watzlawick and Janet Beavin, "Some Format Aspects of Communication," in *The Interactional View,* eds. p. Watztawick and J. H. Weakland (New York: W. W. Norton and Company, Inc. 1977), p. 61.

23 Oliver Wendell Holmes, *The Autocrat of the Breakfast Table* (Boston: Phillips, Simpson, 1858), p. 59.

24 R. D. Laing, *Politics of Experience* (New York: Pantheon Books, 1967), pp. 4-5; see also Dudley D. Cahn, "Feeling Understood as a Research Concept: An Alternative to Empathy," a paper presented at the Central States Speech Association Convention, Chicago, Illinois, April, 1981.

25 D. J. Bern, "Self-perception: An Alternative Interpretation of Cognitive Dissonance Phenomena," *Psychological Review,* 74 (1967), 183-200. See also H. H. Kelley, "Attribution Theory in Social Psychology," *Nebraska Symposium on Motivation,* ed. David Levine (Lincoln: University of Nebraska Press, 1967), 15, 192-240; E. E. Jones and E. Davis, "From Acts to Dispositions: the Attribution Process in Person Perception," in *Advances in Experimental Social Psychology,* ed. L. Berkowitz (New York: Academic Press, 1965), pp. 219-265.

26 See Shirley C. Samuels, *Enhancing Self-Concept in Early Childhood* (New York: Human Science Press, 1977), p. 36.

27 Donald W. Felker, *Building Positive Self-Concepts* (Minneapolis: The Burgess Publishing Co. 1974), p. 2.

28 John J. Sherwood, "Self Identity and Referent Others," *Sociometry,* 28 (1965), 66-81.

29 Mead, H. (1934). *Mind, self, and society: From the standpoint of a social behaviorist.* Chicago: University of Chicago Press.

30 Bandura, A. (1977). *Social learning theory.* Englewood Cliffs, NJ: Prentice-Hall.

31 Robert W. White assisted by Katherine F. Bruner, eds. *The Study of Lives* (New York: Atherton, 1966), p. 74.

32 Erving Goffman, Frame Analysis: *An Essay on the Organization of Experience* (Cambridge: Harvard University Press, 1974), p. 508.

33 Erving Goffman, *The Presentation of Self in Everyday Life* (Garden City, NY.: Doubleday and Company, Inc. 1959), p. 208.

34 Ibid. pp. 22, 30, 67.

35 G. Simmel, "The Secret and the Secret Society," in *The Sociology of Georg Simmel,* ed. K. Wolff (New York: Free Press, 1964), p. 329.

36 Zick Rubin, "Disclosing Oneself to a Stranger: Reciprocity and Its Limits," *Journal of Experimental Social Psychology,* 11 (1975), 233-260.

37 L. A. Hosman and C. H. Tardy, "Self-disclosure and Reciprocity in Short- and Long-Term Relationships: An Experimental Study of Evaluational and Attributional Consequences," *Communication Quarterly,* 38, no. 1 (Winter, 1980), 20-30.

38 L. Rosenfeld, "Self-Disclosure Avoidance: Why I Am Afraid to Tell You Who I Am," *Communication Monographs,* 46, no. 1 (March 1979), 63-74.

39 See Sidney Jourard, *Self-Disclosure: An Experimental Analysis of the Transparent Self* (New York: John Wiley & Sons, Inc. 1971); see also *The Transparent Self* (New York: Van Nostrand Reinhold Co., 1971).

40 I. Altman and D. A. Taylor, *Social Penetration* (New York: Holt, Rinehart & Winston, Inc., 1973).

41 Joseph Luft, *Of Human Interaction* (Palo Alto, Calif.: National Press Books, 1969), p. 6.

42 J. Delia, "Some Tentative Thoughts Concerning the Study of Interpersonal Relationships and Their Development," *Western Journal of Speech Communication,* 44, no. 2 (Spring 1980), 101.

43 Schutz, Firo: *A Three Dimensional Theory,* p. 24.

# CHAPTER 3

# MANAGING MEANING AND LANGUAGE

# GENERAL SEMANTICS AND LANGUAGE

> But then they danced down the street like dingledodies and I shambled
> after as I've been doing all my life after people who interest me, because
> the only people for me are the mad ones, the ones who are mad to live,
> mad to talk, mad to be saved, desirous of everything at the same time,
> the ones who never yawn or say a commonplace thing, but bum, bum,
> bum like fabulous yellow roman candles exploding like spiders across
> the stars and in the middle you see the blue center light pop and every-
> body goes, "Awww!"

A premier example of a run-on sentence! My eighth-grade composition
teacher, Miss Feinstein, would have "bled" all *over* my paper for writing such a
thing, and probably rightfully so! *However,* if we were to translate the sentence into
standard American sentence structure and language use, some of the texture of the
description would be lost and some of its richness destroyed. Jack Kerouac, a no-
table American writer, wrote that sentence in *On the Road*.[1]

## Language is a System of Symbols

The above run-on sentence helps illustrate a basic tenet of general semantics
theory: "An individual's assumptions, beliefs, and attitudes are a function of the
structure of his language, and that his perception and behavior will be affected
more or less in direct relationship to his susceptibility to influence by that language
structure."[2] We are not saying that language determines thought, but we are suggesting that language ability does allow us to represent much of our world.
Language arrests our world or "reality" and lets us conceptualize it, store it, and
later *retrieve* it if we so desire. We, in effect, can "bind time."[3]

Last semester a student and I argued *over* my educational philosophy in relation to an undergraduate course I was teaching. That particular instance doesn't
exist anymore; it's over. It happened last February; time marches on. I am able to
share aspects of that argument and that specific instance with you because I have
represented it with symbols. **Symbols** are signs or words we use to define something. We refer to the actual something, the event, the object as the **referent**.[4] In
this case the symbols I used were words. My language allows me to put the words

together in a fashion that permits you to get a "picture" of a reality that existed last February. Symbols allow me to represent an *event* that occurred in the past. The past isn't lost; I have, in effect, bound time through language.

Remember that my words are not the argument itself. They are a representation of it, much like a city map represents a city but is not the city itself. Ask anyone who has been lost in Chicago with map in hand.

Symbols and language allow us to represent and store realities. Our *knowledge* is a function of our language and symbols. I know what a chair is *even* when a chair is not present. I know what a chair is because I have stored a symbolic representation of one in my brain. Ogden and Richards call the thoughts we have about objects **references**. What I *have* stored is a thought or reference about a chair, not a real chair. The word is not the thing! Sometimes our representations of realities can cause us trouble. Remember, words (symbols) are **arbitrary**; there is not an obvious reason for why they represent what they refer to. There is nothing chair-like in the word *chair;* you can't sit on the word *chair.*

Figure 3.1 Shows Ogden and Richards semantic triangle, which was developed to show the relationship between symbols, references, and referents

Interpersonally we should be aware that different people may represent a single *event* (reality) differently, and a certain amount of interpersonal *sensitivity* may be necessary to understand another's concept of a particular *event.* My brother and I once shared a house with two other friends. They lived downstairs, and we lived in the upstairs apartment. My brother and I enjoy arguing philosophical issues with one another and basically view argument as an intellectual exercise and healthy sibling rivalry. During our friendly "fair fighting," we sometimes raise our voices somewhat above normal levels. Our friends in the apartment below heard us arguing and were convinced we were on the verge of disowning one another and were about to start a subtle family intervention program with us. It took us about two weeks before we could figure out what our friends were up to and another week or so to convince them that argument was a normal state of affairs for us and that we were not having a family crisis. The basic confusion was a problem of different conceptualizations of the reality. Our friends downstairs conceptualized the reality (loud argument) as unhealthy, and we conceptualized arguments (most of them) as healthy. Once we all became aware of our differing representations of the reality, we all breathed easier. The map is not the territory.[5]

**FIGURE 3.1    THE SEMANTIC TRIANGLE**

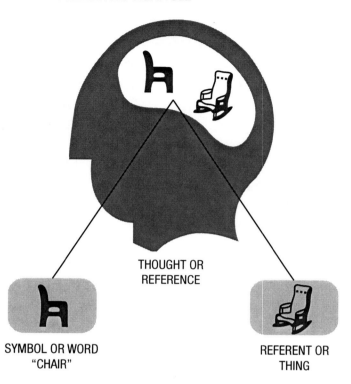

In addition to the problem of different representations of the same reality, realities themselves can change. I recently ran into an old friend we called Marty (short for Martha) whom I had not seen since college. Back in college, her goal was to be a ruthless businesswoman that made tons of money that she would not share with anyone like a husband and, certainly, not children. But here she was in the parking lot of Home Depot getting out of a minivan that contained four well groomed and behaved children, nothing like the person I remembered her to be. Our reunion went something like this:

"Marty?" I said.

"I go by Martha now, Heather! How you doing?" she said while holding one child and unbuckling the car seat of another.

"Fine … Martha, I'm sorry … you just look so different," I said, stumbling over my words. "So, ah, what are you doing now?"

"Oh, I taught first grade until my first was born and I've been a stay at home mom ever since. You?"

"I'm teaching communication."

"No kidding, I just read a book on parent child communication for my 'moms of four or more' book club"

Minivan? Book club? Agonizing reappraisal! When the territory changes, the old map is just no good.

## Semantics Theory Basic Premises: Nonidentity, Nonallness, Self-reflexiveness

General semantics theory provides the student of interpersonal communication with three valuable principles. The first is termed the principle of **nonidentity** (X is not X).[6] The principle of nonidentity corresponds to Korzybski's notion that the "map is not the territory." Remember, the word is not the thing; it is only a symbol and usually quite arbitrary at that.

The second general premise is the principle of **nonallness** (X is not all X).[7] The idea here is that while the map may represent the territory, it cannot possibly represent *all* the territory: " … no matter how much you say about some 'thing,' 'event,' 'quality,' or what not, you cannot say all about it."[8]

The third basic premise is the principle of **self-reflexiveness**.[9] This premise really begins to complicate our lives because it suggests that we necessarily must use language to talk about language. We use language to reflect on language.

## Problems in the Management of Meaning

General semantics theorists have given us a number of working devices or warnings about how our particular language use can affect the meanings we attribute to one another interpersonally. These devices point out the potential for imprecision in the fit between one person's meanings for symbols and another's. Good interpersonal communicators should be sensitive to these kinds of potential problems.

The is problem *is* related to the principle of nonidentity. While we usually use words to communicate, the words are not the things themselves. You can't drive around town in the word *Dodge*.

The *etc.* problem is related to the principle of nonallness. One can never have the last word on something. We humans tend to abstract. That is, we systematically leave out details when we recount experience. There is usually another angle to be explored. Don't presume you have the bottom line!

Our human capacity to abstract sometimes leads us into overgeneralization. The *index* rule cautions us against this. Not all used-car salespeople are alike. It's obvious that we shouldn't generalize. Sometimes we can also make generalization mistakes about individuals. Recall my friend Marty. Marty (college) was certainly not Martha (Home Depot parking lot). My mistake! We need to watch for stereotyping and to appreciate individual differences (both within and between individuals).

*Dating* your language is another form of indexing worthy of a special rule. The date of an event can significantly affect the meaning of an utterance. Take for example the word "sick". When my parents were teenagers in the 1950's and 1960's, sick meant not well. If someone was sick they were ill or under the weather. When I was a teenager in the 1980's and 1990's, "sick" meant gross, disgusting, gag me with a spoon. My daughter, who is a teenager now uses the word "sick" to mean good, bad (which also means good), wicked (also meaning good).

The *either-or* response is a type of overgeneralization usually indicating an individual is concealing differences of degree. Absolute rulers and demagogues use the following device: "You are either for me or against me." When we routinely use words such as *all, nobody,* and *never* ("They're all no good." "You'll never understand."), we are probably guilty of false-to-fact language use. The person guilty of these types of exaggerations runs great risks of creating resentment interpersonally.

## LANGUAGE HABITS

## Codes and Symbols

Different types of social systems or social structures tend to generate different speech systems, ways of talking, or language codes. Our particular language habits sometimes function to label us as members of certain speech communities. People often make initial attributions about us based on our particular language habits.

Not only are attributions made based on language codes, but they are also made on nonverbal codes. Gestures, dress, movements, and facial expressions tend to "place" us as members of a speech community.

## Restricted and Elaborated Codes[10]

Several years ago after moving into a new neighborhood I met two of my new neighbors. They were obviously close friends and were quite nice to me. Parts of our initial conversation went like this.

Gary:     How's about Trucker's tonight?

George:   A little stick, eh?

Gary:     Why not?

George:   Okay, mine or yours?

Gary:     Oh no! Every man for himself … wife, you know.

George:   (to me) Why don't you come along too?

Me:       Sounds great!

I knew I was committed to doing something that night, but for the life of me I had no idea what I would be doing or where. As it turned out, Trucker's was a bar (by another name) with a pool table (stick), and we drove two separate cars to get there. Gary's spouse wanted him home early that night, so he drove his own car.

What I experienced that afternoon was a clear example of a restricted code in operation. In restricted linguistic codes experience is not verbally elaborated.[11] George and Gary as close friends had a lot of shared experience—commonality. Their words functioned indexically. That is, a paucity of words functioned to index a realm of common experience (Trucker's, stick, etc.), to which I was not privy. Generally, but not always, the closer we are to people the more restricted our language codes become. Have you sometimes wondered why outsiders seem awkward!

With elaborated codes, meaning is elaborated verbally in greater detail. With these types of codes the speaker must presume the listener holds a set of experiences different from his or her own.[12] Sensitive interpersonal communication should be elaborative when appropriate.

## Abstraction

The fact that one word can index a realm of experience (as in the previous example) relates to our ability to abstract. Without this ability to abstract much of the interpersonal richness and fun in our lives would be missing. But sometimes abstraction can be a problem.

The heart of the difficulty with language is the confusion of the word with the thing for which it stands. The further we are from this thing—the referent—the more problems of meaning that arise. According to Ogden and Richards, meaning has three elements: a person having thoughts, a symbol, and a referent. The relationship was illustrated earlier with our chair example (Figure 3.1). The relationship between the symbol and the thought is a direct relationship. For example, I know what the word dog means. The relationship between the thought and the referent is also direct: I know what a four-legged canine is when I see one. The relationship between the symbol and the referent is indirect, though (hence the dotted line in the model). The relationship between the symbol and the referent is arbitrary. I could just as easily call a four-legged canine a "berfunkle" or a "perro." Why not? Even though *dog* (symbol) or the animal itself (referent) will elicit the thought (reference) in a person, the relationship between the symbol and referent is indirect. Again, the map (symbol) is not the territory (referent).

**Abstracting** is a process of thinking in which we *selectively leave out* details about concrete or real things. Perception has at least two elements—sensation and interpretation of this sensation. This interpretation is controlled by our individual knowledge, experience, and emotional set. For this reason, as well as because of the limitations of our language system discussed previously, all language contains an element of abstraction.

S.I. Hayakawa (1964) explains abstraction by placing language on a continuum from most concrete to most abstract. This continuum is represented in the **Ladder of Abstraction**[13] (Figure 3.2) in which the lowest rung represents the most concrete words and the highest rung represents the most abstract. This allows us to think of words in terms of low and high-levels of abstraction.

**FIGURE 3.2    LADDER OF ABSTRACTION**

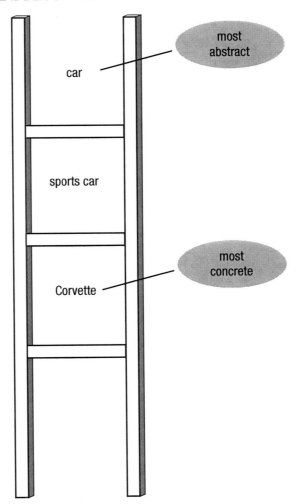

The process of abstraction occurs at different levels. For example, we have cars, sports cars, and Corvettes. The Corvette is a low-level abstraction (most concrete); that is, it is a specific type of sports car, which in turn is a type of car. As we move from lower-level to higher-level abstractions, we tend to consider fewer and fewer details of the specific, original object. Another way of looking at abstraction is to consider firsthand observations as facts, but as facts that may never be described completely. If we move away from firsthand descriptions, we will be in a different order of abstraction—inference. Most simply, an **inference** goes beyond what is observed. If an ambulance is in your driveway when you return home, you may say, "One of my family has been seriously hurt." This is an inference. You must go into the house to see if it is valid. Upon entering the house you may find a close friend excitedly telling your healthy family about his new business venture of converting station wagons into ambulances. The difficulty in co-ordinating and managing meaning between people should become apparent in relation to the abstraction process.

## CONTEXTUAL INFLUENCE ON UNDERSTANDING

### TWO HEAVY-EQUIPMENT OPERATORS

Roy: Put the yellow cat in the garage; leave the other one in the yard, and let's go to lunch.

Bud: Great. Nobody will steal that old sucker.

### TWO FELINE-LOVERS

Sarah:    Put the yellow cat in the garage; leave the other one in the yard, and let's go to lunch.

Robert: Great. I don't think that old timer will be gone when we get back.

The words are similar, but the meanings are clearly different. Roy and Bud are talking about Caterpillar bulldozers; Sarah and Robert obviously are not. Why is it obvious? Because we know the situation and context. Mix the contexts and we can have real confusion.

Sarah: Bud, you wouldn't put that sweet thing in the garage.

Bud: Why not? Nothing that big and ugly is sweet.

Sarah: You can go to lunch by yourself!

If Sarah and Bud are competent interpersonal communicators, they will be able to align their meanings with each other. While this example appears to be simple and straightforward, remember that you had clear clues. It is critical that we consider contextual clues before inferring meanings. Interpersonal communication operates in a multitude of contexts that are not always shared.

A favorite illustration of many teachers regarding coordinating meanings concerns a man staring sadly at a very flat tire. A smiling farmer comes up and asks, "Got a flat tire?" If we take his words literally, his communication appears stupid indeed; and we might answer, "Can't you see birdbrain?" However, a famous psychiatrist interprets "Got a flat tire?" as follows:

> Hello—I see you are in trouble. I'm a stranger to you but I might be your friend now that I have a chance to be if I had any assurance that my friendship would be welcomed. Are you approachable? Are you a decent fellow? Would you appreciate it if I helped you? I would like to do so but I don't want to be rebuffed. This is what my voice sounds like. What does your voice sound like?

There are also multiple levels to meaning. And if that's not enough, there are rule systems that both constitute and regulate our meanings. If we are using different rule systems, the cat may be back in the garage! Interpersonal communication is not always simple. Unfortunately, many people assume that it is.

When interpersonal communication fails or is only half clear, it is usually because we have been unable to coordinate our meanings. To communicate at all hinges upon our ability to infer meanings from contexts, signs, and symbols, and then to create and transmit them in such a way that they coordinate or mesh with the receiver's.

## Levels of Meaning (Meaning Hierarchies)

Our understanding process of behaviors, events, and symbols varies along a hierarchy of meaning.[14] Our meanings change with the levels we use to interpret a symbol or set of symbols. Pearce, Cronen, and Harris illustrate the hierarchy in a manner similar to our Figure 3.3.[15]

**FIGURE 3.3**    THE MEANING HIERARCHY AND ENVIRONMENT—RAW
SENSORY DATA *(WITH APOLOGIES TO CRONEN, PEARCE, AND
HARRIS)*

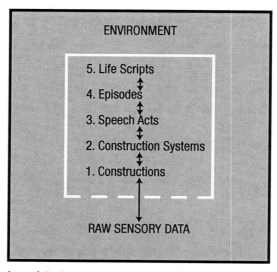

*The Meaning Hierarchy and Environment—Raw Sensory Data (with apologies to Cronen,
Pearce, and Harris).*

We all have hierarchies of meaning. These meaning systems aid us in ordering
and regularizing our environments and, hopefully, in making sense out of them.
The complex environments within which we all must operate are composed of a
pool of raw sensory data. These data have no meaning in and of themselves.
Analyzing environments may, of course, promote understanding; but environments have no inherent meanings—meanings are in us. We interpret the raw sensory data (symbols) in light of our own personal meaning hierarchies. These hierarchies work much like the frame of reference we discussed in the transactional
communication model in Chapter 1. Most of us have reasonably flexible hierarchies that allow us to move through the levels of meaning with relative ease.

The interpretation of our communication environments varies as a function of
where we decide to stop within our personal set of meaning levels. A discussion of
the basic levels of the meaning hierarchy should help clarify this point.

**CONSTRUCTIONS**   The *construction* level (number 1, Figure 3.3) of the hierarchy is basically a perceptual level. We perceive our environment and represent it cognitively. We do more than simply respond in and to our environment; we create representations or *constructions* of it.[16] For example, I can construe (have constructions for) automobiles. I have a perceptual image of 1950s vintage Chevrolets. A 1957 Chevy (referent) need not be physically present for me to have thoughts about it. I have a cognitive construction of the car.

**CONSTRUCTION SYSTEMS**   Constructions produce belief systems. If you construe data in an environment, you generate beliefs about what has been construed. To the extent that I have a construction or constructions for 1957 Chevys, I start developing beliefs about the cars. I can even start developing beliefs about the drivers of the cars: "Mid-fifties Chevys are both engineering and design marvels (belief$_1$); therefore, people who still own and drive such vehicles have both good mechanical and aesthetic senses (belief$_2$)."

What we are trying to illustrate here is a *construction system* (number 2, Figure 3.3)—a set of beliefs generated from an initial construction. Construction systems, therefore, are systems of beliefs that grow out of our constructions of raw sensory data. "Construction systems are the beliefs and purposes produced by constructs, organized into clusters that are related to particular beliefs."[17]

**SPEECH ACTS**   Speech acts (number 3, Figure 3.3) are overt communicative activities. Someone saying something to someone else is a speech act. The acts need not be solely verbal; nonverbal actions directed toward another also count.

Speech acts are the first truly communicative level of the meaning hierarchy. To do a speech act requires a communication action between at least two people. When the owner of a Ford dealership tells an employee to "prep those two new Explorers for the sales floor," a speech act has occurred. For the person to whom the utterance is directed to understand, he or she must have at least a construction for Explorer in order to carry out the task.

**EPISODES**   Episodes (number 4, Figure 3.3) are complexes of speech acts that are viewed as distinct entities by participants. They have been characterized as routines that have special rules for both verbal and nonverbal behavior.[18] "Checking out of the grocery store" might be called a communicative *episode*. There are rules that define and regulate the activity. We usually behave within a general set of rule parameters when purchasing groceries: standing in line, locating your ATM card, stacking groceries on the counter, and so forth.

If we conceptualize the "prep the two new Explorers for the sales floor" utterance under the episode of "selling new Explorers," we realize a set of rules that govern the activity (selling Explorers). People buying their first car are sometimes not as aware of the rule parameters as they should be. They usually become wiser by the time they buy their second car!

**LIFE SCRIPTS**   Life scripts (number 5, Figure 3.3) are sequences of episodes. These sequences function to sustain the general fabric of an individual's expectations. When going to a party composed of good friends, our expectations in terms of how the party will proceed and what will happen are related to the life script we attribute to the party.

If the episode we have termed "selling new Explorers" falls under the life script termed "running a dealership," it is one thing. It is something altogether different if it falls under the life script termed "grand theft, auto."

## Coordinating the Levels

The levels of the hierarchy are related to each other in that higher levels provide contexts for understanding the lower levels. For example, the speech act of a man screaming and waving his arms wildly in the middle of the street qualifies him as little more than a lunatic unless the speech act is given a context. If the episode that contextualized his speech act was jubilation over a Rose Bowl victory, the speech act makes sense; we understand. The act occurred within a context. To the degree that we as observers *don't* realize the context (episode), we see only lunacy.

People vary in their abilities to operate flexibly within hierarchies of meaning. To the extent that a person in an interpersonal communication environment fails to operate at the higher levels of the hierarchy, he or she is not communicatively competent within that particular environment. Cegala, for example, has found that while some people seem to be very *aware* in interpersonal communication settings, they are not very responsive in the settings.[19] They are *aware* in that they have strong explanatory constructs and construction systems, but they fail to contextualize their construction systems within speech acts. Without an ability to operate at the speech-act level, they feel awkward and hence are not very *responsive*. They are quiet!

This is not to say that a lack of communicative competence is always at fault or due to the incompetent person. Recall the earlier example involving my new neighbors, Gary and George. Although I was reasonably responsive—I engaged in speech acts—I was not very aware. I had little idea of what they were talking about because they spoke in a restricted code. I felt quite awkward interpersonally, simply because Gary and George had failed to allow me to index appropriate constructions and construction systems. In this sense I lacked communicative competence within the particular environment—although Gary and George could have helped a bit more. Figure 3.4 illustrates the relationship between communication environments, raw sensory data, and the hierarchy of meaning.

The two triangles in Figure 3.4 represent construct levels and communicative levels of the meaning hierarchy. Communicative levels give context to the construct levels. We get different meanings if we contextualize a construction at the speech-act level as opposed to at the life-script level.

Interpersonal communication is in large part an attempt to coordinate meanings between people. If person A is contextualizing a construction at the speech act level and person B is contextualizing at the episode level, there is room for a major mismatch. The competent interpersonal communicator is able to move through the meaning hierarchy in such a fashion as to best coordinate meanings. The two-headed arrow at the right of Figure 3.4 represents this ability to move through the meaning hierarchy. The two triangles can converge; and as they do, different communicative levels of the hierarchy give contexts to the construct levels of meaning.

It is clear that the management of meaning is no simple task. True interpersonal communication takes effort. In the next section we will talk about two different dimensions, or aspects, of communication and show how they operate within the hierarchy of meaning.

**FIGURE 3.4    THE CONTEXTUAL RELATIONSHIP WITHIN THE MEANING HIERARCHY**

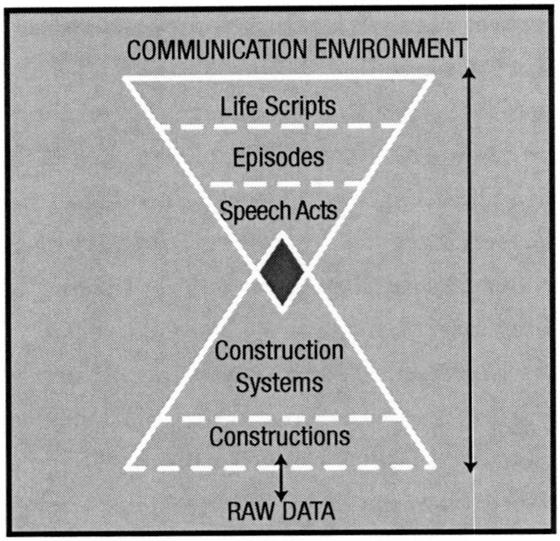

## BASIC AXIOMS OF RELATIONAL COMMUNICATION

Communication scholars agree that there are some simple properties of communication that have fundamental interpersonal implications. The work of Watzlawick, Bavelas and Jackson[20] describe these properties in terms of five axioms that are considered to be self-evident truths.

1.   One cannot not communicate.

2.   Communication refers to content and relationship.

3.   Communication is a series of punctuated events.

4.   Communication employs both digital and analogic communication.

5.   Relationships can be complementary, symmetrical, or transitional.

## One Cannot Not Communicate

Are you communicating when you're asleep? If you're in my classroom you are! You're saying you're bored or just worn out, or you could be ill. Even if you're sick, there's a message involved in your behavior whether I attach that meaning to it or not. Your "fatigue" may be based on the *content* of the course or on your poor *relationship* with the teacher (he's boring). Either way, you are sending a message. The old rule that "one cannot *not* communicate" is probably true.[21]

It seems that even attempted nonbehavior has message impact. Even with silence, others will respond. You may not be communicating intentionally, but others inevitably infer or attribute intentions or meaning to your actions (or nonactions, as the case may be). One of the reasons for this impossibility of not communicating lies in the fact that we use different forms or channels' in our communication behavior. We use language, voice, and action. Simply stated, communication exists in both verbal and nonverbal forms.

## Relational and Content Meanings

The **content** dimension, or raw facts, of communication usually occurs within the verbal band. How we are to understand or "take" the message often occurs nonverbally. We will discuss nonverbal communication in the next chapter.

Try this: "You old bastard."

1. A greeting between close friends.

2. A reference to a rude and insensitive male.

3. A file salesman's remark (bastard file).

4. A reference to a nonstandard auto—hot rod.

5. Born of unwed parents.

Our understanding of the utterance is surely altered by the **relationship** dimension. The *content,* after all, is about someone born of unwed parents, isn't it? Our understanding or interpretation of the statement ranges from an endearing greeting, to a car of dubious origin, to a serious insult—depending on the *relation-*

*ship*. In the example the content (words) remains the same. What distinguishes the utterance as a greeting or an insult is accomplished largely by voice and action.[22]

Most communication has both content and relationship aspects. It is through the manipulation of content and relationship characteristics that we can *move* in and through the levels of meaning in the hierarchy we presented earlier.

Sometimes interpersonal communication is as simple as the previous greeting. When it comes to "I love you," take care. Everything depends on how it is given context within the meaning hierarchy. If it falls within the episode of "one night stand," it is quite different from the life script of "enduring relationship." Consider the utterance "I love you" in Figure 3.5, which traces four hypothetical utterances

**FIGURE 3.5    AN ANALYSIS OF AN INTERPERSONAL RELATIONSHIP *(WITH APOLOGIES TO CRONEN, PEARCE, AND HARRIS)***

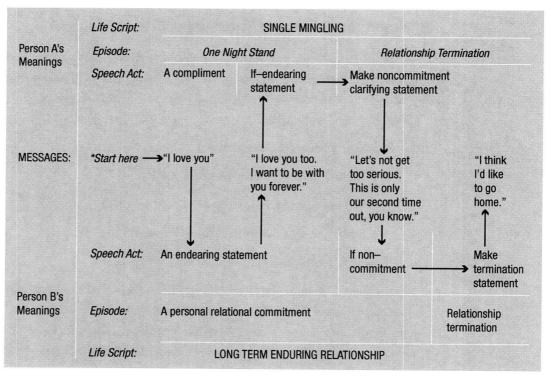

made by two people. As you can see, there is a clear mismatch between person A's and person B's meaning hierarchies. Their life scripts function to contextualize the message differently at first. As they begin to become aware of each other's life scripts and episodic interpretations, their meanings start to align; and, in this case, they realize they were not meant for each other. The ease and facility with which an individual's meaning hierarchy is communicated to others is a major concern in interpersonal communication.[23]

## Punctuation

Mismatches between people in terms of the meaning hierarchy can result in what Watzlawick, Beavin, and Jackson call problems in **punctuation**.[24] Their classic example of the wife who nags and the husband who withdraws is a case in point. When asked, the wife says she nags *because* the husband withdraws. Her nagging (speech act) is intended to stop his withdrawing. On the other hand, the husband says he is withdrawing *because* the wife nags. His withdrawal (speech act) is in response to her nagging. Their problem is that they have both interpreted their communication at the speech-act level, but they have different personal meanings for their behaviors. The wife has *punctuated* the communication from her perspective, and the husband from his.

If the couple were to both step up to the episode level of the meaning hierarchy, their punctuational differences would be made clear. Once the couple saw their behaviors within the episode called "punctuation bind," their problems would cease to exist.[24] Without moving to this level they both suffer from a case of "not being able to see the forest through the trees." A key dimension of interpersonal communication is openness to moving through the meaning hierarchy.

## Digital and Analogic Communication

We should note that digital communication is the primary basis of semantics. **Digital** communication employs arbitrarily assigned symbols—words. Recall our discussion of meaning. There is nothing inherent in the word *dog* that represents the animal. In English we have a convention that relates the symbolic digit, *dog,* to a four-legged mammal that makes a good pet. We could just as easily assign the symbolic digit *perro* (Spanish) or *chien* (French). Words (digital communication) are arbitrary. They bear little resemblance to their referents.[25]

**Analogic** forms of communication bear a closer resemblance to the things they stand for.[26] Analogic symbols are not as arbitrary as digital ones. A Spaniard, a French person, or an American would have no trouble understanding a picture of a dog. The word (analogic symbol) written in different languages could cause some interpretational problems.

Verbal communication, because of its discrete, digital nature, is relatively easy to manipulate. We can move words around in a sentence with ease and thus create nuances in meaning. It is easy to negate facts verbally (digitally). It is easy for the child who has just stolen gum from the candy counter to lie verbally:

Clerk: Young man! Did you just steal gum from the counter?

Young Man: What gum? I didn't steal any gum.

It is not as easy to manipulate the analogic band (nonverbal) of communication. Because analogic communication is not composed of discrete, easily manipulatable communication units, it is usually more difficult to control.[27] It functions to give context or additional interpretation to the digital band.

Clerk: Why can't you look me in the eye when you say you didn't steal gum?

Young Man: (Shuffling feet) I don't know ....

In the greeting "you old bastard," the utterance can be given context analogically. If Max slaps Barry on the back, smiles, and says, "You old bastard," Barry contextualizes (makes sense of) the verbal statement in light of its analogic context. "Backslapping" and "smiling" are analogically associated with friendship behaviors; and, therefore, Barry is able to interpret the sentence as being a friendly greeting rather than an insult. Max and Barry's *relationship* has been defined analogically. Defining relationships between people and between utterances is primarily the domain of analogic communication.[28] Analogic communication can more easily carry emotional content than it can abstract knowledge. Digital communication does better with facts, figures, and definitions of objects, which, of course, can also be critical to a relationship.

## Relationships and Control

Interpersonal communication relationships can be one of at least three types: complementary, symmetrical,[29] or transition.[30]

**Complementary** relationships are characterized by behaviors (verbal, nonverbal, or both) that complement each other. Complementary relationships tend to maximize relational differences. In a two-person (dyadic) complementary relationship, one person must occupy a "one-up" (↑) or dominant, position, while the other occupies a submissive, or "one-down" (↓), position. The following set of utterances might be characteristic of a complementary relationship:

> Boss: Don't leave that towel lying on the counter like that! (↑)
>
> Employee: Sorry, my mistake. (↓)

Value judgments, like good-bad, desirable-undesirable, should not necessarily be placed on either the submissive or the dominant role in complementary interaction. Submission can sometimes even function as a relationship control strategy. Submissive roles can be more powerful than dominant roles in interpersonal relations.

**Symmetrical** relationships are characterized by behaviors (verbal, nonverbal, or both) that reflect each other. Symmetrical relationships are based on equality rather than difference.[31] In a two-person (dyadic) symmetrical relationship both persons engage in similar one-up (↑), one-down (↓), or equivocal (→) communication behaviors. We must again stress that there is nothing inherently desirable or good in symmetrical relationships. Some are quite stable; others can be overly competitive. Consider the following symmetrical utterances:

> Husband:    What do you want to do tonight, dear? (↓)
>
> Wife:   I want to do what you want, honey. (↓)
>
> Husband:    Whatever you feel like is fine with me. (↓)

**Transition** relationships are characterized by communication behaviors (verbal, nonverbal, or both) that are different but not opposite.[32] For example, if one member of a dyad tends to engage in one-up (dominant) communication behaviors, and the other member is equivocal (neither one-up nor one-down), the relationship is probably a transition relationship. Communication behaviors are different, but they are not opposite in this case. As is shown in the following utterances, it is equivocal or "one-across" behavior that allows for the possibility of the transition relationship:[33]

Person A: Go clean up the den, okay? ($\uparrow$)

Person B: Gee, it sure is raining hard today. ($\rightarrow$)

Relationships can be defined by the communication behaviors that seem to occur regularly. A communication behavior within a relationship is usually one of the three previously referred to types: one-up, one-down, or one-across. The three types of interpersonal communication relationships can be defined based on the interaction of the communication behaviors that they entail. Figure 3.6 illustrates these three relationships (symmetrical, complementary, and transition) and their compositions.

A quick reminder: Relationships are also defined analogically. The words alone (digital communication) do not always define the relationship. We (the authors) are forced to operate in a medium (textbook) that is sometimes more digital than we would like. The point we are trying to stress is that very often an "analogic sensitivity" is as important to interpersonal communication competence as is rhetorical sensitivity.

## RULE SHARING

### Symbolic Interaction

We interact with one another symbolically. Most of what we share communicatively with others are symbols. Interpersonal communication is largely a process whereby symbols are shared and exchanged.

**FIGURE 3.6    A COMPARISON OF RELATIONSHIPS BASED ON THEIR RELATIONAL CONTROL CHARACTERISTICS**

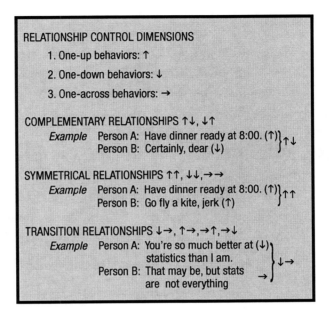

Adapted from Frank E. Millar and L. Edna Rogers, "A Relational Approach to Interpersonal Communication" in *Explorations in Interpersonal Communication*, ed. Gerald Miller (Beverly Hills, Calif.: Sage Publications, 1976).

We have seen that the major functional unit of interpersonal communication is the attribution of meanings to language, voice, and action. We are able to attribute meanings based on the *contexts given* and the *relationships defined.*

It seems clear that interpersonal communication is symbolic communication. We send out symbols (words, gestures, and so forth), which are designed to *represent* things. We try to understand and give meanings to the symbols we receive.

The approach of Symbolic Interaction can be summarized by three premises:[34] (1)Humans act toward things based on meanings they have for them. (2)The meanings we have for things grow out of our social interaction with others.

(3) Meanings are modified, contextualized, and generally manipulated through an interpretive language process used by the individual.

## Rules

We create, modify, interpret, and coordinate meanings interpersonally through the use of rules. To the extent that we share common interpretive rules in making sense of symbols, we *coordinate* our meanings.[35] The rule systems we all employ are composed of at least two general types: regulative rules and constitutive rules.

**REGULATIVE RULES**    Regulative rules function to regulate or guide behavior; they guide sequential communication activities.[36] In terms of our hierarchy of meaning, regulative rules operate only at the *communicative* levels of the hierarchy (see Figure 3.5). They function to regulate communication behaviors—speech acts, episodes, and life scripts.[37] Look at the following interaction sequence:

John:    How are university enrollments looking for the future, Paul?

Paul:    Well, I think overall they're dropping but …

Mary:    Paul, what was the …

Paul:    … in our area we don't seem to …

Mary:    PAUL!

Paul:    What do you want? (irritated)

Mary:    What was the name of that architect we met yesterday?

Paul:    Claude, Claude Davis. (Looks at John) Where the hell was I before all this?

John:    Enrollments.

Paul:    Oh yes, in our area …

Most people recognize Mary as the rule breaker. She's being rude. We recognize her rudeness in that her speech act violates a basic rule: unrelated interruptions of the speaker are insensitive, if not unacceptable, behavior.[38]

**CONSTITUTIVE RULES**    Constitutive rules function to specify how meanings at one level of the hierarchy can be meaningful at another level of the hierarchy.[39] The speech act "thanks" can be viewed as "gratitude" (episode). However, if the utterance is done sarcastically, the episode changes to "ingratitude."

## Coordination of Meanings

The coordination of meanings is essentially an interpersonal process. We all enact episodes to explain or make sense out of communication contexts. The challenge of interpersonal communication is to get different individuals to first enact the same episodes. We have seen how the lack of coordination (episodic mismatch) can lead to potential problems. Recall the "I love you" example in Figure 3.5. Good interpersonal communication works at intermeshing communication behaviors to produce mutually shared episodes. Pearce discusses three methods of coordinating or sharing episodes: casting, mirroring, and negotiation.[40]

**CASTING**    A drama-based analogy can be used in explaining this method of coordination. If an actor has a role he or she wishes to play, other actors are chosen in such a way as to support the primary role. They are cast for *supporting* roles. An individual capable of interpersonally persuading others to "fill out" or operate under his or her episode coordinates meaning by casting. Casting is not always overt. It is sometimes quite subtle and sometimes even humorous.

> If you're not going to play my game, then just don't play.

**MIRRORING**    When a person coordinates conversations by mirroring, he or she "mirrors" or takes on the roles proposed by others. In this respect mirroring is the opposite of casting. "When coordinating by mirroring, persons communicate by seeking to discover what the other person wants them to do and eliciting feedback to see if they are doing well."[41]

> I'm more than happy to play your game. Just tell me what it is.

NEGOTIATION    People who coordinate through negotiation have to be willing to compromise their personal episodes. When negotiation (as an interpersonal coordination strategy) is successful, the resulting episode is usually different from any of the initial episodes the interpersonal communicators brought with them.

> You want this game. I want that one. Let's work out a new game
> we both can play.

## Language is Powerful

When a baby is born, within the first few moments of its life it is given a label (an arbitrary symbol) of boy or girl. If you were asked to list all of the opportunities that come along with the label of boy, you may respond with things like sports ability, strength, higher earning potential, ability to do physical-labor type jobs, ability to be president. If you were asked to list all of the limitations that come along with the label of boy, you may respond with things like can't show emotion, can't wear dresses, can't give birth, can't be a housewife. The same sort of list would be generated when asked to describe the opportunities and limitations that come along with the label of girl.

The concept that language creates opportunities and limitations underscores how powerful language is in structuring our communication and shaping our identity. The communication we take part in shapes our identity and, in turn, our identity shapes the communication in which we take part. The **different-cultures thesis** allows us to view the link between language and gender.[42] Like the example above about the limitations and opportunities given at birth with the label of girl or boy, this thesis states that language will affect the way boys and girls perceive themselves which guides them towards a feminine or masculine culture.

We try to narrow the gap between limitation and opportunity for particular genders by using new labels for things that were traditionally gender specific. For example, if we call the person that puts out fires a fire*man*, we have just created a limitation for girls to hold that position. Therefore, we take part in a form of discrimination against women in the field of firefighting. **Politically correct or PC language** is developed and used in an attempt to remove discriminatory thoughts by removing language that references differences and handicaps.[43] So, fireman be-

*From the time we are born, language shapes our identity and the communication in which we take part.*

comes firefighter, waitress becomes server, policeman becomes police officer and so on.

Language not only creates our personal identities it also shapes the social world around us. Edward Sapir and Benjamin Whorf captured this idea when they created the **Sapir-Whorf hypothesis**.[44] This theory is based on the idea of linguistic determinism which tell us that language determines what we see in the world around us and how we come to understand it. If we come from a family where the word *chair* means the object upon which we sit, then we would describe this word using words like comfortable, wooden, four legs, office. If we come from a family where the word *chair* is used more often to describe the head of a committee then we would describe it using words like important, powerful, seniority. The language system from which we were raised determines how we come to understand things.

For example, I live close to the water and when my nieces and nephews come over I tell them that if they leave the dock without wearing a lifejacket sharks will come out of the water and eat them. Quite a stretch seeing that I live off of fresh water that is only three feet deep, but nonetheless, they believe it. When I tell them of the sharks, they look to their mother for validation; she simply nods her head yes and the story has become a reality.

This is a perfect example of **Symbolic Interaction** at work. Remember that the three premises of Symbolic Interaction are: (1) humans act toward things based on meanings they have for them; (2) the meanings we have for things grow out of our social interaction with others; (3) meanings are modified, contextualized, and generally manipulated through an interpretive language process used by the individual.

The shark story has become so ingrained into the communicative behavior of nieces and nephews at my house that the older kids actually verify the story and make sure that the younger kids never leave the dock without a lifejacket on.

Tricks like this are common and often used to get kids to eat, sleep, take medicine and play nice with their siblings. We think of such instances as harmless white lies that are for the good of the kids. Though we may be getting them to brush their teeth on a daily basis, we are also creating a reality that until proven otherwise will shape the way they behave and communicate. Let's imagine that one of my nephews grew up and was never told that the shark store was just to get him to wear his lifejacket. Picture him, 35 years old, shopping at a grocery story that happens to be near the water, getting some roast beef at the deli and wearing a lifejacket. One would most likely ask, "Why are you wearing a lifejacket in the grocery store?" He would respond, "We are near the water and if I don't have a lifejacket on sharks will jump out of the water and eat me." We would feel sorry for this poor grown man standing in the grocery store with a lifejacket on just because his mean Aunt Heather never told him the shark story was not true.

So why do we have sympathy for grown lifejacket man and hostility for individuals that take part in racist acts? Whether you grew up thinking that sharks would eat you or that you are of a superior race, gender or social class, the language used to describe things, the language you have used to understand your world has created a reality that, until proven otherwise, will guide your behavior. This is just one very simple example of the power of language. The arbitrary symbols we use to describe things known as words can and do have the power to guide behavior.

## SUMMING UP

"An individual's assumptions, beliefs, and attitudes are a function of the structure of his language, … his perception and behavior will be affected more or less in direct relationship to his susceptibility to influence by that language structure."[45] Symbols and language allow us to represent and store realities. Our knowledge is a function of our language and symbols. The Semantic Triangle shows us the relationship between symbols (word or sign) reference (thought) and referent (actual thing).

General semantics provides us with three valuable principles: (1) the principle of *nonidentity* (the word is not the thing); (2) the principle of *nonallness* (the word is not the entire thing); and (3) *self-reflexiveness* (we use language to talk about language). Special problems of the above may be defined as *is, etc., dating,* and *either-or.*

Different types of social systems tend to generate different speech systems, ways of talking, or language codes. Verbal and nonverbal codes usually work together and affect one another. Sometimes they are consistent with one another and thus strengthen a speaker's intended meaning, while at other times they conflict and tend to distort intended meaning. Generally, but not always, the closer we are to people (common experience), the more restricted our language codes become. With elaborated codes the speaker must presume that the listener holds a set of experiences different from his or her own. Sensitive interpersonal communication should be elaborate when appropriate.

Abstracting is a process of thinking in which we selectively leave out details about concrete or real things. Abstraction occurs at different levels. As we move from lower to higher levels we tend to consider fewer and fewer details of the specific, original object (FIDO, Golden Retriever, dog).

Good communication depends upon people being able to coordinate their meanings. This hinges upon our ability to infer meanings from contexts, signs, and symbols, and then to encode and transmit in such a way that they mesh with the receiver's meanings.

Our meaning changes with the level we use to interpret a symbol or set of symbols. Our decoding varies along a hierarchy of meaning thought to include constructions, construction systems, speech acts, episodes, and life scripts. These meaning systems aid us in ordering and regularizing our environments and in making sense out of them. The levels of the hierarchy are related to each other in that higher levels provide contexts for understanding the lower levels. The interpretation of our communication environments varies as a function of where we decide to stop within our personal set of meaning levels. The competent interpersonal communicator is able to move through the meaning hierarchy in such a fashion as to best coordinate meanings.

Even attempted nonbehavior has message impact. People attribute intentions and meanings even to nonactions. One cannot *not* communicate. Most communication has both content and relationship aspects. Both dimensions need to be coordinated.

Symbolic interaction may be summarized by three premises: (1) humans act toward things based on meanings they have for them; (2) the meanings we have for things grow out of our social interaction with others; (3) meanings are modified, contextualized, and generally manipulated through an interpretive language process used by the individual.

We employ both regulative and constitutive rules. Regulative rules operate at the *communicative* levels of the hierarchy and function to regulate speech acts, episodes, and life scripts. Constitutive rules function to specify how meanings at one level of the hierarchy can be meaningful at another level of the hierarchy. "Thanks" can mean gratitude or ingratitude depending on how the episode is interpreted.

Three methods of coordinating or sharing episodes include casting, mirroring, and negotiation. Good communication works at intermeshing communication behaviors to produce mutually shared episodes.

When interpersonal communication fails or is only half clear, it is usually because we have been unable to coordinate our meanings. To communicate at all hinges upon our ability to infer meanings from contexts, signs, and symbols, and then to encode and transmit them in such a way that they coordinate or mesh with the receiver's meanings.

Language is powerful. It creates our personal identities as seen through the different-cultures thesis. The Sapir-Whorf hypothesis tells us that language determines how we see the world and that how we see the world directly impacts our behavior in it. This underscores the idea that language creates our reality.

## NOTES

1 Jack Kerouac, *On the Road* (New York: The Viking Press, 1957), p. 8.

2 Richard W. Budd, "General Semantics: an Approach to Human Communication," in *Interdisciplinary Approaches to Human Communication,* eds. Richard W. Budd and Brent D. Ruben (Rochelle Park, N.J.: Hayden Book Company, Inc., 1979), p. 71.

3 See Alfred Korzybski, *Selections from Science and Sanity,* 3rd ed. (Lakeville, Conn.: The International Non-Aristotelian Publishing Co., 1948).

4 C.K. Ogden and I.A. Richards, *The Meaning of Meaning* (New York Harcourt Brace Jovanovich, 1936; London: Routledge & Kegan Paul, 1936), p. 11

5 See Wendell Johnson, *People in Quandaries* (New York: Harper and Brothers, 1946), chap. 8. See *also S. I. Hayakawaa,* Language in Thought and Action (New York: Harcourt Brace Jovanovich), 1978.

6 Ibid. chap. 8.

7 Anatol Rapoport, "What is Semantics?" *The Use and Misuse of Language,* ed. S. I. Hayakawa (New York: Fawcett, Premier Books, 1962), pp. 19-20.

8 Johnson, People in Quandaries, chap. 8.

9 See Henry Allen, "Phrases To Die For ... OK?" *The Detroit News,* June 6, 1979.

10 See Basil Bernstein, "Elaborated and Restricted Codes: Their Social Origins and Some Consequences," in *Communication and Culture, Readings in the Codes of Human Interaction,* ed. Alfred G. Smith (New York: Holt, Rinehart & Winston, 1966), p. 429.

11 Ibid. pp. 436-437.

12 Ibid. p. 437.

13 Hayakawa, S.I. (1964). *Language in thought and action* (2nd ed.). New York: Harcourt, Brace, & World.

14 Vernon E. Cronen, W. Barnett Pearce, and Linda M. Harris, "The Logic of the Coordinated Management of Meaning: a Rules-based Approach to the First Course in Interpersonal Communication," *Communication Education,* 28, no. 1 (January 1979), 23-28.

15 Ibid. p. 25.

16 George A. Kelley, *A Theory of Personality: The Psychology of Personal Constructs* (New York: W. W. Norton Publishing Co., 1963).

17 Cronen, Pearce, and Harris, "Management of Meaning," p. 25.

18 J. J. Gumperz, "Introduction," in *Directions in Sociolinguistics: The Ethnography of Communication,* eds. J. J. Gumperz and Dell Hymes (New York: Holt, Rinehart & Winston, 1972), p. 17.

19 Donald J. Cegala, "Interaction Involvement: a Fundamental Dimension of Interpersonal Communication" (unpublished paper, The Ohio State University, 1978).

20 Paul Watzlawick, Janet H. Beavin, and Don D. Jackson, *Pragmatics of Human Communication* (New York: W. W. Norton and Co., 1967), p. 49.

21 Robert L. Scott, "Communication as an Intentional, Social System," *Human Communication Research,* 3, no. 3 (Spring 1977), 258-68.

22 See Watzlawick, Beavin, and Jackson, *Pragmatics,* pp. 51-54. See also Jurgen Ruesch and Gregory Bateson, *Communication: The Social Matrix of Psychiatry* (New York: W. W. Norton and Co., 1951).

23 Cronen, Pearce, and Harris, "Management of Meaning," pp. 23-28.

24 Watzlawick, Beavin, and Jackson, *Pragmatics,* pp. 54-59.

25 See S. I. Hayakawa, *Language in Thought and Action;* W. Johnson, People in Quandaries; A. Korzybski, Science and Sanity.

26 Watzlawick, Beavin, and Jackson, *Pragmatics,* p. 62.

27 See Mark L. Knapp and Mark E. Comadena, "Telling It Like It Isn't: a Review of Theory and Research on Deceptive Communications," *Human Communication Research,* 5, no. 3 (Spring 1979).

28 Gregory Bateson, *Steps to an Ecology of Mind* (New York: Ballantine Books, Inc., 1972), pp. 290292.

29 Watzlawick, Beavin, and Jackson, *Pragmatics,* pp. 67-70. See also Gregory Bateson, Naven, 2nd ed. (Stanford: Stanford University Press, 1958).

30 Frank E. Millar and L. Edna Rogers, "A Relational Approach to Interpersonal Communication," in *Explorations in Interpersonal Communication,* ed. Gerald Miller (Beverly Hills, Calif.: Sage Publications, 1976).

31 Watzlawick, Beavin, and Jackson, *Pragmatics,* pp. 68-69.

32 Millar and Rogers, "A Relational Approach," pp. 96-97.

33 Ibid. p. 97.

34 Herbert Blumer, "Symbolic Interaction: An Approach to Human Communication," *in Approaches to Human Communication,* eds. Richard W. Budd and Brent D. Ruben (Rochelle Park, N.J.: Spartan Books, 1972), p. 401.

35 W. Barnett Pearce, "The Coordinated Management of Meaning: A Rules-Based Theory of Interpersonal Communication," in *Explorations in Interpersonal Communication,* ed. Gerald Miller (Beverly Hills, Calif.: Sage Publishers, 1976), p. 25.

36 Cronen, Pearce, and Harris, "Management of Meaning," p. 27.

37 Ibid.

38 See John M. Wiemann, "Explication and Test of a Model of Communicative Competence," *Human Communication Research,* 3, no. 3 (Spring 1977). See also Erving Goffman, *Interaction Ritual* (Garden City, New York: Anchor Press, 1967).

39 Cronen, Pearce, and Harris, "Management of Meaning," p. 26. See also Lawrence W. Rosenfield, "A Game Model of Human Communication," in *What Rhetoric (Communication Theory) Is Appropriate for Contemporary Speech Communication?*, ed. David H. Smith (Proceedings of the University of Minnesota Spring Symposium in Speech Communication, Minneapolis, Minn., May 4, 1968); John R. Searle, *Speech Acts: An Essay in the Philosophy of Language* (Cambridge: Cambridge University Press, 1969), pp. 33-42.

40 Cronen, Pearce, and Harris, "Management of Meaning," p. 25.

41 MacGeorge, ElL., Graves, A.R., Feng, B., Gillilahan, S.J., & Burleson, B.R. (2004). The myth of gender cultures: similarities outweigh differences in men's and Women's provision of and responses to supportive communication. *Sex Roles,* 50, 143-175.

42 Fairclough, N. (2003). "Political correctness": The politics of culture and language. *Discourse & Society,* 14, 17-28.

43 Sapir, E. & Whorf, B

44 Budd, "General Semantics," p. 71.

45 Richard W. Budd, "General Semantics: an Approach to Human Communication," in *Interdisciplinary Approaches to Human Communication,* eds. Richard W. Budd and Brent D. Ruben (Rochelle Park, N.J.: Hayden Book Company, Inc., 1979), p. 71.

# NONVERBAL COMMUNICATION

# IMPORTANCE OF NONVERBAL COMMUNICATION

## Functions of Nonverbal Communication: Expressing Emotion, Conveying Attitudes, Self-presentation, Managing Turn taking

Think about the now famous image of the New York firefighters struggling to raise an American flag at ground zero just after the 9/11 tragedy. This picture was posted to bulletin boards and splashed across the front page of newspapers all across the world. The image needed no caption because the picture spoke for itself. From that picture alone, we sense that *emotion* is being expressed, that there seems to be a struggle, and that attitudes of patriotism are being conveyed. Do the flag or the faces of the men trying to raise it communicate anything? One scholar tells us that two of the main functions or "uses" of nonverbal behavior are for **expressing emotion** and for **conveying attitude**.[1] The men in the photograph of the flag raising at ground zero appear to be fulfilling these functions.

Argyle defines a third function of nonverbal communication as a kind of **self-presentation,** a revealing of one's personality. The more we know about the people in the picture or the circumstances in which they are pictured, the more attributions about the *presentation* we are apt to make. When the firefighters that struggled to raise the flag at ground zero were honored for their patriotic bravery, they wore their dress uniforms. Though an image of them lined up with their awards does not show them in the act of patriotism or bravery, the dress uniforms and medals communicate this for them.

The fourth function of nonverbal communication involves the less dramatic, but important, nonverbal behaviors that usually accompany our verbal messages. We view this function as essentially that of **managing turn taking**—that is, indicating when you want to interrupt another; when you don't want to be interrupted yourself; when you want feedback, more attention, and so on. Voice or paralinguistics is a powerful nonverbal cue, one which we will discuss shortly.

These, then, are the four basic functions or uses of nonverbal communication: (1) expressing emotion, (2) conveying attitudes, (3) self-presentation, and (4) managing turn taking.

## Amount of Nonverbal Communication

It has been said that only 35 percent of your communication is verbal. When you speak face-to-face with a person, that person may be receiving 65 percent of your message by means other than the words you use. They are also interpreting your tone of voice, your gestures, even the way you stand or sit and dress.[2] In one view the relative ability or impact of the facial nonverbals may reach 55 percent and the vocal nonverbals 38 percent.[3] It may be that the blending of channels has more to do with meaning than the simple summing of all the channels.[4] In other words, the verbal is still critical to how we interpret the nonverbal.

When we find that a gesture that means "come here" in the United States means "go away" in Italy, we begin to sense the problem.[5] Perhaps a culture or sub-culture creates its own system of nonverbal communication.[6] There is also evidence that gender differences exist in nonverbal behaviors and that they are in line with societal role expectations.[7]

When combined with the verbal message, nonverbal signals are quite effective in conveying emotional concepts such as love and hate. People display quite different nonverbal responses to various emotional situations. One study found that some people are more sensitive than others to nonverbal signals and that such individuals tend to function better socially and intellectually. The same study also found that young people are less sensitive to nonverbal signals than are older people.[8] No wonder that in some interactions our voices and our actions speak so loudly that our words are often unheard or are not considered important.

In the long run we cannot avoid acting nonverbally. Therefore, we cannot avoid communicating—at least nonverbally. Sometimes our nonverbal behavior may be unintentionally contrary to our verbal message, which is cause for concern. We express our attitudes through our body actions, our voice and articulation patterns, the objects we wear or own, our use of time and space, our language, and, of course, verbal messages. Interpersonal communication, then, includes an almost countless number of verbal and nonverbal channels. Making the nonverbal communication process work for us by improving our understanding of it is the major objective of this chapter.

Watzlawick, Beavin, and Jackson comment clearly on the importance of context and give us, incidentally, a notion of what is included in their definition:

We hold that the term must comprise posture, gesture, facial expression, voice inflection, the sequence, rhythm, and cadence of the words themselves, and any other nonverbal manifestation of which the organism is capable, as well as the communicational clues unfailingly present in any CONTEXT in which an interaction takes place.[9]

They footnote this comment in an amusing but telling way:

The paramount communicational significance of context is all too easily overlooked in the analysis of human communication, and yet anyone who brushed his teeth in a busy street rather than in his bathroom might be quickly carted off to a police station or to a lunatic asylum—to give just one example of the pragmatic effects of nonverbal communication.[10]

The most relevant areas or aspects of nonverbal communication are *body communication* (kinesics), *voice and articulation* (paralanguage), and *environmental aspects* such as space, distance, objects, and time.

## Relationship Communication: Personal Liking, Evaluation of Power, Feedback and Response

The above most relevant areas of nonverbal communication are a large part of what was previously defined as *relationship* communication. We decide at least three important things about people largely on the basis of nonverbal communication. These are (1) personal liking or attraction, (2) evaluation of power relationships, and (3) our feelings about the response and feedback we get from others.

Let's review each of these as nonverbal codes. (1) Sometimes by nonverbal cues alone we might

*Kinesics, or body communication, is one aspect of nonverbal communication.*

feel *attracted toward another.* That person seems a "likeable sort," "a good person," and "easy to be with". That the opposite also happens is all too clear; you may be repelled by someone based on his/her nonverbal cues. (2) Power assessment is our evaluation of another person's status, influence, or clout. Nonverbal cues become important, particularly in the absence of verbal information. Several of these cues will be discussed shortly. (3) Another nonverbal area of this interpersonal decision-making is our perception of a responsive listener, a person who can and will appreciate our positions or our problems. These three nonverbal decisions about people lead us in and out of a lot of communication trouble.

## DIMENSIONS OF NONVERBAL COMMUNICATION

### Kinesics (Language of the Face and Body)

**EXPRESSING EMOTION**   We use body action constantly in our everyday conversations. It is a definite part of our communication system. The way a person walks or sits at a given moment may demonstrate that person's mood more adequately than his or her words do. When we try to avoid looking awkward, it usually communicates even more awkwardness and looks unnatural. In addition, such holding back may lead to poor control of emotions. A lack of action often makes the message less clear. There is no point in trying to avoid body action; there are many good reasons to try to understand it, control it, and use it.

*The Face*   Two scholars who have spent a lifetime studying the recognition of emotions from facial expressions insist that Darwin was correct in claiming that there are universal facial expressions of emotion. Ekman and Friesen identify the following: *happiness, sadness, surprise, fear, anger, and disgust.*[11] Included in this section are pictures and data on four of these basic emotions. The pictures shown are similar to those used by Ekman and Friesen, but are not the originals.[12]

Most facial expressions of emotion, especially in the presence of others, are still somewhat culture-bound. Ekman and Friesen put forth a convincing argument on the practical effects of acculturation as follows:

> "Although the appearance of the face for each of the primary emotions is
> common to all peoples, facial expressions do vary across cultures in at least

**FIGURE 4.1**  *SIMILAR EXAMPLES BUT NOT ORIGINAL PHOTOGRAPHS UTILIZED IN A STUDY OF HOW EMOTIONS ARE JUDGED ACROSS LITERATE CULTURES.*

| | Percentage agreement in how photograph was judged across cultures | | | | |
|---|---|---|---|---|---|
| | UNITED STATES (J = 99) | BRAZIL (J = 40) | CHILE (J = 119) | ARGEN- TINA (J = 168) | JAPAN (J = 29) |
|  Fear | 85% | 67% | 68% | 54% | 66% |
| 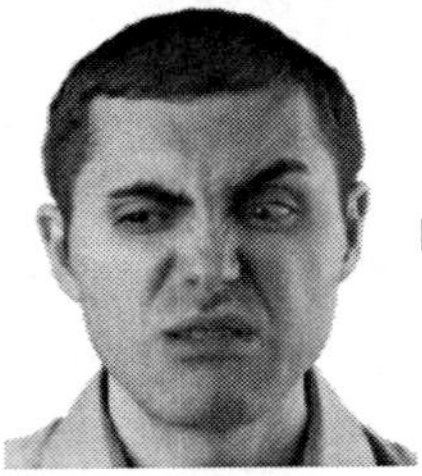 Disgust | 92% | 97% | 92% | 92% | 90% |
|  Happiness | 97% | 95% | 95% | 98% | 100% |
|  Anger | 67% | 90% | 94% | 90% | 90% |

two respects. What elicits or calls forth an emotion will usually differ: people may become disgusted or afraid in response to different things in different cultures. Also cultures differ in the conventions people follow in attempting to control or manage the appearance of their faces in given social situations. People in two different cultures may feel sadness at the death of a loved one, but one culture may prescribe that the chief mourners mask their facial expression with a mildly happy countenance."[13]

They also report evidence from a study of Japanese and American college students that we tend to communicate nonverbally more stereotypically when we are not alone.[14] Of course, we are interpersonally interested in situations in which we are with others. However, if in moments of stress or anxiety we regress, then perhaps these reversions appear interpersonally (universally) as well. Since acculturation is akin to social acting, we may find the culture-bound and stereotypical behavior more useful interpersonally than the true basic portrayals. We cry when we're happy and we cry when we're sad, at least in American culture.

In a study in which emotions of the face were posed and photographed, viewers correctly identified the emotions.[15] We are quite good at stereotypes if they are a part of our culture.

**CONVEYING ATTITUDES**    An **attitude** for our purposes may be defined "as a tendency to respond in a given way."[16] As an example, if an employee's attitude is negative about performing a particular task the boss has told him to perform, there is a tendency for it to express itself nonverbally. The employee may verbally respond with the word "fine" but the rolling of the eyes conveys something much different than "fine".

The eyes, and especially **eye contact,** are considered valuable sources of information as well as conveyors of attitude. Evidence indicates that a man's pupils double in size when shown a picture of a nude woman. Good card players and magicians have an advantage because they know that an opponent's pupils will involuntarily widen when dealt a good card.[17]

Eye contact at close range is needed for this kind of pupil analysis. A longer-range attitude analysis of this notion of eye contact also exists. Teachers of public speaking have been advising it for years. "Be more direct; establish eye contact."[18] On the interpersonal level, a person enamored with another person may spend more time staring at the person than listening to him or her. One researcher has concluded the following:

If the usual short, intermittent gazes during conversation are replaced by gazes of longer duration, the target interprets this as meaning that the task is less important than the personal relation between the two persons.[19]

Argyle makes several other points about eye contact that also suggest the conveying of attitudes.

1.    A looker may invite interaction by staring at another person who is on the other side of a room. The target's studied return of the gaze is generally interpreted as acceptance of the invitation, while averting the eyes is a rejection of the looker's request.

2.    There is more mutual eye contact between friends than others, and a looker's frank gaze is widely interpreted as positive regard.

3.    Persons who seek eye contact while speaking are regarded not only as exceptionally well-disposed by their target, but also as more believable and earnest.[20]

The eyes, as well as the whole face, can be controlled so that all these sultry looks are contrived—well, not entirely. There are natural reactions such as pupil dilation, eye blinks, and certain basic emotions. These are involuntary, but can be considerably controlled by experience or overriding techniques. An airline pilot with faulty landing gear masks his or her natural expressions of fear with a frozen grin; an irritated diplomat affects a slight smile. Some people mask fear with anger, which is often quite convincing.

**REINFORCING GESTURES**    *Reinforcing gestures,* such as clenching a fist or pounding on the table, help convey an attitude or a strong feeling. Such actions usually emphasize a person's words. In disagreeing verbally someone might routinely turn the palms down or out. In appealing for something someone might naturally turn the palms up or in. These types of gestures reinforce through emphasis. Other gestures reinforce through a kind of suggestion. In communicating a scolding attitude, a person might wag a finger in the same stereotypic way a teacher does. No two persons use these reinforcing gestures exactly alike, but the stereotype is usually recognizable. These gestures are also called **emblems.**[21] They are usually translated rather directly as with the hitchhike or A-OK sign.

Description is an obvious function of gestures. All descriptive gestures are also partly reinforcing. The person describing a blind date with gestures communicates more than just size and shape; we might, for example, quickly pick up a message of approval or disapproval. Ekman and Friesen refer to these as **illustrators.**[22]

**SELF-PRESENTATION**     Some of the *gestures* discussed above can develop a consistency approaching a grammar. The early American Indians had an elaborate retinue of nonverbal signs, which for them formed an important language. The deaf have a digital system of hand symbols called signing that carries an amazing amount of concept meaning and conveys attitudes as well. Special signs and symbols have been developed for special groups ranging from athletes and secret societies to subcultures. Some individuals present themselves by more than average hand movements, more than average smiling, rolling of the eyes, unusual gait, and so on. All are ways of presenting ourselves, and all are basically learned.

Gestures often reveal more than one realizes or intends. Observe the gestures of people you know well and see if their specific actions always agree with what you "know" to be their intentions. Would strangers "read" them differently?

Nervous gestures are often annoying to others. The wringing of hands is often a sign of nervousness or indecision. Drumming on the table and kicking the chair are messages that may indicate boredom or impatience.

An important part of self-presentation is **posture,** how we carry ourselves. The way you carry yourself tends to show whether or not you have confidence in yourself. *Posture* affects empathy and what people conclude from a person's signals. Whether you slouch and cower or whether you present yourself with military bearing affects your outlook and sense of power, and your control over yourself is displayed through your posture. A slouching posture can tire a receiver as quickly as it can the sender even though it is not always interpersonally inappropriate. Advice to public speakers makes clear how important posture is to that kind of self-presentation:

> In general, good posture involves the distribution of your body weight in a comfortable
> and poised way consistent with the impression you wish to make as a speaker. You should
> be erect without looking stiff, comfortable without appearing limp. Your bearing should
> be alert, self-possessed, and communicative. Good posture and poise reflect a kind of

cool unconcern. The great danger, as with all stylized body action, is appearing artificial, overly noticeable, or out of place.[23]

**Walking** is not usually a large part of interpersonal communication. However, in conflict interactions, storytelling, cocktail parties, and so forth, we may find it a telling part of self-presentation. Actors have long known the importance of walk to express various moods and degrees of emphasis. The *femme fatale* has a walk that clearly communicates her role; the sneaky villain also has a stylized walk. The child about to be spanked walks quite differently from the way he or she would on the way to the movies.

Take care in your relating and interacting if there is a cultural bias operating. We'll have more to say about these intercultural matters in the environmental dimension of nonverbal behavior.

**MANAGING TURN TAKING**    Unless you are monologuing in what is supposed to be a two-person interaction, you take turns speaking and listening. Much of this is done visually, but it is also done vocally. Some of the signs are obvious, such as holding up your hand or perhaps touching the other person. Some are quite subtle—a nod of the head, a closing of the eyes, a long pause.

How you send and receive these signals are important parts of self-presentation. Some "fighting for the floor" is fun in active conversations, but it quickly becomes disturbing if you are constantly and rudely interrupted. Have you met the verbal person who seems to avoid looking at you (he or she can overlook your signals that way) and is eternally reluctant to give up his or her turn? If this person speaks with long, turn-inviting pauses, but his or her concentration, we presume, makes him or her temporarily deaf (your vocal signs can be overlooked that way), then you've met a real barbarian. Children usually handle this person better than adults. They just push and scream until they get a turn. Of course, children haven't yet learned tact and all the subtle rules and behaviors of turn taking. What, then, are the behaviors or kinesic markers that help us manage interpersonal turn taking?

We have to know (1) how to get the floor and (2) how to hold it; we have to know (3) how to yield the floor; and we have to know (4) how to signal when we would like to skip a turn. This assumes you are not interacting with our barbarian above and that there is some kind of normal give and take expected. The when is probably more important than the how (but that's what this whole book is about).

Some of the visible "I'm yielding" signs are suggested by Scheflen (see Figure 4.2).[24] Most of these would probably be in concert with a changing pitch. If you're having trouble *yielding* the floor, try asking questions. People rarely miss that invitation to speak.

---

### FIGURE 4.2    POSTURAL-KINESIC MARKERS

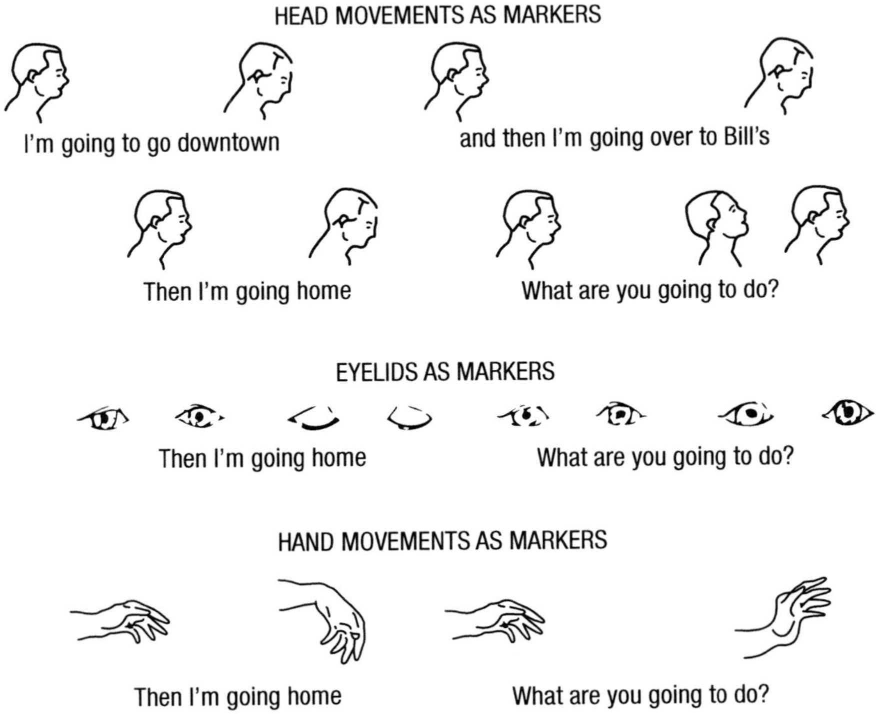

#### HEAD MOVEMENTS AS MARKERS

I'm going to go downtown                    and then I'm going over to Bill's

Then I'm going home                    What are you going to do?

#### EYELIDS AS MARKERS

Then I'm going home                    What are you going to do?

#### HAND MOVEMENTS AS MARKERS

Then I'm going home                    What are you going to do?

From A. E. Scheflen, "The Significance of Posture in Communication Systems," Psychiatry 27 (1964), p. 321; original concept from Ray L. Birdwhistell.

Getting the floor is often only a matter of taking advantage of the invitations charted and discussed in Figure 4.2. However, sometimes you have to become more aggressive kinesically, just as you would have to violently wave a hand to get the attention of a monologuing professor. A pronounced nodding of the head that keeps pace with the speaker's delivery can sometimes get you a turn. The raised index finger is good; the raised palm is blunt but effective if rudeness isn't a problem. More on turn taking will be discussed under paralanguage.

## Paralanguage (Voice and Articulation)

ACROSS THE FUNCTIONS   Can we express emotions through the voice alone? You bet we can. Consider a piercing scream: "Help, murder, rape!" Even without the words, we get the emotional message of *fear*. "Yuck, how awful," we hear as someone observes a gruesome scene. *Disgust* is in the voice.

What do you *hear*? Sadness, anger, disgust? The voice clearly expresses emotions. It is so effective at conveying attitudes that often we don't need the language. Tone, pitch, and inflection say it all. As a matter of fact, when the voice contradicts the words ("She said *NO,* but there was *YES* in her voice"), we tend to believe the voice. The voice is thought to be a harder signal to fake, yet the old radio actors were great fakers. This suggests that voice has a lot to do with self-presentation and that you can do something about it. As in pantomime, there are certain long-standing stereotypes that we take for granted in the use of the voice. We recognize certain radio roles as voice stereotypes—the mean character, the hero, the sissy, and the dunce. The very great danger in using voice stereotypes is that a person might take on an artificial voice permanently. Of course, we all occasionally fail to match the voice we "put on" with the situation in which we find ourselves. Listen to yourself on occasion. If you sound "artsy" when talking about football, your voice habits may be altering your personality in ways that will seriously affect your communication.

The voice contributes much to self-presentation. It may be the single most important code we use. Studies of voice and social status indicate the importance and the communication potential of this nonverbal code. There is evidence that social status can be determined in large part by the signals we receive from the voice alone, apart from language.[25] There is also evidence that Americans tend to downgrade a person who speaks with a foreign accent.[26]

Managing turn taking is another very important function of paralanguage. Following our discussion of visual (kinesic) turn-taking cues, it is clear that they can be and often are done simultaneously. For example, hand signals as a person seeks the floor are probably coordinated with a louder voice. Mark Knapp captures some standard voice (as well as kinesic) behaviors as someone tries to get the floor.

> When the speaker and listener are well synchronized, the listener will anticipate the speaker's juncture for yielding and will prepare accordingly—getting the rhythm before the other person has stopped talking, much like a musician tapping a foot preceding his or her solo performance. If the requestor's rhythm does not fit the speakers, we might observe some stutter starts, for example, " ... I ... I ... wa ..." Sometimes the turn-requesting mechanism will consist of efforts to speed up the speaker, realizing that the sooner the speaker has his or her say, the sooner you'll get yours. ... The most common method for encouraging the other person to finish quickly is the use of rapid head nods, often accompanied by verbalizations of pseudoagreement, such as "yeah," "mm-hmm," and the like. The requester hopes the speaker will perceive that these comments are given much too often and do not logically follow ideas expressed to be genuine signs of reinforcement.[27]

When a speaker pauses, a would-be interrupter often has time to insert a vocalization such as "um," "ah," "uh-huh," or to utilize other behaviors like sighing, coughing, clearing the throat—all clear signs to most people that you would like to interrupt. To *maintain* the floor during necessary pauses, if only to breathe, the speaker might fill up these pauses with these same kinds of vocalizations. If you are *really* serious about maintaining the floor, you would probably also increase your rate and volume and try to avoid any silent pauses.

**VOCAL QUALIFIERS**   You have considerable control over certain characteristics of voice. You can change your *rate* of speaking; you can adjust your *loudness* almost as you would that of a radio; you can speak at different *pitch* levels; and you can alter the overtones or partial tones of your voice, which represent a kind of *quality* control often called *timbre* or *vocal color*. Along with intonation (sounding the vowels), these characteristics are the nonverbal signals that help a listener determine the structure and meaning of what you say.[28]

**Rate**   Test passages have been devised for measuring verbal speed in wpm (words per minute). In general, a rate of more than 185 wpm is considered too rapid for a normal public speaking situation, and a rate of less than 140 wpm is considered too slow.[29] The problem of measurement is confounded by interpersonal interactions where situations, moods, and contexts are considerably more variable than in public speaking settings.

Interpersonally, certain communications may take place at a very rapid verbal rate and others at a slow or mixed rate. A further problem associated with verbal rate is that words are not really separately formed units, but rather tend to flow from one sound to another; this affects both articulation and pronunciation. Take the phrase "Did you eat?" If really speeded up, it becomes "Jeet?" This process is called *assimilation*. The length of sounds or tones is also a factor in verbal rate, as are pauses, phrasing, and general rhythm patterns.

The *duration* of sounds and words normally varies with our moods. We generally use tones of relatively short duration when expressing anger and more prolonged tones for expressing love.

Our use of *pauses*[30] and phrases is a factor in our rate of speaking. The "pregnant pause" is no idle jest; it has much to do with our communication. A phrase is a group of words that forms a thought unit. Pauses occur between words and between phrases, and the number and duration of pauses seriously alter the meaning of what we say. The complexity and nature of our speech material should also affect our decisions regarding the use of phrases and pauses. If you were to use long pauses in a random manner not related to meaning (not an uncommon error), you would then *confuse* your listener. Short pauses generally indicate that there is more to come. If you routinely use a rather intermediate-length pause without consistently relating it to what you are saying, you run the added danger of *monotony*, a tiresome lack of variation. Be sure that your speech pattern of pauses and phrases does not take on a fixed rhythm that interferes with your communication.

Of course, turn taking has a lot to do with our use of pauses. The advice above is great if you don't mind losing the floor while you are in one of your dramatic pauses. Rate by itself does not necessarily affect comprehension. Studies of mechanically compressed speech have indicated this, especially studies using blind people as listeners. We should, however, remember that electronically compressed speech has achieved the state of the art in which all of the *effects* of the vocal qualifiers are carried over—even the pauses. When we increase our rate in normal conversation, that alone carries a message not found in time-compressed speech. In addition, our pitch goes up, articulation suffers, and pauses take on less significance or are lost altogether. It becomes, in large part, a question of self-presentation. A fast rate is done rhetorically with full awareness of the *relationship* risks is one thing. If it's done simply as a bad habit, the risk is others may construe it as compensatory and tactless. They might, given enough samples, also attribute such behavior to a rude, domineering, and self-centered personality. Most fast-rate problems are not relationship problems if the turn-taking rules are remembered.

**Loudness**   Loudness is a measure of the total signal; it can relate to the actual volume of your voice or the intensity of your message. You may think of loudness, generally, as volume; but speech science indicates that volume is related so intimately to pitch that the term loudness may be misleading. Volume is easier to raise as pitch goes up. Furthermore, it is possible to speak with more force or intensity without altering volume proportionately.[31]

We learned earlier that loudness can affect turn taking in conversation. It seems obvious that it can affect your self-presentation. Extreme loudness also has strong *relationship* ramifications for most people. We reserve it for emergencies or issues of great concern—and sometimes for interpersonal conflicts that "get away from us."

There is another side to this loudness question. Sometimes we speak very softly. Among the psychological reasons for a lack of voice projection is a form of avoidance of the speech situation. People tend to *withdraw* from threatening situations. Poor projection is a logical and normal device when you find you cannot run away from an encounter. It may also be a form of *repression*—you hold yourself in check emotionally in order to get through the ordeal. Again, loudness suffers. It is almost as if speaking with a soft, barely heard voice is the next best thing to not being in the situation at all. Your receivers will help you adjust your loudness. Look at them for feedback signs. Are they straining to hear? Are they withdrawing?

Much of what we call *vocal variety* is related to loudness. The force with which you utter certain phrases or words is a form of oral punctuation and can add much to another's understanding of what you say. The manner in which you apply force to what you say is also a factor in vocal variety. You may use a lot of oral exclamation marks, or you may, through the use of intensity, underline many words. Variety, or the contrast between what is emphasized and what is not, is important. An audible whisper can be a powerful nonverbal as well as verbal emphasis in some interactions.

***Pitch*** We can fairly accurately determine sex and, to a point, age through pitch alone.[32] Normal pitch changes as we move from childhood to adolescence to adulthood, and these pitches are generally recognized for what they are. Interestingly, men's voices reach their lowest pitch during middle age and then rise slightly with age.[33] It appears that the same may not be true of women; pitch remains more constant during their adult years.[34]

Utilization of a varied pattern of pitches (versus a Johnny-one-note) is thought to express a more dynamic, extrovert personality. In a study by Addington, this was true of both men and women, although the stereotyped perception for men with considerable pitch variety was described also as "feminine" and "esthetically inclined."[35]

A drop in pitch at the end of a statement frequently indicates a person is ready to yield the floor. If you are maintaining the floor, in part, through rapid rate, your pitch rises. When we speak, we use a variety of pitches. If we were to plot the number of occurrences of the different pitches we use, we would find a central pitch around which the others vary in relatively predictable amounts. The typical musical range may include two octaves. The problem of *optimum pitch* level for a given person—that person's best general pitch level—is a complex one. To find the optimum pitch level often necessitates a compromise between mechanical vocal efficiency and what is generally accepted as being pleasing or appropriate. For example, if a man's optimum pitch is exceptionally high for a man in his culture, he may wish to lower his *habitual pitch* level, the level he uses most frequently, even though he may lose some vocal efficiency by doing so. If pitch is lowered unreasonably, however, the resulting loss of efficiency shows up as inflexible pitch or lack of variety and may reduce loudness.

For most people, optimum pitch should be the habitual or central pitch. Often, optimum pitch is found a little below the habitual or normally used pitch because of tensions that restrict the vocal apparatus. However, young men may strive so deliberately for very low voices that the reverse is occasionally true.

Trying to determine your optimum pitch from the viewpoint of vocal efficiency alone is fun (if not always entirely reliable). With the aid of a piano, determine, in relation to middle C, the lowest and highest note you can sing without a complete loss of quality. This interval is your singing *range*. The next step is to try to find your habitual pitch by using a sample of your normal speech. Hit the piano keys in the vicinity of the optimum pitch already found. At the same time, speak or read until you achieve a kind of blend between your speech and the notes on the piano. You will then have a rough idea as to whether or not your present general pitch is adequate.

*Quality*    Voice quality results from the modification frequency modulation of the vocal-cord tone by the resonators. It is that attribute of tone and sound waves that enables us to distinguish between two sounds that are alike in pitch, duration, and loudness.

Other things being equal, we can easily distinguish the overly nasal, breathy, or harsh voice. In addition, we are able to make nonverbal distinctions of a much more subtle nature. For example, we recognize the voice of a person who is sincerely touched by a tribute or the voice of a person who is suppressing anger. Emotional moods affect voice quality and may have a profound effect upon emphasis and meaning. In this context voice quality is often referred to as *timbre*.

Voice quality is a problem when a person's voice contains consistent deviations that detract from the message or its meaning. Certain organic disorders, such as a cleft palate or nasal obstructions, can cause unusual voice quality. Emotional moods may also result in temporary deviations from voice quality. In addition, voice quality may be affected by the strictly temporary physical problems caused by head colds, sore throats, and the like.

An expert in voice and diction training once said, "Bluntly stated, one may have a dull, uninteresting, or unpleasant voice because his voice is defective or improperly used; but he may also have such a voice because he is a dull, uninteresting, or unpleasant person." Vocal training, like all speech training, cannot take place in a vacuum; rather, it is intimately related to the whole personality. Just as personality affects voice, voice improvement may affect personality.

*Articulation Control* This refers to diction and pronunciation, especially the way consonants are formed or "articulated." It greatly affects the quality of total expression. A *dese, dem,* and *dose* for *these, them,* and *those* says something about the sender apart from the verbal message. What it says may vary considerably with the context. Hollywood will spend much time and money working on the articulation (and dialect) of an attractive, Brooklyn-born future star. It affects self-presentation. Ironically, a standard American dialect may have to be roughened to achieve a self-presentation for a particular role.

To some extent, we adapt our articulation in groups and situations in which a different dialect is spoken, particularly if we are part of such a group. Many students have developed two dialects in order to communicate more easily. Sometimes the use of a second dialect has social and practical advantages.[36] "Ax me a question" may enhance your self-presentation in one group and diminish it in another. Pronunciation is related. In old Milwaukee the word *theater* was typically pronounced "the-*ay*-ter," a compromised carry-over from the German pronunciation of "das Theater" (tay-*ah*-ter). In the Mid-West we hear "the-*uh*-ter." Some localities may say "drammer" for "drama." The extremely valuable dictionary is a little awkward regarding some pronunciations because there are three generally accepted dialects in the United States (eastern, southern, and standard American). The most widespread dialect is standard American, and our dictionaries and national mass media are geared to this dialect.

Our articulation often "gives us away" when we are uptight or suffering unusual anxiety, especially if we are using two dialects of the same language (and most of us are to some extent). That is, we frequently regress to our first learned habits. Articulation control can, therefore, also express emotions. Articulation, diction, pronunciation, accent, dialect—all are related control areas, and all are very sensitive to criticism. Articulation is clearly an important part of our nonverbal (paralinguistic) communication.

## Environmental

The environmental dimensions are the dimensions only slightly less personal than our bodies and our voices and diction, namely *proxemics* (space and distance), *objects* (clothes and things), and *time* (chronemics).

**PROXEMICS (SPACE AND DISTANCE)**    Each of us carries a kind of space bubble around us to mark off our personal territory. It varies in size from person to person and according to the culture from which we come. More hostile people are thought to have larger bubbles. They are more easily angered and upset because it is easier to bruise their larger bubbles. People also have different bubbles for different situations. We "occupy" a certain room of the house; my room, Dad's den, and Mom's living room are pretty special at times. Invasions into another's room often make us quite unpopular. Attitudes are being conveyed here; burst a bubble and you'll find emotions being expressed.

Cultural influence is considerable. Individuals in Latin American and Arab cultures tend to stand close together when they talk. Most North Americans like to talk at arm's length. What most Latin American and Arab cultures consider normal distance is considered intimate or hostile by most North Americans. The possibility of poor, or at least confused, interpersonal communication is obvious. Within our own culture, these appropriate distances change according to the message and how well we know the listeners. We tend to stand farther away from strangers than from friends. Of course, we are apt to stand closer when saying "I love you" than when saying "Hello there!" We also use our voices differently according to distance, message, and mood. Edward Hall has proposed a scale that helps identify the relationships (Figure 4.3).[37] Figure 4.4 depicts the various speech situations which a person might encounter.

## FIGURE 4.3

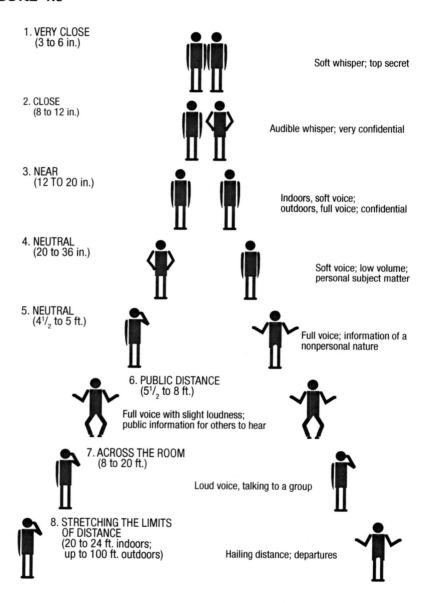

1. VERY CLOSE
   (3 to 6 in.)

Soft whisper; top secret

2. CLOSE
   (8 to 12 in.)

Audible whisper; very confidential

3. NEAR
   (12 TO 20 in.)

Indoors, soft voice;
outdoors, full voice; confidential

4. NEUTRAL
   (20 to 36 in.)

Soft voice; low volume;
personal subject matter

5. NEUTRAL
   ($4\frac{1}{2}$ to 5 ft.)

Full voice; information of a
nonpersonal nature

6. PUBLIC DISTANCE
   ($5\frac{1}{2}$ to 8 ft.)

Full voice with slight loudness;
public information for others to hear

7. ACROSS THE ROOM
   (8 to 20 ft.)

Loud voice, talking to a group

8. STRETCHING THE LIMITS
   OF DISTANCE
   (20 to 24 ft. indoors;
   up to 100 ft. outdoors)

Hailing distance; departures

Adapted from Hall, The Silent Language, pp. 208-209.

# FIGURE 4.4

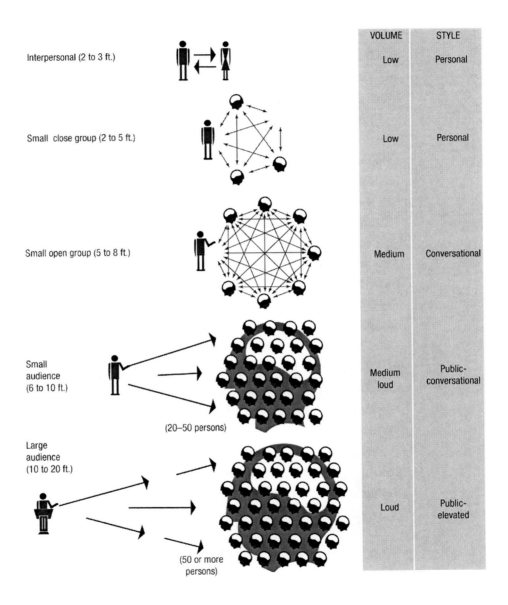

| | | VOLUME | STYLE |
|---|---|---|---|
| Interpersonal (2 to 3 ft.) | | Low | Personal |
| Small close group (2 to 5 ft.) | | Low | Personal |
| Small open group (5 to 8 ft.) | | Medium | Conversational |
| Small audience (6 to 10 ft.) | (20–50 persons) | Medium loud | Public-conversational |
| Large audience (10 to 20 ft.) | (50 or more persons) | Loud | Public-elevated |

© Raymond S. Ross

**OBJECTS (CLOTHES AND THINGS)**   Research suggests that individuals who appear attractive to the receivers of communication are more successful interpersonally. In one clever study, a young woman was dressed and made up attractively for one group of receivers and then was dressed and made up to look unattractive to a similar audience. The young woman was judged to be more believable and was generally found to be more persuasive and more desirable when presented attractively.[38]

We cannot change everything about our physical appearance through clothing, grooming, and "things" that we put on, hang on, glue on, tie on, or splash on (rings, wigs, eyeglasses, girdles, lipstick, aftershaves). However, we can do a lot; but it is sometimes a short way from appropriate to inappropriate.

Right or wrong, many stereotypes are associated with clothes and things. Research helps us define even these. Persons who wear bizarre clothes are considered more radical, activist, and more likely to experiment with drugs. People who wear more conventional dress are associated with everyday jobs and "traditional fun."[39] The problem is in knowing what kinds of clothes and things are conventional, in style, or expected of us. That happens to be the problem of all interpersonal communication, whether nonverbal or verbal. Some life scripts include dress codes that prescribe what it takes to be "consistent and acceptable." The point is that the nonverbals of clothes and things make a big difference in the way we are seen totally—that is, socially, vocationally, sexually, and so on. Note in Figure 5.29 how meanings change when dress code objects are in or out of line with their historical period.

Does a firefighter's uniform make him or her brave? Proud? It might! Our self-presentations are thought to affect our attitudes and our self-concepts—the way we see ourselves. A change to party clothes after a long day on the job has made many of us feel "like a new person."

**TIME (CHRONEMICS)**   Most Americans are serious, if not neurotic, about being *on* time. We also take *leaving* time very seriously and are quick to attribute messages and attitudes to "time" behaviors. Some Americans have more casual attitudes about time than others. As an example, some students are routinely late for all their classes, and their reasons have nothing to do with their regard for the other students, the professor, or the course. Then again, people tend to read lateness as some kind of negative attitude.

Cultural differences point out the importance of time as nonverbal communication. Navajo Indians have great interest in immediate or *now* time, but little interest in future time. Their language has no words for "future" or "late." Iranians have less interest in *now* time, but great interest in past time.[40] An appointment in our culture for 10:00 A.M. on Tuesday means just that (give or take five or ten minutes). However, the Navajo might hear only Tuesday; South Americans might hear the message as any time between 10:00 and 11:00 A.M. Of course, even these cultures have succumbed to more technical time demands such as airline departures, radio and television programming, timed laboratory experiments, and the like. An invitation to drop by *any time* (rather than a specific day and time) is usually interpreted as "don't bother," unless there is a very close personal relationship that allows predictions of *appropriate* time. The same general invitation in another culture may literally mean that any time is appropriate.

To complicate matters even more, our meetings, and especially those in business, are usually single-issue or problem-oriented (monochronistic). Not so across the cultures. A Latin American may have several unrelated issues in mind and, in fact, have several other meetings scheduled at approximately the same time. This can be most frustrating for individuals who expect to spend only a few minutes in a meeting and subsequently feel trapped for hours. We are told that this system of multiple issues in one meeting works well even for business people once everyone starts with the same assumptions. The point is that we *don't* start with the same assumptions, and it's easy to feel insulted or to insult others.

In our culture we are more time-specific, and when we don't follow the general rules, we are perceived as sending a message. Others will attribute meanings to our deviant behavior. A long-distance phone call in the middle of the night typically has a different urgency than one during the day. Being thirty minutes late for a forty-five-minute job interview invites all kinds of negative inferences from the waiting person. Seldom are we in trouble for being early, but we may get into trouble for being late. Almost every interview form includes an evaluation of the subject's dependability, which often translates into his or her attitude toward being on time. Our general culture tends to stress promptness. Television viewers complain by the thousands when a scheduled program is delayed by a news special or a game that runs into overtime.

Lateness suggests low regard for the receiver, the situation, or the message. The late person who remains silent runs some interpersonal risks. If a person has no really good reason for being late and no one really cares, perhaps it doesn't matter. Students say that about some large lecture classes with no attendance requirement. However, in small classes in which relationships are more personal, a routinely late person (fifteen to twenty minutes) is inviting negative attributions about such behavior. I called one such student aside and asked for an explanation. The apologetic student explained that her previous class was across the campus and that her professor routinely went overtime. Fair enough, but why didn't she tell me? She didn't think it mattered. When I suggested that I was concerned that she was expressing low regard for the course or me, she was absolutely flabbergasted and replied that it was one of her favorite courses.

Even if an explanation for unusual tardiness is weak or nobody's business, some apology is in order: "I'm sorry, I can't explain right now." It cuts down the number of negative attributions possible and keeps the communication door ajar. We can often save strained interpersonal relations by giving good reasons when we are late.

The bell at the end of the class defines staying time in a classroom situation. However, in less formal business and social settings there is more leeway. What is an appropriate amount of time for a business meeting? Usually not all day, as the case may be with the Latin Americans discussed previously. Typically we specify the time span: "Let's take an hour and discuss this matter." or "Have you got a couple of hours at lunch tomorrow?" Some of these luncheons may go on for three or four hours, I'm told, indicating that someone didn't know when to leave.

Social events or drop-in visits offer still more leeway. To be fashionably late for a cocktail party is no big deal, but to be an hour late for a dinner party might really be rude. Apologies are in order. But how long does one stay? Leave time also varies culturally. However, this problem is tricky enough just in our culture. I once went to a Sunday morning champagne brunch (11:00 to 1:00 on the invitation) that lasted all day. No one left, and the host was delighted. Usually when you're the last one at the party, unless you've received a sincere request to stay and not just a "social grace" invitation, it's time to leave.

## PERSPECTIVES

Our nonverbals of whatever kind, conscious or unconscious, may be characterized as follows:

1.  They always communicate something.

2.  They are believed.

3.  They are bound to the situation.

4.  They are seldom isolated.

5.  They affect our relationships.

### They Always Communicate Something

Assuming some kind of human interaction, *one cannot not behave;* and since behavior is nonverbal communication, *one cannot not communicate.* A blank stare communicates something to the receiver, even if it is just confusion. This is not always appreciated by less sensitive personalities. These behaviors may be consciously or unconsciously conveyed; but one way or another, they communicate. They communicate emotion and attitudes, they communicate who we are, and they help us manage interpersonal interactions.

### They Are Believed

Perhaps nonverbals should not be believed, but this tendency exists. Con men have taken advantage of this fact from the beginning. Nonverbals may be hard to fake for most of us, but not for good actors. When what you say disagrees with how you look or sound, people tend to believe the nonverbals.

### They Are Bound to the Situation

You hear that a good friend has just been given a clean bill of health on a suspected cancer. "Oh that's just great," you reply. The tone and inflection of your voice, the expression of your face, the body posture you assume—all tend to agree on the message. A drunken driver has just demolished your parked car. "Oh that's just great," you comment - only this time these identical words are accompanied by a slap to your head, a roll of the eyes, and a voice that clearly conveys displeasure. The nonverbals in this case are clearly the ones to be believed. When it comes to basic emotions, the face is thought to be most believable. Two distinguished scholars insist it is, even across cultures and even where there is no television to teach the stereotypes.[41]

## They Are Seldom Isolated

It is very difficult for most of us to be very angry and yet control our actions and voices so that we appear calm. A glisten of perspiration, a faster eye blink, a slight tremble, dryness in the voice—these and more give us away. Even when we are laughing on the outside (and crying on the inside), the character of our laughter probably gives us away. These other nonverbals tend to be related, consistent, and supportive of one another. When they are not, suspicions about intent are raised. Except in pictures or audiotapes, nonverbals are difficult to isolate. In addition, nonverbal behaviors can have multiple meanings, some obvious, and some very subtle indeed.

Unless you are in a laboratory looking at very limited and controlled facial expressions, you perceive a total impression that includes all of the verbals as well as all of the nonverbals. It also includes the setting and psychoenvironment as discussed in previous chapters. Despite all of the importance of the nonverbal messages, the lesson here should be clear: Don't ignore the verbal; it's still the major part of most interpersonal interactions. To concentrate on only one isolated movement, expression, or tone is a poor way to manage meanings.

## They Affect Our Relationships

As we said at the beginning of this chapter, we decide three important things about people largely on the basis of nonverbal communication. These are personal liking or attraction, evaluation of power relationships, and our feelings about the response and feedback we get from others.

## SUMMING UP

It has been said that only 35 percent of our communication is verbal; 65 percent of our messages may be given by means other than the words we use, such as our tone of voice, our gestures, and the way we stand, sit, and dress. The four basic functions of nonverbal communication are: (1) expressing emotion, (2) conveying attitudes, (3) self-presentation, and (4) managing turn taking. We decide at least three important things about relationships largely on the basis of nonverbal communication: (1) personal liking or attraction, (2) evaluation of power relationships, and (3) our feelings about the response and feedback we get from others.

Dimensions of nonverbal communication include kinesics (language of the face and body), paralanguage (language of the voice), and environmental (language of space, objects, and time). There are universal facial expressions of emotion: happiness, sadness, surprise, fear, anger, and disgust. However, most facial expressions, especially in the presence of others, are still somewhat culture-bound. The eyes are considered valuable sources of information as well as conveyors of attitude.

To help manage turn taking, we must know how to get the floor, how to hold it, how to yield it, and how to signal when we'd like to skip a turn.

Voice may be the single most important nonverbal code we use. It is often so effective at conveying emotions and attitudes that we don't need verbal language. Tone, pitch, and inflection say it all. Vocal qualifiers over which we have some control are rate, loudness, pitch, quality, and articulation.

Space and distance (proxemics) are the personal space or territory we deem acceptable. Our preferences are culture-bound. Space and distance are closely related to the message, situation, and mood. We adapt our voices in rather set ways to these aspects. E. T. Hall suggests an eight-point scale from three inches to one hundred feet. Another scale suggesting proper volume and style according to type of communication (interpersonal, small group, audience) was shown in this chapter.

Object language uses the influence and display of material things. It includes the clothes we wear, and the jewelry, cosmetics, and so forth that make a statement. The key word is appropriate.

Our nonverbals of whatever kind, conscious or unconscious, may be characterized as follows: they always communicate something, they are believed, they are situation bound, they are seldom isolated, and they affect our relationships.

## NOTES

1 M. Argyle, *Bodily Communication* (New York: International Universities Press, 1975). See also M. Argyle, The Psychology of Interpersonal Behavior, 2nd ed. (New York: Penguin Books, 1972), p. 47.

2 Randall Harrison, "Nonverbal Communication: Exploration into Time, Space, Action, and Object," in *Dimensions in Communication,* eds. J. H. Campbell and H. W. Hepler (Belmont, Calif.: Wadsworth Publishing Co., Inc., 1965), p. 101.

3 Albert Mehrabian, *Nonverbal Communication* (Chicago: Aldine·Atherton, 1972), p. 182.

4 Timothy G. Hegstrom, "Message Impact: What Percentage Is Nonverbal?" *The Western Journal of Speech Communication,* 43, no. 2 (Spring 1979), 134-42.

5 William Kloman, "E. T. Hall and the Human Space Bubble," *Horizon,* 9 (Autumn 1967), 43.

6 Marianne laFrance and Clara Mayo, "A Review of Nonverbal Behaviors of Women and Men," *The Western Journal of Speech Communication,* 43, no. 2 (Spring 1979), 96-107.

7 Ibid.

8 Robert Rosenthal and others, "Body Talk and Tone of Voice—the Language without Words," *Psychology Today,* September 1974, 64-68.

9 Paul Watzlawick, Janet Beavin, and Don D. Jackson, *Pragmatics of Human Communication* (New York: W. W. Norton & Company, Inc., 1967), p. 62.

10 Ibid.

11 Paul Ekman and Wallace V. Friesen, *Unmasking the Face* (Englewood Cliffs, N.J.: Prentice-Hall, Inc., 1975), pp. 22-23.

12 Ibid. p. 25.

13 Ibid. pp. 27-28.

14 Ibid. p. 23.

15 Henry E. Garrett, *Great Experiments in Psychology* (New York: Appleton-Century-Crofts, 1941), p. 330. See also J. Frois Wittman, "The Judgment of Facial Expression," *Journal of Experimental Psychology,* 13 (1930), 113-51; D. Dusenbury and F. H. Knower, "Experimental Studies of the Symbolism of Action and Voice-I: A Study of the Specificity of Meaning in Facial Expression," *Quarterly Journal of Speech,* 24, no. 3 (1938), 435.

16 Raymond S. Ross and Mark G. Ross, *Understanding Persuasion,* 4th ed. (Englewood Cliffs, N.J.: Prentice-Hall, Inc., 1994), p. 87.

17 Eckhard H. Hess, *The Tell-Tale Eye* (New York: Van Nostrand Reinhold Company, 1975), p. 15. See also E. Hess, "Attitude and Pupil Size," *Scientific American,* 212 (April 1965), 46.

18 Raymond s. Ross, *Speech Communication,* 5th ed. (Englewood Cliffs, N.J.: Prentice-Hall, Inc., 1980), p.137.

19 Michael Argyle, *The Psychology of Interpersonal Behavior* (New York: Penguin Books, 1967), pp. 105-116.

20 Ibid.

21 P. Ekman and W. V. Friesen, "The Repertoire of Nonverbal Behavior: Categories, Origins, Usage, and Coding," Semiotica, 1 (1969), 49-98.

22 Ibid.

23 R. S. Ross, (2008). *The Speechmaking Process,* 12th ed. P. 242.

24 A. E. Scheflen, "The Significance of Posture in Communication Systems," *Psychiatry* 27 (1964), 321; original concept from Ray L. Birdwhistell.

25 James D. Moe, "Listener Judgments of Status Cues in Speech: A Replication and Extension," *Speech Monographs,* 39, no. 2 (1972), 144-47.

26 Anthony Mulac, Theodore D. Hanley, and Diane Y. Prigge, "Effects of Phonological Speech Foreignness upon Three Dimensions of Attitude of Selected American Listeners," *Quarterly Journal of Speech,* 60, no. 4 (December 1974), 411-20.

27 Mark L. Knapp, *Essentials of Nonverbal Communication* (New York: Holt, Rinehart & Winston, 1980), p. 133.

28 Arthur Wingfield, "Acoustic Redundancy and the Perception of Time-compressed Speech," *Journal of Speech and Hearing Research,* 18, no. 1 (1975), 96-104.

29 Grant Fairbanks, *Voice and Articulation Drillbook* (New York: Harper & Row Publishers, Inc., 1960), 115. Some authorities argue that since listening rates may range from 400 to 800 wpm, a public speaking rate of 200 wpm is not unrealistic.

30 Norman J. Lass and Marcia Paffenberger, "A Comparative Study of Rate Evaluations of Experienced and Inexperienced Listeners," *Quarterly Journal of Speech,* 57, no. 1 (1971), 89-73.

31 However, accuracy of perceived emotions on voice cues alone varies. See J. R. Davitz and L. Davitz, "The Communication of Feelings by Content-free Speech," *Journal of Communication,* 9 (1959), 6-13. See also J. R. Davitz, *The Communication of Emotional Meaning* (New York: McGraw-Hill Book Company, 1964).

33 N. J. Lass and others, "Speaker Sex Identification from Voiced, Whispered and Filtered Isolated Vowels," *Journal of the Acoustical Society of America,* 59 (1976), 675-78.

33 E. D. Mysak, "Pitch and Duration Characteristics of Older Males," *Journal of Speech and Hearing Research,* 2 (1959), 46-54.

34 R. E. McGlone and H. Hollien, "Vocal Pitch Characteristics of Aged Women, *Journal of Speech and Hearing Research,* 6 (1963), 164-70.

35 D. W. Addington, "The Relationship of Selected Vocal Characteristics to Personality Perception," *Speech Monographs,* 35 (1968), 492-503.

36 Mildred C. Matlock, "Teaching Standard English to Black Dialect Speakers," *Michigan Speech and Hearing Association Journal,* 10, no. 2 (1974), 91-99.

37 E. T. Hall, *The Silent Language* (New York; Doubleday and Company, Inc., 1973), pp. 208-209.

38 J. Mills and E. Aronson, "Opinion Change as a Function of the Communicator's Attractiveness and Desire to Influence," *Journal of Personality and Social Psychology,* 1 (1965), 73-77. See also R. N. Widgery and B. Webster, "The Effects of Physical Attractiveness upon Perceived Initial Credibility," *Michigan Speech Journal,* 4 (1969), 4-15.

39 For more on these matters see Mark L. Knapp, *Essentials of Nonverbal Communication,* pp. 113-19.

40 For more on cultural differences see Hall, *The Silent Language.*

41 Ekman and Friesen, *Unmasking the Face,* p. 23.

# LISTENING

# RELATIONSHIP CHARACTERISTICS

Consider this conversation from Jim's perspective.

Jane: In my thinking I've come to the conclusion that certain narcotic drugs should be legalized in the same way alcohol is legal. I guess what I'm really talking about are marijuana derivatives.

Jim: (thinking) *How can she possibly argue that?*

Jane: Furthermore, I think ... (talk, talk, talk).

Jim: (thinking) *THC (active ingredient in marijuana) is a central nervous system depressant and as such is the functional equivalent of other CNS depressants.*

Jane: But you know ... (talk, talk, talk).

Jim: (thinking) *... like barbiturates ...*

Jane: My argument seems to be losing ... (talk, talk, talk).

Jim: (thinking) *... seconal, phenobarbital, amytal ... dangerous stuff.*

Jane: So anyway, I guess I really have to come off my initial argument.

Jim: (talking) How can you make such a claim? THC is a CNS depressant, the functional equivalent of barbiturates. We might as well make seconal legal? Could you imagine that? A bunch of seconal "heads" running down everything in sight with their cars.

Jane: (puzzled) Yeah, I know. In fact that's just what I'm saying. Weren't you listening?

Jim: (embarrassed) Oh, sorry ...

Jane: Really ...

In this example Jim has failed to be a good listener, but what happened to him is common. We get so *ego-involved* with an argument that we spend the lion's share of our nontalking time in developing and rehearsing our counter-arguments. In doing so we sometimes fail to grasp the texture or logic or history of the initial argument. We don't listen; we may not even be hearing.

Failure to listen adequately has relational implications. In the example, Jim is telling Jane nonverbally that he didn't listen. Jane might interpret this as insulting or condescending on Jim's part. With the characteristics of the relationship gone awry, much of the potential interpersonal richness of the relationship may be lost. An unproductive and unwanted conflict may even result—all this because of Jim's listening mistake. Therefore, listening has clear relationship implications. We can unintentionally "put someone down" by our failure to listen. Sometimes we fail to realize this when we are insensitive to relational cues and find ourselves in a real communication bind.

Listening is critical to interpersonal competence. The key to communicative competence and good listening is in being a **participant observer**. In our example, Jim was participating. He certainly had a *line* to say, but he put himself in *wrong face* because the line was inappropriate. Jim uttered an inappropriate line because he failed to *observe* the interaction. He lacked reflexive listening skills. Had Jim been both participating and observing his interaction, he would have seen that Jane was working her way out of her initial claim. If Jim had listened more carefully, the interpersonal encounter would have been better coordinated; and he probably would not have the relationship problems that he now has.

## THE IMPORTANCE OF LISTENING

"LISTEN, MY CHILDREN ... "

"First listen, my friend, and then you may shriek and bluster." (Aristophanes)

"Hearing is one of the body's five senses. But listening is an art." (Frank Tyger)

"Hear twice before you speak once." (Scottish saying)

"The funny thing about human beings is that we tend to respect the intelligence of, and eventually to like, those who listen attentively to our ideas, even if they continue to disagree with us." (S. I. Hayakawa)

"While the right to talk may be the beginning of freedom, the necessity of listening is what makes the right important." (Walter Lippman)

"Speech is difficult, but silence is impossible." (Chinese proverb) "Shut up, he explained!" (Anonymous)

"The listener is always right." (Carroll C. Arnold)[1]

From our discussion of the verbal and nonverbal (content and relationship) aspects of interpersonal communication, it is obvious that not all of the coordinated management of meaning is verbal. In fact, communication surveys show that we spend 60 to 75 percent of our time not talking.[2] In fact, according to Ford, Wolvin, & Chung,[3] as college students you spend so much time listening that learning how to do it properly could greatly benefit you academically. Stuart Chase argues that listening is the other half of talking, and if talking is going to work, we need to "beef up" listening—which is talking's counterpart.

> Americans are not good listeners. In general, they talk more than they listen. Competition in our culture puts a premium on self-expression, even if the individual has nothing to express. What he lacks in knowledge he tries to make up for by talking fast or pounding the table. Many of us, while ostensibly listening, are inwardly preparing a statement to stun the company when we get the floor.[4] There is hope! We have evidence that listening can be *improved* through understanding the process and acquiring better attitudes about social interaction and listening itself. Listening training improved the listening ability among elementary school students.[5] College students improved their listening comprehension through a program first designed for industry.[6] Oral reading seems to help.[7] There is *even* evidence that improving our listening skills may improve our reading skills.[8]

Good listening habits are important. William Work, who synthesized much of the research cited above, reminds us that to a large extent *we are what we listen to.*

> Nutritionists tell us that we—quite *literally*—are what we eat (and drink and breathe). In terms of our physical being, this is true. In terms of our psychic selves, we—quite *literally*—are what we hear and read and view. As our social structures and systems become more complex, each individual becomes more dependent on the ability to process information effectively. Competence in listening and speaking is central to the achievement of that end. Being a good listener will not guarantee "success" or happiness or the securing of one's life goals, but for most, poor listening will stand in the way of their attainment.[9]

**FIGURE 5.1    STEPS TO GOOD LISTENING**

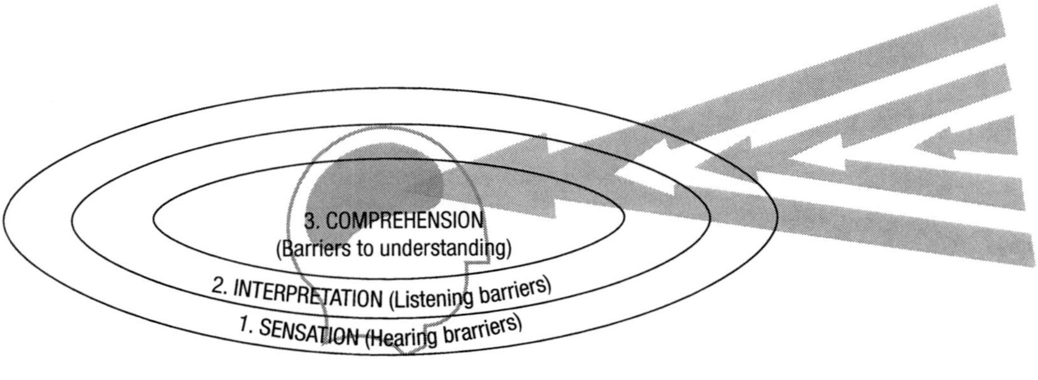

3. COMPREHENSION
(Barriers to understanding)

2. INTERPRETATION (Listening barriers)

1. SENSATION (Hearing brarriers)

## LISTENING MODELS

If we can become better listeners by understanding the listening process, then the model shown in Figure 5.1 may help us attain that goal. Listening is perception, and you will recall that perception was defined as having two broad components: sensation and interpretation. We have to bring our past experiences, attitudes, and emotions to bear on the sensations of which we are aware to make any sense or *interpretation* of them. Our interpretation can, of course, be unlike the one intended by the sender. Therefore, the third step, *comprehension,* is shown in the Ross model.

### The Ross 3 Step Model

The oral messages entering the model in Figure 5.1 illustrate that some messages are never heard because they never reach the sensation circle or *level.* Other messages may only reach the interpretation circle and perhaps never be totally understood. Even the messages that penetrate the comprehension circle may not be totally understood. The arrows also remind us that we are dealing many times with several messages simultaneously or at least in very close succession. They may compete with and distort one another. Some of these messages, because of their complexity or perhaps emotionality, may need more time to go through the steps and overcome the specific barriers found at one or more of them. "I don't think I heard you." "What did you call me?" "That's heavy; run it by me again."

It seems clear that all of the steps can be operating at the same time and with more than one message. It is no surprise that we often have tragic listening breakdowns. A KLM pilot of a jumbo jet at Teneriffe Airport in the Canary Islands apparently never heard his instruction to "stand by for takeoff." The pilot of a Pan American aircraft also missed something in the listening process and taxied beyond the runway exit leaving the Boeing 747 in the path of the Dutch jet as it took off without permission. On that day misunderstanding resulted in an aviation disaster—581 people lost their lives.

For purposes of clarity, we will discuss each of the three steps in this model separately and describe the special barriers attendant upon each one.

In step one of Figure 5.1, **sensation,** we are really talking about hearing. Of course, our perceptions are related, and hearing is frequently affected by our other senses. We see as well as hear another person. **Hearing barriers** include items such as noise, hearing impairment, fatigue, sensory distraction, and sender deficiency. These barriers are reasonably obvious. If someone is operating a jackhammer or beating a drum, you may lose the verbal signal merely because of noise. People often

*Hearing barriers include noise, hearing impairment, fatigue, sensory distraction, and sender deficiency.*

have hearing losses of which they are not aware. We all have learned that we hear poorly when we are tired. Sensory distractions are also caused by competing noises and sometimes by other verbal messages. Distraction can also be caused by the other senses. A foul smell, temperature extremes, an attractive face—any of these can be barriers to hearing. Sender deficiency refers to a very poor speaker—one who lacks volume, projection, or is so dull as to make hearing actually difficult. When electronics are involved, as they were in the Canary Islands plane tragedy, still more problems of noise and sensory distraction are obvious.

We can think of step one as mainly auditory sensation, keeping in mind that all of our other senses also contribute to what we finally come to understand. Listening, then, is dependent upon our sense of hearing and our ability to hear despite barriers. Assuming we have overcome the barriers and are willing to stay attentive, we are finally hearing but not yet seriously listening.

In step two, **interpretation,** we are talking about the beginning of listening, which is the assigning of meaning to what we hear. We may never fully comprehend or understand the message, but we are receiving part of it. Our understanding of the message may be quite different from what the sender intended. This leads us to the interesting problem of **listening barriers.** All of the *hearing* barriers of step one also affect step two. The barriers can best be expressed as bad listening habits. Listening barriers include criticizing the person instead of the message, permitting negative stereotypes to intrude, prejudging, seeking distractions, and faking attention. These bad habits are worth more discussion. Are you guilty of any of them?[10]

**CRITICIZING THE PERSON INSTEAD OF THE MESSAGE**    Try to disregard a person's appearance or interpersonal mannerisms when they offer you an excuse for not listening. This often takes real effort!

**PERMITTING NEGATIVE STEREOTYPES TO INTRUDE**    If we hear something that challenges our most deeply rooted prejudices, our brains may become *over-stimulated* in a direction that leads to bad listening. We mentally plan a rebuttal to what we hear, develop a question designed to embarrass the talker, or perhaps simply turn to thoughts that support our own feelings on the subject at hand. This is a kind of closed-mindedness that may cause us to daydream, yawn, or get so upset that we confuse the message. Letting emotionally loaded words blur the message also belongs in this category.

**PREJUDGING**    Sometimes we may jump to the conclusion that we understand the other person's meaning before it is fully expressed. Worse yet, prejudging often means preparing and rehearsing answers to questions or points before fully understanding them. This all too common bad habit communicates poor meaning coordination at best and rudeness at worst.

**SEEKING DISTRACTIONS**    A dandy way to avoid listening is to actively seek out distractions—looking out the window for something, anything that might be more interesting; concentrating on another person who excites you; daydreaming or actually causing distraction.

**FAKING ATTENTION**    *This is also* called sleeping with your eyes open! You only pretend to listen, and your act gets quite good. You smile, nod, blink, and so forth; you may even fool another person for awhile. That's why this habit is so cruel. You may be fooling (and cheating) both yourself and others.

In step three, **comprehension,** we are talking about *understanding* what you are listening to. Listening is clearly a vehicle for building communicative competence. Understanding is really the link between people's direct perspectives and metaperspectives on experience. To the extent that you understand my direct experience of you and vice versa, we have understanding.

With understanding we are better able to sense the characteristics of the episodes within which our speech acts occur. Understanding helps us determine when our friends are asking for advice, help, or just looking to "blow off some steam" communicatively. With an understanding of the episodes people are working from, we better coordinate our communication behaviors. Listening is, therefore, a key to understanding.

We can probably do a better job of listening if we remember *why* we are listening. We are not always involved in deep, evaluative listening, or even in informational listening. We often listen for fun and recreation—for enjoyment. We can be a poor listener and a poor conversationalist as well if we push all social discourse into content analysis. Sometimes people talk just for the sheer joy of it, and *that,* not the words, is the real message. Good listeners must be sensitive to this kind of communication behavior. Does "How are ya?" from a person you pass on the street call for a ten-minute response—or is it simply a form of recognition? How about "nice day." "Like heck it is. What do you mean by that?"

This model is also known as *SIER 4 Stage Communication Construct.* SIER is an acronym for the four words shown in Figure 5.2.

**FIGURE 5.2     SIER 4 STAGE COMMUNICATION CONSTRUCT**

SIER can be utilized either as a diagnostic or planning tool. For a desired effect, lowest level stages require fulfillment in an ascending order.

SIER can be used in 3 time frames:

1. PAST TENSE—diagnostic—determine cause of communication breakdown.
2. PRESENT TENSE—diagnostic—ongoing determination of successful fulfillment.
3. FUTURE TENSE—planning—complete preparation of all necessary stages.

SIER can be utilized by both a sender or receiver of messages to maximize their complete communication needs.

**REACTION:** What is the reaction or response of the receiver(s)? How does it match with the sender's objective?

**EVALUATION:** How is the message evaluated or judged by the receiver(s)? Is there acceptance or rejection, liking or disliking, agreement or disagreement, etc., on the part(s) of the receiver(s)? Is it similar to sender's objective?

**INTERPRETATION:** How is the message interpreted by the receiver(s)? What meaning is placed on the message? How close (similar) is the interpreted message meaning to the intended message meaning?

**SENSING:** Is the message received and sensed by the intended receiver(s)? Does the message get into the stream-of-consciousness of the intended receiver(s)?

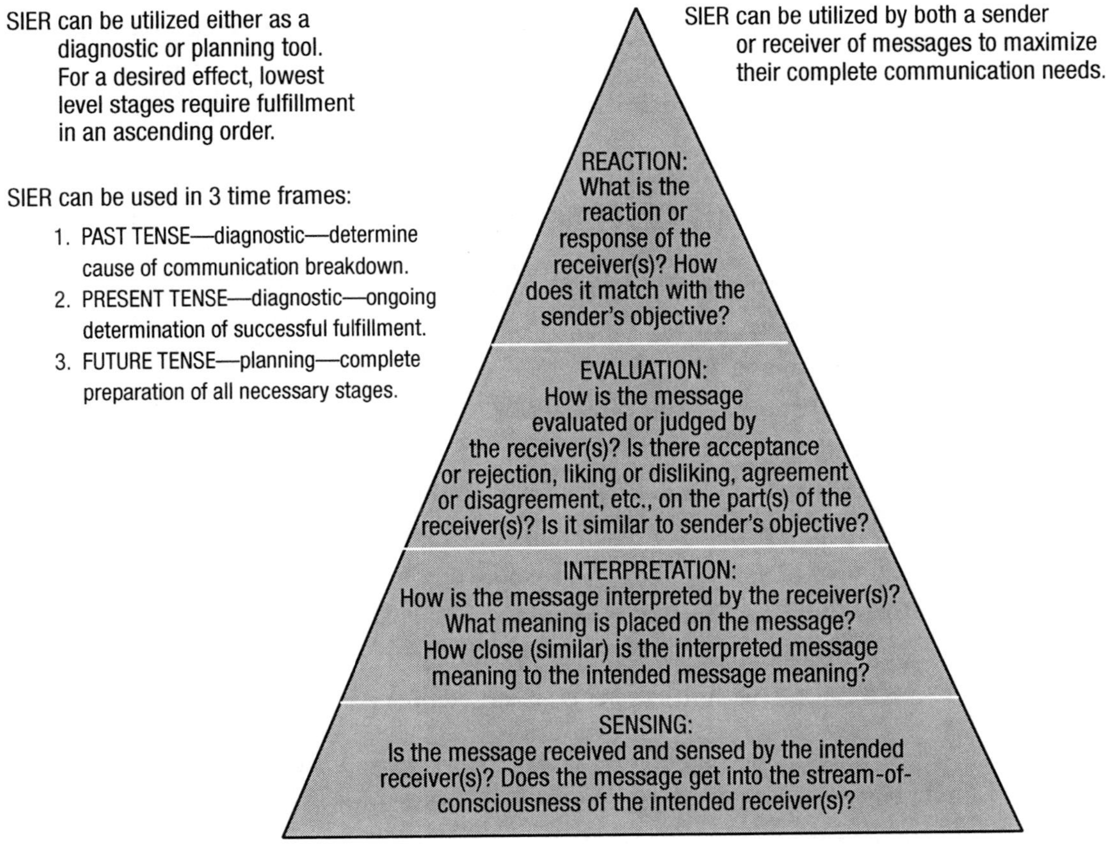

Lyman K. (Manny) Steil, University of Minnesota and President, Communication Development, Inc.

According to its author[11] it can be utilized to advantage by both senders and receivers of messages; it can be used as either a diagnostic or a planning tool. To achieve desired effects, the lowest level stages require fulfillment first. The model can be used in three time frames:

1. *Past tense*—diagnostic—determine cause of communication breakdown. Was it a sensing problem, one of misinterpretation, one of sender or message evaluation, or one of misreading the receiver reaction signs? Perhaps it really was understood.

2. *Present tense*—diagnostic—ongoing determination of successful fulfillment through all of the stages.

3. *Future tense*—planning—complete preparation of all necessary stages. An anticipation of problems of hearing, message difficulty, receiver bias and sophistication, and unusual or novel reactions attendant upon special situations and/or receivers.

## IMPROVING LISTENING HABITS

Good listening improves understanding. To *comprehend* interpersonal communication we must actively listen. A key, then, to improving our listening habits is to make listening an active process.

Listening involves more than just sensation and interpretation. It is not just hearing, nor is it a passive process. Good listening takes concentrated effort, and, frankly, most of us don't give listening the effort it deserves. We are bad listeners, and we view this as a real problem that needs some consistent effort. There are a number of specific ways to enhance comprehension through listening.[12] Some of these ways are reviewed here.

### Reflect the Message to the Talker

Reflecting messages is also known as *feedback*. Listening as an active process involves communicating. Feedback is information sent from listeners to speakers about the direct experience of the listener: "This is what I understand you to be saying." Feedback thus becomes a method for enhancing the agreement between the direct perspective of the listener and the metaperspective of the speaker—*understanding.*

Using reflective feedback also aids listeners in determining or understanding the general intent or purpose of an interpersonal communication encounter. It aids the listener in detecting the episode from which the speaker is operating. Reflective feedback aids speakers and listeners in the general management of meaning. By reflecting a speaker's message, we are, in effect, examining (and confirming) the linkages between words (symbols) and their referents.

## Be a Participant-Observer

In our interpersonal endeavors most of us have no problem being a participant. It's being an *observer* too that creates problems. Being able to participate and observe allows us, in a sense, to review our previous behaviors. Being able to see our behaviors as an interaction sequence gives us a clearer picture of our intentions and purposes in the interaction. An early awareness of our intentions within an interpersonal communication setting puts us on more stable communicative ground in the management and coordination of our behaviors.

## Be Aware of Your Biases and Attitudes

Our constructs and construction systems tend to predispose our thinking. A conscious awareness and exploration of biases and attitudinal sets can help us adjust interpersonally if necessary.

## Prepare to Report

If you think of having to report what you've heard to someone important to you, you are apt to listen more carefully. The threat of embarrassment is at work here.

## Analyze Your Listening Errors

We all misperceive at times. Reflecting back on the types of communication behaviors we engaged in when listening errors were made can be quite enlightening. We can learn from our mistakes if we view them in light of the communication contexts in which they occurred.

Ten keys to effective listening are shown in Table 5.1.

Over one hundred years ago in George Eliot's *Felix Holt,* The Reverend Rufus Lyon counseled the hot-tempered hero as follows: "Therefore I pray for a listening spirit, which is a great mark of grace. ... The scornful nostril and the high head gather not the odors that lie on the track of truth."[14]

Pflaumer reviews an ideal listener for us as one who:

keeps an open, curious mind

listens for new ideas

relates what is heard to what is known

is self-perceptive and listens to others from that self

pays attention to what is said

does not blindly follow the crowd

maintains perspective

looks for idea organization and arguments

listens for the essence of things

stays mentally alert, outlining, objecting, approving

is introspective but critically analytical

attempts to understand values, attitudes and relationships

focuses on the speaker's ideas

listens with feeling and intuition.[15]

## SUMMING UP

Failure to listen adequately has relational implications. We can unintentionally put someone down by our failure to listen. The key to communicative competence and

## TABLE 5.1    10 KEYS TO EFFECTIVE LISTENING[13]

These keys are a positive guideline to better listening. In fact, they're at the heart of developing better listening habits that could last a lifetime.

| Ten Keys to Effective Listening | The Bad Listener | The Good Listener |
|---|---|---|
| 1. Find areas of interest. | Tunes out dry subjects. | Opportunizes; asks, "What's in it for me?" |
| 2. Judege content, not delivery. | Tunes out if delivery is poor. | Judges content, skips over delivery errors. |
| 3. Hold your fire. | Tends to enter into argument. | Doesn't judge until comprehension is complete. |
| 4. Listen for ideas. | Listens for facts. | Listens for central themes. |
| 5. Be flexible. | Takes intensive notes using only one system. | Takes fewer notes. Uses 4–5 different systems, depending on speaker. |
| 6. Work at listening. | Shows no energy output ; fakes attention. | Works hard, exhibits active body state. |
| 7. Resist distractions. | Is easily distracted. | Fight or avoids distractions, tolerates bad habits, knows how to concentrate. |
| 8. Excercise your mind. | Resists difficult expository material; seeks light, recreational material. | Uses heavier material as exercise for the mind. |
| 9. Keep your mind open. | Reacts to emotional words. | Interprets color words; does not get hung up on them. |
| 10. Capitalize on fact; thought is faster than speech. | Tends to daydream with slow speakers. | Challenges, anticipates, mentally summarizes, weighs the evidence, listens between the lines to tone of voice. |

good listening is in being a participant-observer—that is, observing one's own behavior as well as others' behaviors while at the same time being an active participant.

The importance of listening is reflected by surveys that indicate that people may spend as much as 60 to 75 percent of their time listening. Americans are not thought to be good listeners. There is evidence that we can improve our listening habits through better understanding process and through developing better attitudes toward the task of listening.

A three-step listening model is discussed; the three steps are sensation, interpretation and comprehension. The *hearing* barriers to sensation are noise, hearing impairment, fatigue, sensory distraction, and sender deficiency. The *listening* barriers to interpretation are insisting the topic is stupid or uninteresting, criticizing the person instead of the message, permitting negative stereotypes to intrude, prejudging, seeking distractions, and faking attention. Some of the barriers to *comprehension* are intelligence, reading ability, vocabulary, thinking ability, and experience.

SIER, a 4-stage communication construct, is described. The four stages are sensing, interpretation, evaluation, and reaction. It can be utilized by both senders and receivers and can be used in three time frames—past, present, and future.

A key to improving our listening habits is to make listening an active process, which includes the following: (1) Reflect the message to the talker; (2) Be a participant-observer; (3) Be aware of your biases and attitudes; (4) Prepare to report; and (5) Analyze your listening errors. The use of reflective feedback aids both speakers and listeners in the general management of meaning. By occasionally reflecting a sender's message, we are examining and confirming the linkages between words and referents. Participant-observers see their behavior as an interaction sequence involving intentions and purposes. An early awareness of such intentions, relevant to the setting, should make us better listeners.

Ten keys to *effective* listening are shown plus the habits of both good and bad listeners. The ten keys are:

1.  Find areas of interest.

2.  Judge content, not delivery.

3.  Hold your fire.

4.  Listen for ideas.

5. Be flexible.

6. Work at listening.

7. Resist distractions.

8. Exercise your mind.

9. Keep your mind open.

10. Capitalize on fact that thought is faster than speech.

Listening is an integral part of the processes of interpersonal communication and perception. It is the most used of our communication skills. It may be defined as a conscious, cognitive, active effort using mainly the sense of hearing (reinforced by the other senses), which in turn leads to interpretation and understanding.

## NOTES

1 William Work, "Eric Report," *Communication Education,* 27, no. 2 (March 1978), 146.

2 Ralph G. Nichols and Leonard A. Stevens, *Are You Listening?* (New York: McGraw-Hill Book Company, 1957), pp. 6–8.

3 Ford, W., Wolvin, A., & Chung, S. (2000). Students' self-perceived listening competencies in the basic speech communication course. *International Journal of Listening,* 14, 1-13.

4 Stuart Chase, "Are You Listening?" *Reader's Digest,* December 1962, p. 80.

5 Susan Fleming Blackburn, "The Construction, the Implementation, and the Evaluation of a Title I Primary Grade Listening Program," "Eric Report," *Communication Education,* 27, no. 2 (March 1978), 150.

6 Deane Ford Schubach, "An Experimental Evaluation of a Program for Improvement of Listening Comprehension of College Students," "Eric Report," *Communication Education,* p. 151.

7 Margaret Weidner, "Reading Achievement of Grade Four Students," "Eric Report," *Communication Education,* p. 150.

8 Robert Lee Lemons, Jr., "The Effects of Passive Listening and Direct Training in Listening upon the Reading and Listening Skills of a Group of Black Fourth Graders," "Eric Report," *Communication Education,* p. 149; Thomas G. Sticht and others, "Auding and Reading: A Developmental Model," "Eric Report," *Communication Education,* p. 149.

9 Work, "Eric Report," *Communication Education,* p. 152.

10 These bad habits are adapted from R. G. Nichols and L. A. Stevens, *Are You Listening?* (New York: McGraw-Hill Book Company, 1957), pp, 104–12 and L. Barker, *Listening Behavior* (Englewood Cliffs, N.J.: Prentice-Hall, Inc., 1971), pp. 61–66.

11 Lyman K. (Manny) Steil, University of Minnesota, and President, Communication Development, Inc.

12 Carl H. Weaver, *Human Listening, Processes and Behavior* (Indianapolis and New York: The Bobbs Merrill Co., Inc., 1972), p. 99.

13 Sperry is Sperry Univac computers, Sperry New Holland farm equipment, Sperry Vickers fluid power systems, and guidance and control equipment from Sperry division and Sperry Flight systems. Used with permission of Sperry Corporation.

14 George Eliot, *Felix Holt, the Radical: The Personal Edition of George Eliot's Works* (New York: Doubleday, 1901), p. 70.

15 Elizabeth M. Pflaumer, "Listening: A Definition and Application" (paper delivered at the International Communication Association Convention, Atlanta, Georgia, April, 1972), p. 7. (Rewritten for rhetorical purposes.)

# CHAPTER 6

# COPING WITH CONFLICT

## THE ANATOMY OF CONFLICT

Conflict is a hazard of living, much of it unavoidable—you can't win 'em all. However, we can learn to cope with conflict. Before we discuss the rules of conduct, let's examine what typically is at the root of the matter.

A very large part of **interpersonal conflict** involves our concern for the relationship with another person. Will the message or content part of our interaction threaten the relationship? **Interpersonal conflict** is a verbal or nonverbal expression of a struggle that is a result of the individual's inability to agree on an avenue to best meet their goals and needs.  Conflict becomes interpersonal because of the role of interdependence.

To blurt out your strong political feelings to a dorm acquaintance is one thing. To do the same with an employer of a different persuasion (but with whom you have a satisfactory relationship) might be quite another matter. Much depends on the employer; some people seem to have a greater tolerance for differences of opinion and conflict. So much depends upon the situation. Are you blurting out your feelings on or off the job? Are these shows of feeling job relevant or recreational? The message content might concern an issue or goal of varying importance to you and the receiver. Perhaps you've used strong language on an issue of only minor concern to you but of major concern to the receiver. I was once reported to the ombudsman for using the word *damn* in class. Two religious-sect students were very concerned about obscenity and had a narrower definition of obscenity than I. I made my peace with them, enabling us to continue our student-teacher relationship. We also must consider the content and relationship concerns in terms of *others* who may be involved. In this case the others were the rest of the class, some who would have forgone the relationship; however, most sensed the multiple conflict and adapted.

Conflict is inevitable but, as we shall see, not always the end of the world. So much depends on how we manage it. Some experts even think conflict is part and parcel of real intimacy.[5] What causes close relationships to fall apart is an unwillingness to face conflicts constructively. They are faced destructively or simply avoided for as long as possible.

Conflict almost always involves perceptions of incompatible goals and/or threats to a relationship.[6] That communication is at the heart of the matter is clearly stated by Simons: "Communication, ... is the means by which conflicts get socially defined, the instrument through which influence in conflicts is exercised, and the vehicle by which partisans or third parties may prevent, manage, or resolve conflicts."[7] Much of what we assume about the nature of conflict and its relational effects is incorrect. This chapter will dispel some of the myths you may have about conflict, provide a thorough understanding of the nature of conflict, and offer ideas about how to most effectively deal with conflict.

## Myths About Conflict

**CONFLICT IS ALWAYS BAD.**  One of the most common myths about conflict is that it is inherently bad.  We assume that when people in a relationship have conflict that this is a sign of a bad relationship. This implies that the only way you can have a perfect relationship is if it is conflict free.  Research shows that when asked to think about relational conflict people tend to think negatively, comparing it to things like war and disease.[1] This negative image of relational conflict is false. Though constant bickering may be the sign of larger relational problems, there are many positive aspects to relational conflict. It is very healthy for relational partners to get feelings and ideas out in the open through free expression. Relational partners that are able to confront and solve conflict actually have stronger relationships than those that have no conflict at all.[2] Also, individuals that are able to deal with conflict sensitively are viewed as communicatively competent.[3]  Though starting a little conflict will not necessarily lead to a better relationship, the idea that conflict is always bad is just a myth.

**CONFLICT IS DUE TO MISUNDERSTANDING AND MISCOMMUNICATION.**  This myth stems from the idea that conflict is due to individuals' inability to accurately communicate their goals to one another.  This is often times not the case.  There are many situations when people are able to clearly communicate their goals to each other, yet disagree. For example, I often have communication with my husband about the proper direction of the silverware in the silverware basket of the dishwasher. I think the tips should go up for maximum cleaning. My husband thinks the tips should go down to avoid injury when emptying the basket.  Now, after several years of marriage, when I open the dishwasher and find the silverware tips down, I don't mumble something like, "How much clearer can I be with him? The tips go up!" There has been no unclear communication or misunderstanding. Both my husband and I have been explicitly clear about our opinions on the silverware direction, and we both clearly understand each other; we just simply disagree. There is no longer a point to argue about it (or sneak into the kitchen and change the direction of the silverware while he is sleeping) because we have agreed to disagree.

**CONFLICT CAN ALWAYS BE RESOLVED.** This myth is based on the notion that if we get really skilled managing conflict, we will be able to resolve all conflicts. There are, in fact, several skills that will be suggested later in the chapter to help you manage conflict most appropriately; however, there are no magic skills that can solve all conflict. You just read about the reality of my silverware situation. No amount of better listening or clearer communication will resolve the difference of opinion between my husband and me. Our silverware beliefs are so deeply ingrained that we have to agree to disagree and move on to resolvable conflicts.

*A number of myths surround conflict, including that it is always bad or is due to miscommunication or misunderstanding.*

**CONFLICT CAN BE AVOIDED.** This myth is based on the old adage of "If you can't say anything nice, don't say anything at all" (quote by the mothers of all of your authors). From the time we are small children we are taught that conflicts are bad, so don't start one. Conflict, however, is impossible to avoid. Therefore, if not having anything nice to say leads to you saying nothing at all, there is a chance the conflict will go away,[4] although there is a greater chance that this will lead to significant relational problems. It is an inaccurate perception that conflict is bad and should be avoided. Conflict is natural and even individuals in the happiest of relationships still have conflict, even about things like silverware direction.

Whether we are acting on myth or fact, conflict is bound to affect the way we behave.

## Constructive and Destructive Behaviors

**Destructive behaviors** tend to be self-centered while **constructive behaviors** are relationship centered. If the issue means absolutely everything and the relationship means very little, perhaps the message strategy doesn't really matter. If the conflict escalation isn't completely destructive, it might at least clarify the issues.

Message strategies that include name calling, threats, deception, sarcasm, and other similar behaviors are clearly destructive and elicit reactions of hurt, fear, confusion, and distrust. They expand and escalate the conflict, as Deutsch would say.[8] Sometimes these behaviors are aimed more at the relationship than at the issue. "He irritates me so much that I'll vote the opposite way," whatever the issue. The bumper sticker, "Draft my ex-wife, PLEASE" has little to do with the draft.

Behavior even concerning a relatively unimportant issue (for you) involving a relatively unimportant relationship might inadvertently turn out to be **destructive**. A young professor was moving to Detroit. This fact was unknown to a third person joining the two old friends.

| | |
|---|---|
| New person: | Did I hear you say Detroit? |
| Young professor: | Yes, I'm ... (interruption) |
| New person: | Boy, that place is the pits. |
| Old friends: | See you around. |
| New person: | Hey, don't leave. I need your help. |

Constructive and socially sensitive approaches to conflict (or any other interaction) involve some context and situation analysis before proceeding. Some topics are, after all, superficial and lack rhetorical impact anyway. The new person above described Detroit in terms of gut feelings and first impressions, which are not necessarily communicative fare. More will be said of sensitivity in the next section.

**Constructive conflict** is open, but it is *relationship* as well as content centered; and it seeks an atmosphere of trust.[9] It also seeks a forthright but supportive, rational, problem-solving kind of issue confrontation. At the same time it is sensitive to psychological adjustment mechanisms used by all people to take the heat out of frustration and conflict.

> Messages intended to seek another's opinion, state one's own opinion, or obtain or give restatement reflect such an orientation (problem-oriented) and were positively associated with conflict resolution.[10]

In a sense, you get what you give. "Just as hostile behavior is likely to draw a hostile response, positive (favorable) messages are likely to elicit positive responses … positive messages by either member of a dyad are likely to prevent or reduce a potentially destructive cycle of conflict."[11]

## Adjusting to Frustration and Conflict

Part of the constructive coping approach to interpersonal conflict is to first understand the psychological nature of frustration and conflict and how we humans normally adjust to it. **Frustration** results when an external barrier stands squarely between you and your need or goal.

The barrier may be a thing or condition which you can literally attack. For instance, you can kick the tire that goes flat on your way to an important meeting, swear at the parking ticket that calls for a court appearance, break the putter that "makes" you bogie the hole, blow the horn as you are hopelessly caught in a gigantic traffic jam on the expressway while taking a child to the hospital. There is a suggestion that frustration may lead to aggression in the preceding examples. Indeed, a *frustration-aggression hypothesis* has been postulated.[12]

When the barrier is a person such as a policeman, a boss, a teacher, parents, or others who are typically difficult to attack physically or socially, then

*Adjusting to frustration and conflict using the constructive approach involves understanding the psychological nature of frustration and conflict.*

we have the problem of what to do with our aroused emotion and aggression. Since direct confrontation of the barrier is not always possible, this aggression is often taken out on or displaced to an innocent person, pet, or object. Barriers inherent in all societies, such as rules, laws, and customs, often lead us to displaced aggression. Sometimes a nonsense telephone call or an unloved, uninvited guest in the middle of a favorite television program causes this phenomenon to occur. A classic example of displaced aggression is reported by Miller and Bugelski in which boys at a camp had their weekly night at the movies interrupted by a long testing session. Pre- and post-ratings showed significantly increased hostility toward minority groups, when in fact the testing had nothing to do with the minority groups.[13] There is historical evidence that lynching increased when the farm value of cotton decreased.[14] Of course, frustration does not always lead to aggression. When people are involved, a lot depends on how we attribute the intent of the deed that irritated us. Rough shoves by a berserk fan at a big game may be aggravating, but not as intensely aggravating as it would have been if it had happened in a more serene, uncrowded environment. As we get older and wiser we hopefully go through a more sophisticated process of attributing intentions and analyzing situations.

Communications and information that redirect our attributions of intentional irritations or barriers usually reduce our aggressive inclinations. Even children sort some of this out when appropriate communications are forthcoming. When third graders building block towers had them unceremoniously kicked over by a sixth grader, they quickly developed aggressive feelings. However, they were less hostile when they were told that the culprit was sleepy and upset, a constructive approach.[15]

When personal limitations make one's self the barrier, frustration may become very intense and lead to disillusionment and regression, as well as aggression. The would-be nuclear physicist who has no aptitude for equations, the would-be basketball player who doesn't have the necessary height, the would-be artist who simply doesn't have any talent—all are examples of frustration born of personal limitations or perhaps inflated levels of aspiration. When we encourage or persuade people to assume unrealistic levels of aspiration and achievement completely beyond their capabilities or the realities of the environment, we can expect them to fill the gap with a great deal of frustration. To be self-motivating, plans, promises, and goals must be pragmatically realistic. Otherwise, we may find people actually regressing in terms of their goals or becoming so disillusioned that they simply give up.

Some **psychological conflict**, or internal conflict (you vs. you), besets all of us with varying levels of intensity. It typically takes place when we have to make choices between needs that are incompatible or mutually exclusive. Two or more motives block each other as it were. You hate your boss, but you need the job. You want to play golf, but you have to go to class to pass the course. You love your husband *and* your boss. The last example is a case of what is called **approach-**

**approach** conflict, a choice between two or more positive, usually incompatible goals. A second form is called **approach-avoidance** conflict and is illustrated by the man who loves his wife but can't stand his children, or the paper lion who wants to play football but is terrified at the thought of getting hurt. A third form is called **avoidance-avoidance** conflict; you give your hard-earned money to the thief or risk getting hurt. Whenever we are coerced into doing something disagreeable through threats or punishment, the method is only as good as the strength of the psychological barrier (self-preservation-avoiding bodily harm), and we experience conflict and frustration.

## FORMS OF ESCAPE

When the choices are not only incompatible but also intensely fear provoking (attack the enemy or suffer a coward's fate), people may resort to various forms of psychological escape.

*Mental Paralysis*    One form of escape is **mental paralysis,** which leads to no action at all. For example, a man freezes on the battlefield, appears to be in a stupor, or actually collapses from emotional fatigue. In less critical situations a person may simply appear disinterested, terribly tired, or lazy, when in fact that person is going through intense emotional conflict. Thus, no decision or no action is a form of adjustment (avoidance). Choosing the lesser of two or more evils is conflict producing for even the best of us. This form of escape is neither uncommon nor typically successful in the long run.

*Alternation*    A second form of escaping conflict is **alternation,** a kind of psychological plasticity involving vacillation and irresolution in which one alternately tries to satisfy each of the conflicting goals or needs. This kind of adjustment often explains unpredictable and contradictory human behavior. A priest who believes in birth control may find himself trying to appease the needs of the papal encyclical one moment and the needs of his assumed social conscience the next. A female executive climbing the corporate ladder and fighting for equal employment opportunities for a woman who finds herself wanting to have children but does not believe in day care may, also, find herself being contradictory or speaking out of "both sides of her mouth". Adjusting to intense conflict is a sticky, complex business.

A third form of escape from psychological conflict is escape in the literal sense. When taking part in **literal escape,** you walk away from a marital confrontation by going fishing; you resign from the church; you quit school. These actions avoid an outward or even physical conflict—temporarily in some cases, permanently in other cases. Sometimes we escape by pretending a need is nonexistent. What discrimination? What problem? What contradiction in my behavior? We repress one or more of our need systems, which usually have a way of reemerging as all real needs do. This is not to say that we cannot profit emotionally from a stolen day on the golf course when the demands of the daily grind exhaust the best of us.

**ADJUSTMENT MECHANISMS**    Adjustment mechanisms are unconscious defense systems used by the mind to relieve ego tensions caused by conflict and frustration. They help us believe that a need does not exist or that it has been satisfied. They distort reality to defend and to take pressure off the ego.

Only when a particular defense mechanism is used consistently and becomes a chronic pattern of behavior should it be considered abnormal. Most of us could not get through a normal week without resorting to some mild defense mechanisms. They are like pressure valves which take the steam and heat out of failure, guilt, insecurity, and general stress. They are thus normal in mild degree, unconscious, and important considerations for those who would constructively cope with interpersonal conflict. Some of the more important mechanisms follow.

*Rationalization*    **Rationalization** is a less painful explanation or alibi for unacceptable behavior. The classic example is Aesop's fable of the fox and the grapes. After repeated leaps at the succulent, hanging grapes, the defeated, frustrated fox remarks that they are sour grapes anyway. *"Sour grapes"* has become an idiom for rationalization. Undoubtedly the fox was better able to live with himself after this mild distortion. Many people who receive deserved traffic tickets for moving violations have been known to offer lengthy explanations of how they were victims of circumstances. As long as these alibis do not become chronic behavior, and as long as they are not heatedly given to the arresting officer, they probably take the sting out of a trying and frustrating experience. It is, of course, modest self-deception. Interpersonally we can recognize this internal conflict in people who use contradictory evidence to justify their beliefs, see nothing wrong with oftimes blatant inconsistencies, often become irritated when their arguments are questioned, or are eternally seeking or inventing alibis for their beliefs or behaviors.

It is often temporary or special-issue related, but it complicates interpersonal communication. Good listeners cope best with this defense mechanism. If you know you are in a "sour grapes" or defeated mood, it is probably a good idea to seek friends who will understand.

*Compensation*    **Compensation** is the process of substituting one goal-seeking pattern of behavior for another pattern that has been frustrated. Demosthenes, frustrated by stuttering, worked very hard (recall the pebbles in the mouth) to overcome his disorder and eventually became the premier Greek orator. When people substitute new need-satisfying patterns for frustrated ones, it is important to their personal adjustment and to society's adjustment that the new endeavor is not equally or more frustrating than the first. Had Demosthenes been equally frustrated in his oratory, he might have become even less secure and compensated in less useful ways. Some people compensate by seeking attention for its own sake, engaging in excessive fantasy, and even eating too much. There are jokes about the frustrated lovers who buy red convertibles!

Since defeats and failures are part of living, we can expect to meet compensatory behavior in our interactions. We may quickly recognize compensatory communication when the source of the conflict or frustration is obvious. A student frustrated by a failed exam may pour out criticisms of the course, the instructor, the exam, and so forth in an effort to ease the pain. He or she might also brag about other glories and brilliant behaviors in an effort to substitute superiority for inadequacy. In some cases, and frequently because of intense inferiority feelings, compensatory behavior takes the form of verbal or even physical aggression. Communication and persuasion become most difficult.

*Projection*    The store security guards had been secretly observing a woman who they were convinced was shoplifting. They had not detained her because they were not quite sure they could make their case stick. While pondering their next move, they were shocked to have the woman approach them and proceed to upbraid them for not arresting the several shoplifters she had observed in the store.

**Projection** is the attributing or transferring of guilt and unpleasant motives to others. Other typical cases are the loafer who accuses others of loafing, and the cheater who accuses others of cheating. Perhaps certain "do-gooders" are projecting onto others the sin that tempts them. Typically, the negative traits being projected to others are unrecognized by the guilty person. Projection helps explain much apparent contradictory behavior in people. It is a psychological mask which lets us hide behind accusations against others which are the same as the guilt-laden defects which we are not always consciously aware of in our own behavior.

*Repression*    **Repression** is the excluding from consciousness or screening of those motives or desires considered unacceptable, repugnant, or threatening. We escape an emotionally difficult situation by pretending it does not really exist. In psychoanalytic theory repression also refers to the ejecting from consciousness of painful or guilt-laden experiences. We don't *really* remember mildly crunching somebody's fender in the parking lot. We weren't *really* cheating—just kind of checking the other person's procedures. We didn't *really* shout at Mom—well anyway, she knows we love her.

All repression isn't bad. Some modest "counting to ten" when faced with an interpersonal conflict may save you embarrassment or perhaps the interaction itself. We all repress some anxiety in tense situations. Beginning speakers do this, and it works for awhile, perhaps long enough for experience and success to offset it. However, constant repression is seldom a satisfactory psychological adjustment. Realistic confrontation and compromise of our conflicts and frustrations are pragmatically the best policies.

*Contraposition (Reaction Formation)*    **Contraposition** refers to a mechanism whereby repressed desires are replaced by their direct opposites. This mechanism is demonstrated by the person who "protests too much." An example is the father who can't stand his mentally challenged stepson and unconsciously wishes to be rid of him, but expresses this negative wish through lavish gifts and unusual concern for the child's well-being. Freud calls this behavior *reaction formation*. Freud also suggests that romantic notions of chastity and purity may mask crude sexual desires, that piety may conceal sinfulness, and that altruism may hide selfishness.

It is evident that some interpersonal communication analysis which misjudges the interactants' motives can be 100 percent wrong.

***Regression***    **Regression** is a return to past behavior that was once satisfying or at least attention getting. When Rick is born, five-year-old Jack finds his status shaken and returns to thumb sucking or even bed wetting. When fifty-year-old Ed is suffering leadership anxiety, we notice an almost imperceptible stamping of the foot. Seventy-year-old George handles conflict by referring to the "good old days." My first automatic transmission made my new car a real joy until the first giant traffic jam threatened my new car. Suddenly I was trying to shift again. Double panic set in when the old, friendly clutch was missing. Now that we're back to straight sticks, I occasionally forget to shift. The fellow with the lampshade on his head is usually exhibiting some kind of regressive behavior whether from conflict, frustration, or too much boilermaker punch—a kind of returning to the womb.

More seriously, regression frequently translates interpersonally into a louder voice, faster rate, verbosity, and an unwillingness to give up the floor. There is, however, a beta hypothesis involved. One may do exactly the opposite, particularly if there is a role or status difference between the interactants. This is not to say that every verbal, aggressive person is suffering from some kind of latent frustration or conflict. As we discussed earlier, attractive verbal people take into account the people, situation, and context. Some cultures are thought to be more verbal than others, other things being equal.

***Other Defense Patterns***    In addition to the adjustment mechanisms discussed above, there are several others worthy of mention.

IDENTIFICATION—a form of status seeking or protection through over identification with a group.

FANTASY—daydreaming or seeking imaginary satisfactions in place of real ones.

NEGATIVISM—a chronic state of opposition, often to all kinds of authority.

CONVERSION—the changing of mental conflicts and frustrations into physical symptoms.

ACTING-OUT—permitting the expression of forbidden desires.

## BUILDING COMMUNICATIVE COMPETENCE

When our psychological or internal conflict (you vs. you) becomes external through communicative behavior (you vs. other), communication competence is paramount for a positive outcome.

### "Saving Face"

On a recent Friday night Jean, a friend of mine, and I went to a tavern owned by another friend, Joe. He had specifically invited us because he was featuring a live musician. When we arrived, Joe was waiting at a table with a full pitcher of beer for us. He was obviously enjoying his hired talent. The music was not exactly my cup of tea, but it was played with precision and finesse. After we sat down, our interaction went something like this.

*Line*

1. Joe:   (smiling) Quite a sound, huh? You gotta go to New York to hear stuff like this.

2. Me:   He does play with precision, Joe.

3. Joe:   I know. He's cheap too.

4. Me:   Where did you find him?

5. Joe:   He plays on Sundays at our church. Jean, what do you think?

6. Jean:  I think he stinks …

7. Joe:   (mouth drops open … silence)

8. Jean:  He's playing too slow … needs to step up the tempo. The selection of material itself is wrong. This is a bar, Joe, not Sunday school.

9.  Me:    Uh, Joe, you've gotta understand. Jean and I have been arguing about art and aesthetics all night; we're kind of hypersensitized.

10. Jean:   That's true, but this stuff obviously is not for here.

11. Me:    Have another beer Jean (laughing and rolling my eyes at Joe).

12. Joe:    (hurt) I'm really sorry.

My latter utterances were designed to save face for Jean. I was trying to put her lines into a context for Joe (an episode). In line 9 I was telling Joe that Jean's lines were occurring within the episode of a "good argument over art" rather than within the episode of "an insult." That attempt failed to work because of Jean's line 10. I then tried to integrate Jean's behavior within the episode of "drinking too much" for Joe. I don't think that worked either—that excuse rarely does.

Goffman talks about self-presentation in terms of "face work."[23] Goffman would say Jean was in **wrong face** because her line was inappropriate. It failed to coordinate with the episode that Joe was creating.[24] Joe can be said to be **out of face** because he doesn't have a line that can coordinate with Jean's.[25] He says nothing and apparently feels hurt. My communicative work can be classified as an attempt to **save face** for Jean by creating an episode for Joe that might allow him to voice a line that would coordinate.

Doing "face work" in self-presentation is just what we mean when we talk about coordinating meanings. The competent interpersonal communicator needs to be sensitive to his or her self-face and others' faces. Having communicative competence obviously doesn't assure us that our lives will be stable and conflict free.

## Communicative Competence

**Communicative competence** lies partially in realizing the complexities in our communicative lives—the multitude of meaning structures that we and others create. The other part of *interpersonal competence* lies in action—our ability to present ourselves and our ability to *mesh* (coordinate) our self-presentation with others.

**Self-presentation** is really a meaning management process. We encode symbols that are illustrative of *our* personal meanings for phenomena. Our personal

*Communicative compentence requires understanding of the other person through coordination of direct perspectives and metaperspectives.*

meanings for things are functionally related to our *selves*. The encoding of symbols, in this sense, is actually a presentation of self. When we read the words of Ernest Hemingway, for example, we learn something about the man (self). How can this be? The symbols we use are reflective of our selves. Even in reading textbooks, the reader can make some inferences about the characteristics of the author. By this point in this text you should have some ideas about the personality characteristics of your authors.

When two people interact, there are two self-presentations. To the extent that these self-presentations mesh or coordinate, they create a common episode. The episode could be argument, endearment, compliment, conflict, or confusion. Our ability to coordinate our self-presentation in such a fashion as to create common episodes clearly relates to our communicative competence. In talking about communicative competence, Wiemann says that "the primary function (of conversational encounters) is the establishment and maintenance of self and the social identities of the participants."[26]

## Perspectives on Experience

R. D. Laing argues that our interpersonal behavior is largely a function of how we experience or perceive the communicative relationship.[27] Laing contends that a person experiences a communication encounter in two ways—from a **direct perspective** and a **metaperspective**. If we are talking, I experience your language and actions (behavior) directly. We can see other people's behavior but not their experience. If I am sensitive, I can also infer your direct experience of me. When I infer your experience of me, I am working at the *metaperspective* level. For example, when my business agent sends me a letter demanding copy for the publisher and I think she's being pushy *(direct perspective),* and she realizes that I think she's being pushy *(metaperspective),* we have understanding.[28] If we don't have this understanding or conjunction between direct and metaperspectives, it becomes difficult to coordinate our meanings or negotiate the episode.

Communicative competence requires understanding (the coordination of direct perspectives and metaperspectives). In the "face work" example Jean lacked understanding of Joe. Joe was hurt by Jean's comments *(direct perspective),* and Jean failed to realize the impact of her lines on Joe *(metaperspective);* hence Jean lacked understanding.

## Role Taking and Role Enactment

We all play roles in the episodes within which we operate. I play one role when listening to music with friends and another when I am in the classroom.

The social contexts within which we operate vary along a continuum that goes from very informal to very formal.[29] (See Figure 6.1.)

**FIGURE 6.1**

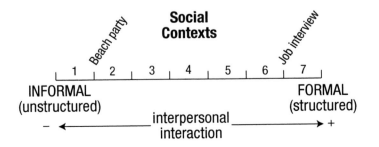

A night on the beach with friends might be very informal and unstructured: "See you when it's convenient." A job interview, on the other hand, might be very formal and very structured: "You'll meet the chairman at 9:00, the dean at 10:00, and the vice-president at exactly 12:10." In general, the more informal the social context, the more *interpersonal* the communication experience. Informal social contexts require more face work and more coordinated meaning management.

Our role playing within contexts is made up of two parts—role taking and role enactment.[30] **Role taking** refers to the internal process we go through in making inferences about self and others.[31] As we become sensitive to a particular episode, we begin to categorize self and others. This categorization leads to expectations of behavior. Sensitive role taking aids the interpersonal communicator in assessing the range and nature of the communication obligations of any particular interaction. In our earlier example Jean was not sensitive to nor willing to take a role that complemented the episode Joe was developing in relation to the music in his bar. What resulted was a lack of coordination, poor face work, and a shorter, more difficult evening.

Dynamic role taking operates in an adaptive context. In interpersonal communication there is a lot of give and take as we coordinate our actions. Therefore, we must be adaptive. We must adapt to the context, situation, or episode. We need other people's cues to assess ourselves. Our ability to self-assess enhances our ability to take roles appropriate to an episode.

**Role enactment** is the verbal and nonverbal behavior that results from our role taking.[32] It is the essence of interpersonal communication. In our Jean and Joe example Jean's role enactment (lines) was not appropriate for Joe's episode. What resulted was misinterpretation or, at best, a meaning mismatch. Jean was in wrong face and Joe was out of face.

## On Becoming a Participant Observer

**PERSPECTIVE TAKING**    We can ask people about our direct perspectives: "What do you mean when you say that?" We can also ask people about our meta-perspectives: "How am I coming off to you? Am I getting across?" Sometimes we should simply ask for clarification or confirmation; sometimes we should analyze how we're communicating.

Learning to become a good participant observer is the beginning of perspective taking and the heart of building communicative competence. Doing participant observation is no easy task. It takes practice. It requires listening, reflexivity, and empathy to accomplish the observation part, and it requires an adaptive and responsive posture to do the participant part. One secret of the participation observation strategy is to let your physical being become a type of gauge. Your body must, in effect, take readings on your participation. Then you are ready to reflect on or observe these readings and use them adaptively to create new, coordinated participation behaviors.

**CAREFUL LISTENING**    Many times it's better to be quiet for awhile and listen. It's surprising how clear things become when you're not so busy talking. As we have learned in Chapter 5, observe your listening habits.

**REFLEXIVITY**    *Reflexivity* refers to looking back on previous communication behaviors. If we take the time to think back and review what's been said, we often see a structure or regularity to our interaction that was previously overlooked. This structure/regularity can give us some clues about the types of episodes we've been enacting and perhaps the types of episodes we should enact in the future.

**EMPATHY**    *Empathy* is the essential part of what Laing calls understanding. It refers to putting yourself in the experiential stance of the other. It's taking the meta-perspective. "Put yourself in the other person's shoes."

## COPING BEHAVIORS

### Types of Sensitivities: Noble Selves, Rhetorical Reflectors, Rhetorically Sensitives

Rhetorical sensitivity is a particular attitude toward encoding spoken messages. It represents a way of thinking about what should be said and then a way of deciding how to say it.[16]

It is, according to Hart and Burks, " … that type of … sensitivity which … makes effective social interaction manifestly possible."[17]

It is our view that **rhetorically sensitive** (RS) people are interpersonally attractive. They judge encounters carefully before taking a stand on an issue, they distinguish between "content" and "relational" communication, and they know when to "speak up" or to "shut up."

People not rhetorically sensitive have been described as **"noble selves"** (NS) and **"rhetorical reflectors"** (RR). The noble selves have been characterized as persons who see "any variation from their personal norms as hypocritical, as a denial of integrity, as a cardinal sin."[18] Rhetorical reflectors have been described as persons who "have no self to call their own. For each person and for each situation they present a new self."[19] They empathize with (or at least appear to empathize with) and reflect each situation in which they find themselves.

The rhetorically sensitive person seeks to moderate these extremes. They are not braggarts, but neither are they chameleon like, fearfully reflecting and hiding in each encounter. The attitude might be scaled as shown in Figure 6.2.

**FIGURE 6.2    SENSITIVITY TOWARD HOST INTERACTIONS, WHERE (NS) IS NOBLE SELF, (RR) RHETORICAL REFLECTOR, AND (RS) IS RHETORICALLY SENSITIVE**

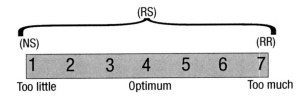

## Situations and Contexts

The research into rhetorical sensitivity suggests that the notion captures the special situations and contexts in which people find themselves. For example, nurses with high rhetorically sensitive scores tend to work in rehabilitation programs, outpatient clinics, and psychiatric wards. The rhetorical reflectors work, as one might predict, with extended care and intensive care patients. The nurses with higher noble-self scores tend to be the supervisors.[20]

In a study of military personnel, officers were found to be more rhetorically sensitive than sergeants. The sergeants tended to be noble selves; the enlisted men were mostly rhetorical reflectors.[21]

Rhetorical sensitivity, then, is an effective matching of message sending to the requirements of the receivers and the situation *and* context. In a study of hundreds of students in a speech fundamentals course where audience analysis was heavily stressed, rhetorically sensitive scores were significantly higher at the end of the semester. This was not true of control subjects in other university courses.[22] Rhetorical sensitivity is a measure of a person's audience analysis efforts and willingness to carefully consider the psychological environment before encoding messages. It is the ability to accurately judge public and interpersonal encounters and to sense when to be a reflector and when to be a noble self.

It is our position that a rhetorically sensitive person will have more interpersonally satisfactory experiences. The specific attributes of such a person should be especially valuable in heading off unnecessary interpersonal conflicts or coping with them when necessary. Our first suggestion is to take as your general perspective one of being rhetorically sensitive.

## On Rhetorical Sensitivity

**ADAPTING TO SPECIFIC AUDIENCES, RECEIVERS, CONTEXTS, AND SITUATIONS**   The rhetorically sensitive person appreciates that his or her self-concept is understood by others through interaction with others in contexts and situations that are meaningful to them. The RS know that "talk is not everywhere valued equally."[33] To adapt is to be an appropriate social actor, one who can live with reasonable role taking.

**EVALUATING MESSAGE RELEVANCE**   A prudent evaluator of message relevance, the RS evaluates the purpose of his or her information in any interaction. If it has little rhetorical purpose and threatens the relationship, the RS will consider silence. The RS assesses when to speak up and when to shut up. The RS does not run from a fight, but considers whether the issue is relevant and worth the effort. If so, the RS works diligently to couch it prudently and persuasively.

**CONSIDERING CONTENT AND RELATIONAL DIMENSIONS**   As one who considers the content and relational dimensions of his or her communications, the RS is aware that how you say something is sometimes more important than what you say. The RS is not opposed to "straight talk" but is opposed to "letting it all hang out." The RS is opposed to manipulation, but not to ethical strategies that enhance an interaction. In the words of Hart and Burks,

> "Is it inappropriate to choose carefully among alternate strategies so that my words will have the greatest social impact possible? Or is it really so wrong to stop a moment, to sift through the myriad verbalizations that can make social an idea, and to choose those rhetorical forms that appear best suited to the situation at hand?"[34]

## Managing Conflict Fairly

**RECOGNIZE ADJUSTIVE BEHAVIOR**   It's easy to be unfair, unkind, and subjective. In discussing the adjustment mechanisms we learned how we all occasionally succumb to conflict and frustration. We expect some tolerance from others when we temporarily "lose it," and we usually intend to extend it to others. The problem is that we don't always take the time or have the time to painstakingly analyze every interpersonal interaction or every hidden hang-up, real or fancied, which confronts us.

However, before we can get to the issue or **content** of a conflict, we often have to deal with the **relationship** dimension. We need not ignore all rationalizations, compensations, regressions, and so forth. We cannot and, as we shall see, sometimes should not. Nevertheless, an objective and sensitive analysis often calls for considerable discounting, since its message is more ventilation than substance.

If communication is the means by which conflicts become socially defined, then it is imperative that we don't let normal adjustment tendencies misidentify the real conflict. This coping perspective includes the ability, ideally, to know when to take a person *literally* and when not to. The situation often helps locate the tolerance line. Chapter 3 discussed this problem of language and meaning.

Being tolerant of adjustive behavior even when it provokes anger is perhaps what the Christian adage meant by turning the other cheek or what the old adage of "counting to ten" means. The advice of a popular communication teacher Irving Lee was to "stay angry, but look again at what you are responding to." Don't just count to ten or turn the other cheek, but rather look again objectively to see if your anger is justified. According to Lee, in three out of every four times a person becomes angry a second look will show that he or she is overreacting or is not justified in feeling angry. "When angry look again."[35]

During a long, hot summer a young police officer weary and angry over innumerable car thefts in his precinct saw a person removing a wheel from a car. His blood boiled as he reached for his gun. He called upon all of his training and experience to pause and look again; he knew the man, it was his own car, and he was replacing a flat tire! A possible tragedy was avoided because a young police officer fought his emotions long enough to "look again." Before you blow your cool, run it through one more time. Is it what it appears to be? Is it really worth the extent of your anger?

A forthright problem-solving approach to conflict doesn't work well until you get past the relationship problems, many of which are intensified by insensitivity or lack of knowledge about the adjustment mechanisms. From a sender's perspective the problem is essentially the same. It's just as easy initially to overlook how our overcompensation might make a mess of an interaction and contribute to the real conflict.

Managing conflict fairly calls for an understanding and a tolerance of the defense systems used by others to protect their self-concepts and to relieve ego pressures. It also calls upon us to manage our own defense mechanisms so that we don't compound an already difficult interaction.

**FIGHT FAIRLY**    One way to know what is fair is to discuss what is unfair. In their book *The Intimate Enemy: How to Fight Fair in Love and Marriage* psychotherapist

*In kitchen-sinking, the fight becomes a heated exchange of insults, with each side using every argument possible—even if the argument has nothing to do with the conflict.*

George Bach and colleague Peter Wyden review a great many unfair fighting techniques or "crazy-makers."[36] Several are relevant to the kinds of interpersonal conflicts we are talking about. Even after appropriate excuses for adjustment behavior, these are really unfair.

**KITCHEN-SINKING**    **Kitchen-sinking** throws every argument into the fight but the kitchen sink. This type of unfair fight ends up being a heated exchange of insults. Several things are brought up that really have nothing to do with the conflict at hand.

**GUNNYSACKING**    **Gunnysacking** saves up all manner of grievances and complaints that are "toted along quietly in a gunny sack … (till) they make a dreadful mess when the sack finally bursts." Bach and Wyden catch this crazy-maker with the following episode.

A wife arrives twenty minutes late for a meeting with her husband Bill and an important friend. Bill is furious.

He:    Why were you late?

She:    I tried my best.

He:    Yeah? You and who else? Your mother is never on time either.

She:    That's got nothing to do with it.

He:    The hell it doesn't. You're just as sloppy as she is.

She:    (getting louder) You don't say! Who's picking whose dirty underwear off the floor every morning?

He:    (shouting) I happen to go to work. What have you got to do all day?

She:    (shouting) I'm trying to get along on the money you don't make, that's what.

He:    (turning away from her) Why should I knock myself out for an ungrateful bitch like you?[38]

Some conflict was legitimate; she was late. But check the gunnysacking and some kitchen-sinking—the mother-in-law complaint, and the masculinity grievance, the money complaint …

**BELTLINING**    **Beltlining,** as in boxing, strikes a blow at or below the beltline—a foul in some cases, painful at best. We all have a psychological beltline or tolerance level for some interpersonal pain. Communications can be more prudently transmitted when we know where those beltlines are. If a boxer had his trunks up around his neck, we'd think it an unfair fight, yet some people face conflict situations in much the same way, making a low blow out of the mildest of admonitions. Unless you are in therapy, it's a sure way to become embroiled in a dirty fight (or to be ignored).

All of us need to check the beltlines of others and perhaps adjust our own from year to year and situation to situation. In dealing with intimates and friends we are advised to give some clue indicating where our beltlines are so we do not deceive others. If Mom and Dad don't want your visiting girl friend in your bedroom in their house, they should make that beltline clear before she arrives at the door. Conflicts are easier to cope with when we know what they are about and where the sensitivities lie.

**MONOLOGUING**    **Monologuing** is incessant talking, a verbosity which tolerates no real feedback. Wendell Johnson in discussing the "Language of Maladjustment" describes an extreme case.

> One of the most striking cases I have ever known is that of a lady who seems to have no terminal facilities whatever. It is quite probably that she could talk all day; I have never felt up to making the experiment. An interesting thing about her speech is that a little of it is not unpleasant. Listening to her talk is somewhat like watching a six-day bicycle race; the first few laps are even a little exciting, perhaps. It is the five-hundredth lap that gets you. She seems to be motivated by a profound sense of frustration in her social and professional activities; in any prolonged monologue she eventually settles down to a steady outpouring of criticism and pained astonishment concerning her real and imagined rivals. In common parlance, she is a "cat." Her denunciations of other people, given usually in confidential tones, seem to serve as a crutch with which she supports her own tottering self-esteem.[39]

Certainly all verbose people are not monologuers. Even the more quiet among us can become overtalkative given the right issue or frustration. The normally verbose know they talk a lot; and they, therefore, work at being and frequently are excellent listeners. The persistent and chronic monologuers may have a more serious maladjustment problem according to Wendell Johnson. His descriptions may help us recognize in ourselves and others when we are reflecting a personal quandary and fighting unfairly.

> The disorienting language of verbose individuals will usually be found
> to express, in more or less conspicuous degrees, idealism, frustration,

and the varieties of aggression that take the form of criticism, vengeful-
ness, and vigorous self-defense. It expresses, also, a naive faith in words,
something quite remindful of primitive word magic.[40]

According to Bach and Wyden monologuers are enormously resented. They
have only limited constructive advice for victims of monologuing: walk out, cover
your ears, hold up your hand, reward acknowledgements.[41] They have found that
the best training for monologuers is to let them see and hear themselves and their
victims on television. It's one way to get them to absorb feedback.

**SANDBAGGING   Sandbagging** sets up or traps someone into saying something that is later held against him or her. It is often a phony plea for openness. You
comply by laying out the administrative heads in your organization and are subsequently attacked by the sandbagger who supports Uncle Lou and the administration. Sometimes sandbagging can be more subtle: A con man listens patiently and
attentively until you put your foot in your mouth or buy the swamp land and essentially sandbag yourself. Women used to complain loudly about being sandbagged (or compromised) by unfair men. Of course, with enlightenment it's impossible to be sandbagged in these matters.

## Preparation and Practice

**PREPARATION PERSPECTIVES**   Sometimes conflict is dumped in your lap.
You arrive at the office and an act of God has cut off all of the power and heat.
Now that's not an interpersonal conflict. However, if you are in a leadership role,
it can quickly become one if people feel that you should have anticipated such a
calamity and had auxiliary power and heat available. Interpersonal conflicts are
sometimes like that too. They catch us by surprise but, perhaps, they shouldn't as
often as they do. "I didn't know she was unhappy." "I had no idea I was being unkind." "He just up and left me." All are familiar lines to marriage counselors.

This is not a recommendation to seek or create conflicts, but it is a suggestion
to be alert to small ones and to confront them before they become large ones. If
you have some kind of comprehension of an interpersonal conflict and are convinced that you must confront, then consideration of the following general questions should help you prepare for such an encounter.

***How Critical is the Conflict?***    Must it be confronted immediately? Should it be? Has your irritation magnified the problem? Is it really your business? Have you "looked again"? Remember Irving Lee's findings that when we are emotional and angry, three out of every four times a "look again" proves we were wrong or at least not totally justified in our anger.

***Is It Primarily Relational or Content Oriented?***    All interpersonal conflicts are in part relational, but some are entirely so. Other times an issue is the primary cause of conflict with some relational consequences. An argument over twin or double beds may be content for some, but lovers would, we're sure, find it relational as well. In fact, the beds may be a secondary issue from the start. It is not always easy to assign weights to content and relational matters, but we should try. If a friend is constantly monologuing using the same tired issues, it is probably relational. Perhaps you have taken the issues too seriously and your friend hasn't; perhaps you need some new friends …

***Is the Receiver Aware of the Conflict?***    The earlier marriage counselor examples make this point of awareness. "I had no idea she was unhappy" We may be very aware of another's behavior that is bothersome and frustrating to us; but if, thanks to the silence of others and ourselves, that person is unaware of a problem, we have a conflict with a very special twist—a twist that we must consider before engaging in systematic confrontation. The approach to this encounter should vary depending upon whether the "other" is an intimate, a casual friend, a superior, a subordinate—in short, the way in which the relationship is important to you.

***Is There a Role Difference?***    In Utopia all people are equal and their roles in society make no difference. Presidents and kings are viewed in the same way as the rank and file. It is a cruel illusion. Many needless conflicts are spawned by innocents who confuse "equal under the law" with "equal in all ways." Without arguing intelligence, it is clear that some people have better reaction times, retention skills, and abilities to abstract complicated data. That can make for a role difference, but so can the less easy to swallow assigned or elected roles. In the military it is clear—RHIP,

Rank Has Its Privileges. That's why we have NCO (noncommissioned officers) Clubs and Officers' Clubs. That's why the president of a major corporation or government agency has a chauffeured car and others do not. Like it or not, role difference makes a difference. It is an issue you must address pragmatically as you assess the criticality of the conflict and the approach or strategy you will use in confronting it. More will be said of these strategies in the chapter on interpersonal influence.

*Am I Prepared to Lose?*    A really mean question! You should, after all, think positively and have faith that people will see things *your* way after honest discussion; or if not your way, surely they will see some other way mutually acceptable to all. After sitting in on arbitration cases it became obvious to me that some conflicts don't get resolved at all, and that third parties sometimes simply hand down resolutions and decisions. There are winners, there are losers, and there are times when we're not sure whether we've won or lost.

It pays to calculate your risks in these matters. If I lose, will my relationship suffer? How will I maintain contact? Will I be able to confront this conflict again perhaps with more success next time? Am I destroyed? Does a loss mean my job? Can I live with it?

In small group conflicts if rational, problem-solving and aggressive, rhetorically-sensitive arguments don't resolve anything, we frequently resort to votes. We can sometimes calculate those risks by anticipating voting behavior. We may be surprised when we lose, but we are usually psychologically *prepared* for a defeat. We'll have more to say about group conflicts in a later chapter.

Coping with conflict is serious business and calls for thoughtfulness, awareness, and a willingness to confront it intelligently, fairly, and systematically. An agenda for conflict coping or fair fighting follows.

**BEHAVIOR AND PRACTICE**    *Personally Define the Problem.*    Personally define the issue or behavior that bothers you. This includes all of the perspective questions suggested in the previous section. Is it critical? Is it relational? Is it understood? Is there a role difference that matters? After these considerations you're ready to *state the conflict specifically.* Try to keep it singular; don't kitchen-sink or gunnysack on this one. You'll only deceive yourself. Explain to your own satisfaction how it really affects you. Check your thinking by *trying it out on a trusted friend*. Stand still for feedback; it may also be a test of your friends. If it washes here, you are ready to consider an appropriate style of communication as you approach the confrontation.

## Conflict Management Styles

**AVOIDANCE—I LOSE, YOU LOSE.** In this case you have little concern for the relationship; and if the conflict impinges only slightly on your personal goals, your style might very well be a low-profile one. You can take or leave your boss as a friend, and it's a short term relationship anyway. You are aware that he or she has matrimonial problems which you feel may be hurting his or her effectiveness as a supervisor, but they don't particularly affect your personal goals in or out of the organization. This is not much of a conflict for you, and you're not sure about the organization. This may be the time for an avoidance or impersonal style.

**COMPETING—I WIN, YOU LOSE.** With this approach you have much concern for the conflict and minimal concern for the relationship. The senior pilot in the aforementioned example was backed into this one. His argument was a short one given the emergency.

Two union business agents representing the plumbers and the carpenters have a conflict over who has jurisdiction over the installation of bathroom wall fixtures in an apartment complex. Both groups can't do the work. One will win and one will lose if it takes arbitration.

**COMPROMISING—I WIN AND LOSE, YOU WIN AND LOSE.** This is a compromise style wherein your concerns are typically low or mixed. As in the jurisdictional conflict above, it is a popular backup style even when one or both concerns are very high. During the protest years of the 1960s the president of a major university was faced with "non-negotiable demands" from a large group of very militant, emotional students. He commented in retrospect, "I gave up on your rational, problem-solving approach (collaborating); and I couldn't give the university away (avoidance) or (accommodating); confrontation (competing) was to incite a riot ... I sought whatever viable solutions of the moment I could negotiate (compromising)." The compromise style is not always an easy one and not always the best, long-term resolution of a conflict. In the case above, the university and the students were protected; and eventually the president was able to assume a successful, rhetorically sensitive, collaborative, problem-solving style.

**ACCOMMODATING—I LOSE, YOU WIN.**    In this situation the concern for the relationship is unusually high, and the concern for personal goals is either low to begin with or is surrendered for the sake of the relationship.

A useful, but tricky, style … sometimes. You are smitten with an incredibly attractive person who literally takes your breath away. You discover that he or she has strong political leanings which are the opposite of yours. Unless your politics are truly at the 9 on the scale, you would probably use a style that accommodates the relationship and yields on the political conflict. Depending upon how the relationship develops, you might move to any of the other styles. You might, of course, really change your politics, but you won't change the other person's if you stay accommodating.

You love your parents and you want desperately not to hurt them, but they simply can't agree to your having a roommate of the opposite sex. You could forgo the roommate (accommodating) or at least assume that style. If you try collaboration, the rational approach, and it fails, you may find yourself in an argumentative style, competing. Of course your parents may go the compromising way, "Okay, but not in our house," or perhaps avoid it all together, "It's your life" (or is that also compromising?). We said this was a tricky style. The point is that it's just a style we're talking about, not necessarily perfect solutions to interpersonal conflicts.

**COLLABORATING—I WIN, YOU WIN.**    Here one has much concern for the relationship and much concern for personal goals. It is an enlightened style based on the assumptions that conflicts are natural in the human experience; conflicts are amenable to rational, cooperative problem solving; and a sensitive openness is the necessary first step. More will be said of these assumptions in the section on reviewing positive attitudes about conflict in this chapter.

The problem with ideal styles is that situations, contexts, and circumstances are not always ideal. The roommate problem might be amenable to this mutual-exploration style, but it could be a disaster if Mom and Dad really have strong opinions about this sort of thing. If they won't even participate in such a problem-solving discussion, you've obviously struck out.

Another set of constraints on the collaborative approach is the ethics, oaths, agreements, and business and professional obligations to which you have previously agreed. The doctor who is asked by a friend to provide illegal drugs is going to have to be hardheaded about the law and his or her code of ethics. Professionals and others in the public eye have confrontational constraints and aggressive obligations both legally as public figures and morally in terms of their ethical codes. The organization person is tied (or ought to be) by constitutions, bylaws, labor agreements, affirmative action, the Internal Revenue Service, and other laws of the land. Some have argued that the bureaucratic constraints are so great that the synergistic (a working together) striking of a business deal is a thing of the past.

In addition to requiring participation, the collaborative style is usually very time consuming. Don't be in a hurry.

Part of your style decision should be based on the typical styles used by the other or others involved in the conflict. If you know you are going to have to interact with a confirmed competitor—that is, an aggressive, "tell it like it is" approach to conflict resolution—your starting point may be a little (or a lot) short of collaboration.

*Decide Your Communication Style.*   We discussed earlier your concern for the content versus the relationship. It could also be stated as your concern for your personal goals in the conflict versus your concern for the relationship (in any given conflict).

Borrowing from Slake and Mouton[42] and the Jay Hall revision[43] we get a characterization of the styles available.(See Figure 6.3) The horizontal scale allows you to assess just how important your personal goals are in any given conflict. The vertical scale allows you to assess just how important the relationship is to you in any given conflict. There are eighty-one intersections, but the four styles typified by the corners plus a central compromise style, are enough to make the point. Your analysis of your specific conflict should help you choose an appropriate style. Ideally you should seek a  collaborative, problem-solving style, but some conflicts quickly call

**FIGURE 6.3**    INTERPERSONAL CONFLICT STYLES

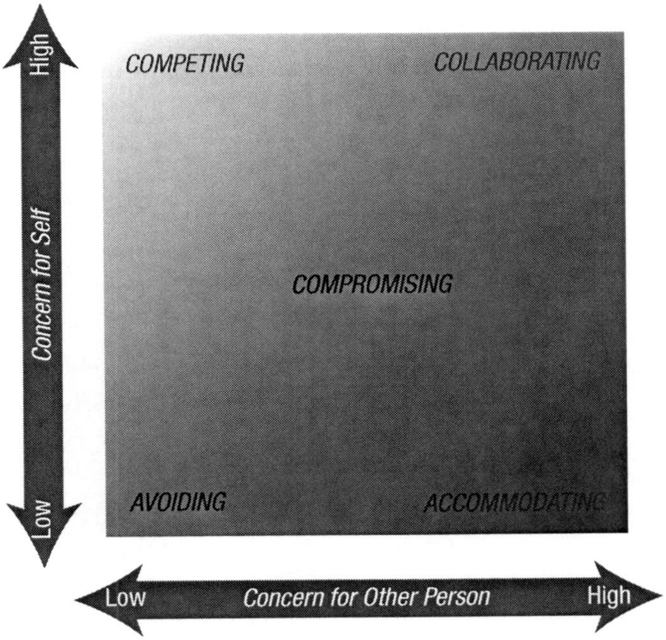

for backup styles when collaboration fails. Sometimes the time factor is enough. A conflict between two pilots on a damaged aircraft calls for quick assessment of what to do; but when time runs out, the senior officer turns to an aggressive competitive style: "We're going to abort. Prepare for an emergency landing." This happens despite the pilot's concern for the relationship between him or her and the crew.

## Conflict Strategies

In one interesting study of styles (or strategies) of resolving relational conflict five types along with their representative tactics were delineated (See Figure 6.4). Except for number five, they all seem a little harsh, but all were found to be used

## FIGURE 6.4    INTERPERSONAL CONFLICT STRATEGIES

1. **Strategy of Manipulation**

   Be especially sweet, charming, helpful and pleasant before bringing up the subject of disagreement

   Act so nice that he/she later cannot refuse when I ask him/her for my own way

   Make this person believe that he/she is doing me a favor by giving in

2. **Strategy of Non-negotiation**

   Refuse to discuss or even listen to the subject unless he/she gives in

   Keep repeating my point of view until he/she gives in

   Argue until this person changes his/her mind

3. **Strategy of Emotional Appeal**

   Appeal to this person's love and affection for me

   Promise to be more loving in the future

   Get angry and demand that he/she give in

4. **Strategy of Personal Rejection**

   Withhold affection and act cold until he/she gives in

   Ignore him/her

   Make the other person jealous by pretending to lose interest in him/her

5. **Strategy of Empathic Understanding**

   Discuss what would happen if we each accepted the other's point of view

   Talk about why we do not agree

   Hold mutual talks without argument

*From M. Fitzpatrick and J. Winke, "You Always Hurt the One You Love: Strategies and Tactics in Interpersonal Conflict," Communication Quarterly, 27, no. 1 (Winter 1979), p. 7.*

with some success across a variety of contexts.[44] We do not offer them as recommendations, however. Knowing the basic styles and being able to use those most appropriate to the requirements of each specific conflict are your best perspectives.

You should also be ready to switch styles when necessary and perhaps reassess your personal concerns for certain goals and certain relationships.

**REVIEW POSITIVE ATTITUDES ABOUT CONFLICT.**    Just to make sure your courage is up, your head is on straight, and you are not acting emotionally, try these attitudes for reassurance.

1.    Conflict is serious business but a natural hazard of living.

2.    When conflict is resolved effectively and with rhetorical sensitivity, such an experience can preserve or enhance a relationship.

3.    A positive, rhetorically sensitive openness is usually the first step toward conflict resolution.

4.    "When angry look again." If your anger is truly justified, it is human to admit it and to seek feedback from the appropriate respondent—but "look again."

**MAKE AN APPOINTMENT.**    Now that you have worked your way through your personal definition of the conflict (including the style decisions, and assuming it's still of enough concern to confront an important someone about), you are ready to get on with the discussion. But is the other person (or persons) ready? One way to find out is to test these waters by asking if there is a convenient time for your adversary to discuss your problem. Make a date as it were.

During one year I lost both of my parents. On my first day back to school after the second funeral, an unannounced student rushed into my office literally screaming about a class schedule problem. I had to call on my last ounce of professionalism to resolve the conflict. Of course the student didn't know about my problems, and besides, I was being paid to solve the student's problems. I really think, however, that had I a knife in my chest and blood on my shirt, this particular student would have been summarily unimpressed and would still have shouted, "Dr. Ross, I have a problem!"

Appointments can help conflicting parties arrive at a psychologically constructive time for heavy discussions. They needn't be all that formal either. "Son, I'd like to talk to you about your problems in graduate school. Can we find a time to discuss some of these things?" To plunge in without this kind of consideration often is understood as "Son, you're fouling up in graduate school, and we're going to talk about it right now!" It's easy to see why some people never even get to a real confrontation of a conflict. They alienate one another in the preliminaries. Don't overlook this step in preparing your conflict-coping agenda. It's kind, rhetorically sensitive, and makes for a more systematic discussion.

**CONFRONT THE CONFLICT.**    It's your day in court. State your conflict as you have personally defined and rehearsed it. Keep it singular and explain how it affects you. Don't monologue, keep it brief, and avoid kitchen-sinking and gunnysacking.

Next, seek agreement on your statement, not the right and wrong of it, but just the statement itself. Are you agreed that you are talking about the same problem? If you are the one on the receiving end, a good technique is to repeat it: "I hear you saying that you feel you were discriminated against in the last round of promotions because of your sex." Control your emotions and stay on the topic. It's easy to stray:

"Are you an officer in NOW?" If you are serious about resolution, don't trap or sandbag.

Now allow response time. The person reacting to the statement has a right to reply or, in some cases, to ask for a delay if more time or information is needed. If and when the discussion proceeds, don't monologue, but rather solicit feedback. Keep your analysis rational and stick with your decision on communication style unless it proves to be obviously out of sync with the situation. Be open and positive.

If you resolve or partially resolve the conflict, review your joint understanding. Thank your interactant particularly when there were good faith, constructive efforts made to at least try to reach a solution.

---

**FIGURE 6.5    A WORKING OUTLINE FOR CONFLICT SITUATIONS**

> **CONFLICT: PREPARATION AND PRACTICE**
> I. Preparation Perspectives
>     A. How critical is the conflict?
>     B. Is it primarily relational or content oriented?
>     C. Is the receiver aware of the conflict?

       D. Is there a role difference?

       E. Am I prepared to lose?

II.     Behavior and Practice

       A. Agenda building

          1. Personally define the problem.

          2. Analyze how it affects you exactly.

              a. Consider your adjustment behavior (mechanisms).

              b. Use fair-fight, constructive techniques.

                  (1) Don't kitchen-sink.

                  (2) Don't gunnysack.

                  (3) Don't beltline.

                  (4) Don't monologue.

                  (5) Don't sandbag.

          3. State your problem.

              a. Singularly

              b. Specifically

              c. Fairly

          4. Try it on a friend.

       B. Decide on an appropriate communication style.

          1. 1/1, avoidance or impersonal tolerance

          2. 9/1, aggressive, argumentative, confrontational

          3. 5/5, viable solution

          4. 1/9, human accommodation

          5. 9/9, collaboration, problem solving

       C. Review positive attitudes about conflict.

          1. Conflict is serious business, but a natural hazard of living.

          2. When conflict is resolved effectively, with rhetorical sensitivity, such an experience can preserve or enhance a relationship.

            3. A positive, rhetorically sensitive openness is usually the first step toward conflict resolution.

            4. "When angry look again." If your anger is justified, it is human to admit it and to seek feedback from the appropriate respondent.

       D. Make an appointment.

          1. A mutually convenient time

2. A psychologically constructive time

E. Confronting the conflict

   1. State the conflict singularly, specifically, fairly.

   2. Seek agreement on the statement.

      a. Control emotions.

   b. Stay on the topic.

      c. Don't sandbag.

   3. Allow response time (or delay).

      a. Don't monologue.

      b. Solicit feedback.

      c. Keep analysis rational.

      d. Be open, positive, and rhetorically sensitive.

   4. If resolved or partially so, review your joint understanding.

THANKS!

## SUMMING UP

Conflict is a hazard of living. A large part of interpersonal conflict involves your concern for the relationship with the other person. Will the message or content part of your interaction threaten the relationship? Conflict almost always involves perceptions of incompatible goals and/or threats to a relationship. There are several myths about the nature of conflict: (1) conflict is always bad; (2) conflict is due to misunderstanding and miscommunication; (3) conflict can always be resolved; and (4) conflict can be avoided Destructive behaviors tend to be self-centered, while constructive behaviors are relationship centered. Name calling, threats, deception, and sarcasm are destructive and elicit reactions of hurt, fear, confusion, and distrust. Constructive conflict is open, but it is relationship as well as issue centered; and it seeks an atmosphere of trust. It seeks a forthright but supportive, rational, problem-solving kind of issue confrontation.

Frustration results when an external barrier stands between us and our needs or goals. Psychological conflict takes place when we have to make choices between needs that are incompatible or mutually exclusive. To escape frustration and conflict we may resort to a kind of *mental paralysis* or avoidance behavior. Another way to escape is through *alternation,* a kind of psychological plasticity involving vacillation and irresolution in which we alternately try to satisfy each of the conflicting goals or needs. A third way is *literal escape*—that is, we simply walk away from the conflict and hope it will go away. Adjustment mechanisms are unconscious defense systems used by the mind to relieve ego tensions caused by conflict and frustration. They distort reality to defend and take pressure off the ego. They include rationalization, compensation, projection, repression, contraposition, regression, and others. They are normal in mild degree.

"Rhetorical sensitivity is a particular attitude toward encoding spoken messages. It represents a way of thinking about what should be said and then a way of deciding how to say it."[45] It is a type of sensitivity that makes effective social interaction possible. Rhetorically sensitive (RS) people judge encounters carefully before taking a stand on an issue. They distinguish between content and relational communication, and they know when to speak up or shut up.

People not rhetorically sensitive have been described as noble selves (NS) and rhetorical reflectors (RR). The noble selves may be characterized as individuals who see any variation from their personal norms as hypocritical, as a denial of integrity, as a cardinal sin. Rhetorical reflectors are described as persons who have no self to call their own. For each person and situation they present a new self. They reflect each situation in which they find themselves.

Goffman talks about self-presentation in terms of "face work" (as in saving face). The competent communicator needs to be sensitive to his or her self face and others' faces. When two people interact, there are two self-presentations. If these coordinate, they create a common episode. A primary function of interpersonal encounters is the establishment and maintenance of self and the social identities of the participants.

Our interpersonal behavior is largely a function of how we experience or perceive the communicative relationship.[46] We experience communication from a direct perspective and a metaperspective. When one infers another's direct experience of oneself (my notion of what your notion is of me), one is dealing with the meta-perspective level.

Role taking is the internal process we go through in making inferences about self and others. Sensitive role taking aids in assessing the range and nature of the communication obligations of any particular interaction. Role enactment is the verbal and nonverbal behavior that results from our role taking. It is the essence of interpersonal communication.

We become participant-observers through careful listening, reflexivity (a looking back or reviewing), empathic understanding, and taking both a perspective and metaperspective view. (What do you mean? How am I coming over?)

We cope with conflict better if we are rhetorically sensitive. This includes an ability to adapt to specific audiences, receivers, contexts, and situations; being a prudent evaluator of message relevance; and consideration of the content and relational dimensions of conflict communications.

We can manage conflict fairly if we first learn to recognize adjustive behaviors. Managing conflict fairly calls for an understanding and a tolerance of the defense systems used by others to protect their self-concepts and to relieve ego pressures. It also calls upon us to manage our own defense mechanisms. Dirty fighting techniques include kitchen-sinking, gunnysacking, beltlining, monologuing, and sandbagging. Assessing a conflict situation should include the following questions: (1) How critical is the conflict? (2) Is it primarily relational or content? (3) Is the receiver aware of the conflict? (4) Is there a role difference? (5) Am I prepared to lose? Preparation behavior for conflict situations should include the following: (1) Define the issue or behavior that bothers you and state the conflict specifically; (2) Decide your communication style; (3) Review positive attitudes about conflict; (4) Make an appointment; and (5) Confront the conflict systematically. Some useful principles to help you through trying times include: (1) Conflict is a natural hazard of living; (2) When conflict is resolved with rhetorical sensitivity, such an experience can preserve or enhance a relationship; (3) A positive, rhetorically sensitive openness is usually the first step toward conflict resolution; and (4) "When angry look again"; if your anger is justified it is human to admit it and to seek feedback from the appropriate respondent.

# NOTES

1 Buzzanell, P.M., & Burrell, N.A. (1997). Family and work place conflict: Examining metaphorical conflict schemas and expressions across context and sex. Human Communication Research, 24, 109-146.

2 D.H. Solomon, L.K. Knoblock, & M.A. Fitzpatrice, "Relational Power, Marital Schema, and Decisions to Withold Complaints: An Investigation of the Chilling Effects of Confrontation in Marriage," Communication Studies, 55 (2004): 146-67.

3 Lakey, S.G., & Canary, D. J. (2002). Actor goal achievement and sensitivity to parther as critical factors in understanding interpersonal communication competence and conflict strategies. Communication Monograph, 69, 217-235.

4 Petronio, S. (2002). *Boundaries of privacy: Dialectics of disclosure.* Albany, NY: SUNY Press.

5 A. M. Greeley, Sexual Intimacy (New York: Seabury Press, 1973). See also I. Altman and D. A. Taylor, *Social Penetration: The Development of Interpersonal Relationships* (New York: Holt, Rinehart & Winston, 1973); M. L. Knapp, *Social Intercourse: From Greeting to Goodby* (Boston: Allyn and Bacon, Inc., 1978).

6 For another view see J. H. Frost and W. W. Wilmot, *Interpersonal Conflict* (Dubuque: Wm. C. Brown Publishers, 1978), p. 9.

7 G. R. Miller and H. S. Simons, eds., *Perspectives on Communication in Social Conflict* (Englewood Cliffs, N.J.; Prentice-Hall, Inc., 1974), p. 3.

8 M. Deutsch, *The Resolution of Conflict: Constructive and Destructive Processes* (New Haven; Yale University Press, 1973).

9 A. C. Filley, *Interpersonal Conflict Resolution* (New York: Scott, Foresman & Co., 1975).

10 E. R. Alexander, "The Reduction of Cognitive Conflict," *Journal of Conflict Resolution,* 23 (1979), 137.

11 W. R. Cupach, "Interpersonal Conflict: Relational Strategies and Intimacy," (paper presented at the annual convention of the Speech Communication Association, New York, November, 1980), p. 7 (parentheses ours).

12 John Dollard and others, *Frustration and Aggression* (New Haven, Conn.; Yale University Press, 1939). See also R. R. Sears, E. E. Maccoby, and H. Levin, *Patterns of Child Rearing* (New York: Harper and Row Publishers, Inc., 1957).

13 Neal E. Miller and Richard Bugelski, "Minor Studies of Aggression: II. The Influence of Frustrations Imposed by the In-Group on Attitudes Expressed Toward Out-Groups," *Journal of Psychology,* 25 (1948), 437-42.

14 Carl I. Hovland and Robert R. Sears, "Minor Studies of Aggression; VI. Correlations of Lynchings with Economic Indices," *Journal of Psychology,* 9 (1940), 301-10.

15 S. K. Mallick and B. R. McCandless, "A Study of Catharsis of Aggression," *Journal of Personality and Social Psychology,* 4 (1966), 591-96.

16 R. P. Hart, R. E. Carlson, and W. F. Eadie, "Attitudes Toward Communication and the Assessment of Rhetorical Sensitivity," *Communication Monographs,* 47, no. 1 (March 1980), 2.

17 R. P. Hart and D. M. Burks, "Rhetorical Sensitivity and Social Interaction," *Speech Monographs,* 39, no. 2 (June 1972), 75.

18 D. Darnell and W. Brockriede, *Persons Communicating* (Englewood Cliffs, N.J.: Prentice-Hall, Inc., 1976), p. 176.

19 Ibid. p. 178.

20 Hart, Carlson, and Eadie, "Attitudes Toward Communication," p. 2I.

21 Dudley D. Cahn and Gary M. Shulman, "An Exploratory Study of the Relationship between Rhetorical Sensitivity, Leadership Effectiveness and Rank in Military Organization," *Michigan Speech Association Journal,* 15 (1980), I-II.

22 Ladene Schoen, "A Study of the Audience Sensitivity and Rhetorical Sensitivity of Students Enrolled in Speech 0200, Basic Speech, at Wayne State University and Implications for Pedagogy," (unpublished doctoral dissertation, Wayne State University, 1981). i

23 Erving Goffman, "On Face Work," *Psychiatry,* 18 (1955), 213-3l.

24 Ibid. p. 214.

25 Ibid.

26 John M. Wiemann, "Explication and Test of a Model of Communicative Competence," *Human Communication Research,* 3, no. 3 (1977), 196.

27 R. D. Laing, *The Politics of Experience* (New York: Pantheon Books, 1967), p. 4. See also Stephen W. Littlejohn, *Theories of Human Communication* (Columbus, Ohio; Charles E. Merrill Publishing Co., 1978), pp. 208-12.

28 Stephen W. Littlejohn, *Theories of Human Communication* (Columbus, Ohio: Charles E. Merrill Publishing Company, 1978) pp. 209-10.

29 T. R. Sarbin and V. L. Allen, "Role Theory," in *The Handbook of Social Psychology, Volume L 2nd* ed., eds. G. Lindzey and E. Aronson (Reading, Mass.; Addison-Wesley, 1969), pp. 492-94.

30 Ibid. pp. 489-99.

31 Ralph H. Turner, "Role-Taking, Role Standpoint, and Reference-Group Behavior," in *Role Theory Concepts and Research,* eds. Bruce J. Biddle and Edwin J. Thomas (New York: John Wiley & Sons, Inc., 1966), p. 152.

32 Sarbin and Allen, "Role Theory," pp. 489-91.

33 G. Philipsen, "Speaking 'Like a Man' in Teamsterville; Culture Patterns of Role Enactment in an Urban Neighborbood," *Quarterly Journal of Speech,* 61, no. 1 (February 1975), 13-22.

34 R. P. Hart and D. M. Burks, "Rhetorical Sensitivity and Social Interaction," p. 90. For a detailed discussion of five constituent parts of a rhetorically sensitive attitude see R. P. Hart, R. E. Carlson, and W. F. Eadie, "Attitudes Toward Communication and the Assessment of Rhetorical Sensitivity."

35 Irving J. Lee, H*ow to Talk with People* (New York Harper and Row Publishers, Inc., 1952), pp. 113-20.

36 Dr. George R. Bach and Peter Wyden, *The Intimate Enemy* (New York: William Morrow and Company, Inc., 1969), p. 135.

37 Bach and Wyden, *The Intimate Enemy,* p. 3.

38 Wendell Johnson, *People in Quandaries* (New York: Harper & Brothers, 1946), pp. 245-6.

39 Ibid. p. 248.

40 Bach and Wyden, *The Intimate Enemy,* p. 142.

41 Robert R. Blake and Jane S. Mouton, *The Managerial Grid* (Houston: Gulf Publishing Company, 1964), p. 10.

42 Jay Hall, *Conflict Management Survey* (Woodlands, Texas: Teleometrics International, 1969).

43 M. Fitzpatrick and J. Winke, "You Always Hurt the One You Love: Strategies and Tactics in Interpersonal Conflict," *Communication Quarterly,* 27, no. 1 (Winter 1979), 3-11.

44 Hart, Carlson, and Eadie, "Attitudes Toward Communication," p. 75.

45 Laing, *The Politics of Experience,* p. 4.

46 Steven M. Alderton, "A Processerol Analysis of Argumentation in Polarizing Groups," in *Dimensions of Argument* (Salt Lake City, Utah: University of Utah Press, 1981), pp. 693-704.

# CHAPTER 7

# INTERPERSONAL POWER AND INFLUENCE

As we have seen in the last chapter, conflict is a definite. It's natural and unavoidable. To gain even greater insight into the concept of conflict it is helpful to begin to understand the concept of power. **Power** is what gives one person the ability to control the behavior of another. As you can imagine, power has a tremendous influence on the outcome of conflict. We consider **interpersonal influence** to be a change, attributable to another person, in someone's thinking, feelings, or behavior. Though the idea of one person being able to influence another's behavior can be a frightening thought, it is reality. Power and influence are just as natural and unavoidable as conflict.[1]

The following chapter will discuss where power comes from and why we are susceptible or not susceptible to power.

## SOURCES OF POWER

The best place to start in understanding power is a discussion about where power comes from. Why do certain people have it, and others don't? Why do we allow some people to have power over us, and why are we able to have power over others? The influence we have over others in making decisions, behaving, and winning arguments comes from six sources of power.[2] Keep in mind, these sources of power do not stand alone, and they are undoubtedly not the only ones.[3]

### Referent Power

You have **referent power** when others wish to be like you or to be identified with you. The general premise behind this source of power is that if we want to be like another person, we just need to believe and behave like them. Referent power is grounded in an individual's charisma or a combination of attractiveness and prestige. There is a direct, positive correlation with increase in attractiveness and prestige and increase in ability to influence others. The more common ground or identification you have with someone such as similar attitudes and beliefs, coupled with raised levels of likeability and respect, the greater your referent power.

A good example of an individual with referent power is an older sibling. The younger sibling respects the older sibling; and due to their strong sense of identification or common ground (they most likely have very similar beliefs and attitudes), the younger sibling aspires to be like the older one. A good example of not necessarily wanting to be *like* another person but wanting to be *identified with* another person is the world's best party guest. We all know "that guy or gal" who lights up the room when he/she arrives, someone that oozes charisma and is the life of the party. We find ourselves wanting to be with "that guy or gal".

Referent power is not unlike *ethos,* a term used by Aristotle to designate an audience or group member's perception of the speaker as ethical and credible. In regard to ethical proof, Aristotle set forth the general rule that "there is no proof so effective as that of the character."[4] Character power is related to Aristotle's notions of good will, good moral character, and good sense, as receivers perceive these. In modern times source credibility has been discussed in terms of good intentions, trustworthiness, and competence or expertise.

Ethical proof refers to credibility that is established or reinforced by the sender's ethical characteristics (as perceived by group members) and behavior during the interaction. In its most general sense ethical proof refers here to the group's impressions of honesty, character, wisdom, and good will.

## Legitimate Power

You have **legitimate** power when others believe you have the right to control their behavior due to your position or status and the influence that comes with it. This source of power is grounded in the idea that certain people should have power over certain others because of the position they occupy. "Because I said so" is a very strong argument from a mother with an angry look on her face. As children we believe our parents have the right to control our behavior because of their position of parent. Other common examples of individuals with legitimate power are teachers, police officers and employers. Legitimate power only works if we respect the person in power. We wouldn't have the need for prisons if all law enforcers had true legitimate power. All of my students would have A's in my class if I had true legitimate power as their professor. How well one "wears" legitimate power has a lot to do with how influential they are interpersonally.

## Expert Power

You have **expert power** when others see you as having advanced expertise or knowledge. Expert power is case sensitive. We are rarely viewed as all knowing in all situations. Therefore, expert power can shift from person to person depending on the situation. When people perceive someone with expertise and knowledge as being unbiased or having no personal gain or interest in the matter, the level of influence will increase. Expert power only works if the expert or knowledge holder has something that others need. You may be the world's foremost expert on gum chewing, but you most likely do not hold much influence over the majority of individuals. "You're only as good as your information."

## Persuasive Power

You have **persuasive power** when you are perceived as having a heightened ability to communicate logically and persuasively. The perception of excellent communication skills leads to the ability to influence the behaviors and attitudes of others. A good example of this power is that of my siblings and me when I was an undergraduate in college. I have always had the "gift for gab". As a small child people would say "get this girl into law school or on the used car lot because she sure can sell it." When I chose Communication as my major in college with a focus on persuasion, the belief about my "gift" was made that much more concrete. Consequently, when my siblings had something bad to tell my parents or needed to ask for money, they would come to me for a script to recite, leading my parents to go easy on them or fork over the cash. This gave me great persuasive power in my family because everyone knew I would win any argument and could get people to think I knew everything about anything. However, just because someone has the "gift for gab" doesn't mean he/she inherently possesses persuasive power. Communication elements such as vocabulary, language choice, and message organization are thought to reflect on the source. Studies show that, other things being equal, people who exhibit a greater linguistic diversity in terms of verb tenses, adjectives, adverbs, and connectives are perceived as more credible. Inarticulate people are rated low in terms of competency, dynamism, and social status.[5] Nonfluent, inarticulate language generally decreases one's credibility.[6] The same can be said of poor use of voice. As we learned earlier, receivers attribute a person's social status from voice cues alone.[7]

Of course, a showy display of language can work against us, hurting not only credibility but also clarity. Many special aspects and conditions affect people's perceptions of credibility. Although a convicted, hard core, experienced car thief may not meet the classical tests of credibility (good will, good moral character, good sense), if this person were to speak, however profanely and poorly, about the secrets of the trade, he or she might indeed be perceived as having a special credibility. After all, this person is an expert, and perhaps the language is appropriate (or at least less important) to this expertise.

## Reward and Coercive Power

This type of power is grounded in the ideas of positive and negative reinforcement, or what we know as rewards and punishments. You have **reward power** if you have the ability to reward others. Parents have reward power over children with allowances professors have reward power over students with grades, and bosses have

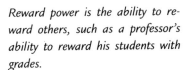
*Reward power is the ability to reward others, such as a professor's ability to reward his students with grades.*

reward power over employees with wage increases. Reward power only works if individuals are motivated by the reward you have to offer. Rule of thumb: If a student is not motivated by grades, a professor doesn't have much power over that student's behavior regarding the class.

You have **coercive power** if you have the ability to administer punishment or take away rewards. If you have reward power, you most likely have coercive power as well. Coercive power only works when the punishment is actually acted out. The simple threat (if not seen as a strong one) will not influence compliance. Rule of thumb: Be sure that your teenaged daughter actually wants to go on the family vacation before you think threatening her with not going on the trip will give you coercive power and motivate her to comply with curfew rules. You are only as powerful as the other individual is compliant. Compliance and its relation to social influence will be discussed in the next section.

## UNDERSTANDING SOCIAL INFLUENCE

Here we are most interested in interpersonal influence, dyads, and small groups. However, there is also a giant interest in influence at a large-group level in such fields as politics, advertising, marketing, and propaganda. Many of the concepts and theories are similar, but the applications are often quite different. In large-group, the idea that social influence models the audience is typically viewed as a statistical concept, a numerical averaging of the demographics (age, income, residence, education, and so forth). An advertiser knows (or tries to know) the target audience going in and expects to lose on some dimensions but win big on others. In the Presidential primaries of 2008 John McCain practically ignored young voters (ages 18 – 24) as a target audience. It was analyzed as an unstable voting group that was strongly opposed to his candidacy. Pragmatic, perhaps, but it worked on the overall short-term strategy.

Interpersonal persuasion is different because we are dealing with living, breathing people, not statistical profiles. Feedback is faster and more personal. It is interactive and usually quicker to accommodate change. This is not to say that one doesn't run into individuals who hold hard attitudes on issues of special interest and are very difficult to persuade. This often leads to interpersonal conflict as we learned in Chapter 6. Perhaps there are times, issues, and personalities that, like the propagandists, we shouldn't even try. In any event, our focus in this chapter is on personal interaction rather than on the audience as a statistical concept.

## Attitudes

**DEFINITIONS**     We previously defined *interpersonal influence* as a change in one person's thinking, feelings, or behavior that is attributable to another person. The *change* we are discussing is what attitudes are all about. An **attitude** may also be thought of as a tendency to respond in a given way. More specifically, it is the "predisposition of an individual to evaluate some symbol or object or aspect of the world in a favorable or unfavorable manner."[8]

Fishbein and Ajzen view attitude as " ... the sum of a person's salient beliefs about an object's attributes ... multiplied by his evaluations ... of these attributes."[9] Attitudes are thus made up of beliefs and evaluations of the beliefs. To the extent that the belief system is engaged deeply, the attitude becomes more motivating. In other words, the more primal the beliefs and the more applicable they are judged to be (evaluation), the more ego-involved or motivating the resulting attitude.

We have *ranges* of acceptance such as positive, negative or neutral. These ranges have also been referred to as *latitudes* of attitude.[10] This is an important notion in assessing and effecting social influence. An attitude object could also be a product, thing, or social issue.

A lightly held attitude, such as a preference for one brand of coffee over another, suggests only a modest personal involvement. A commitment to one's religion, family, country, or life style may be quite another matter. Attitudes about these may be the result of a much more deeply engaged belief system. These attitudes may involve us very personally. They help define our self-concept. They involve our ego. The point is that a single point on a numerical scale seldom best represents attitudes. The degree of involvement (belief system engagement) is difficult to ascertain from a single point on a numerical scale. For example, suppose a person, Sue, checked a 3 on the issue shown in Figure 7.1.

It sounds as though she would be somewhat difficult to influence. She might very well be influenced if that were really the only position she favored. Suppose, however, that there was a range of numbers that fit her attitude. Perhaps she could

**FIGURE 7.1**

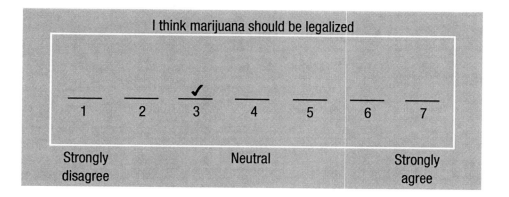

also live with positions 2 and 4. These we can label *acceptable* positions. Perhaps she found positions 5, 6, 7, and 1 unacceptable or *objectionable*. We now have more attitude information. (See Figure 7.2.)

While position 3 is the *most* acceptable, her range includes the neutral position. Persuasion now looks more promising. We are beginning to get an idea of just how strong the belief system that underlies her attitude is.

**FIGURE 7.2**

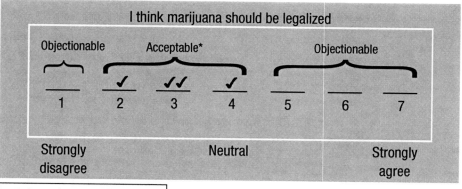

## FIGURE 7.3

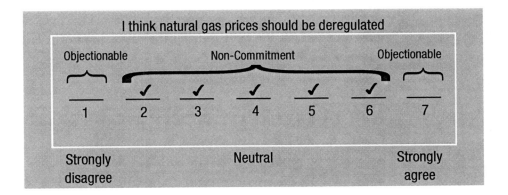

Suppose Sue had a large range or latitude of *noncommitment* as shown in Figure 7.3. Assuming she has enough interest or ego involvement to receive persuasion, we could assume she'd be easy to persuade in either direction. However, if Sue's range of acceptance was very narrow, and her most acceptable position was still position 4, she might be very difficult to persuade. She has rejected all the other positions, as illustrated in Figure 7.4.

## FIGURE 7.4

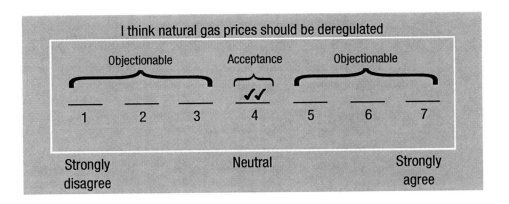

In general, the larger the range of rejection (objectionable positions), the more ego defensive Sue becomes and the more difficult to influence she becomes. The larger the range of acceptance or noncommitment, the less Sue's ego is involved; and the easier it is for her to change her attitude. In simpler terms, the larger the range of rejection, the more difficult the persuasion is; the larger the range of acceptance or noncommitment, the less difficult the persuasion. A large range of rejection predicts ego defensiveness.

**FUNCTIONS THAT ATTITUDES SERVE**    Attitudes appear to function differently for the individual, depending on the situation he or she is in. If we understand why people hold the attitudes they do, we are better prepared to predict how and when the attitudes might change. People may hold similar attitudes but for quite different reasons. One person's attitudes toward liberalizing marijuana penalties might be based on the practical problems of enforcing the current law; another's attitude might be based on a difference in life style.

Below are three general functions that attitudes serve:[11]

*1. A referencing function*    "People need standards or frames of reference for understanding their world, and attitudes help to supply such standards."[12] We gain prepackaged norms and attitudes from our larger value systems and culture. These supply reference points for better comprehending a very complex world. When we are exposed to new knowledge that affects us, we often find in our attitudes a handy frame of reference for categorizing and understanding it.

We also reference such things as pleasure and pain, good and bad, reward and punishment. These are very practical attitudes. We adjust and modify this referencing function in very utilitarian ways. We tend to classify such things as high grades, money, and special privileges as favorable and their opposites as unfavorable. We also acquire some of our attitudes in whole or in part because of this practical referencing function.

*2. A self-identification function*    Our attitudes help us define ourselves and know who we are. Some attitudes give positive expression to our value systems. We gain identity as well as satisfaction from the expression of some cherished attitudes. Our prayers in church, our oaths of office or allegiance, even the clothes we wear—

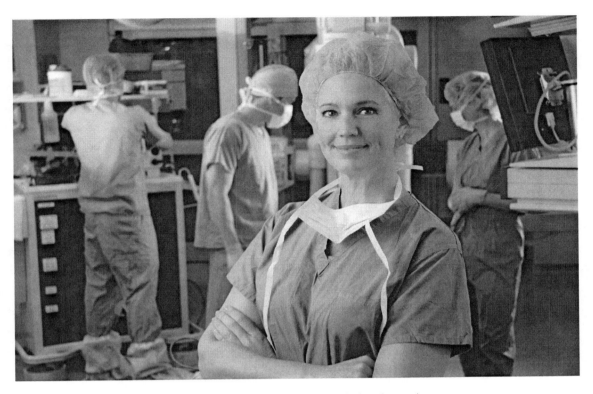

*Our attitudes, actions, and the clothes we wear all help us assert and identify ourselves.*

all help us assert and identify ourselves. When our feelings and actions contradict our beliefs, we often have trouble with this function.

### 3. An ego-defensive function
We often develop attitudes thought to protect our egos from conflict and frustration. These attitudes help us reduce anxieties and adjust to threats. They can help us survive temporarily trying times by taking the heat out of conflict, the pain out of frustration. When such attitudes are totally unrealistic and persistent, they can hurt us by delaying objective solutions to problems and slowing our social adjustment to the real world.

Sooner or later we all feel the pressure of differences between our personal needs and the demands of society. When we become ego-defensive and find it difficult to compromise or adjust our attitudes, we may adjust in other ways. We may distort reality to take pressure off our egos. We may lash out. We may retreat to states of repressed hostility.

All people are subject to these physical and emotional happenings. Evidence suggests that persons suffering from emotional disorders represent extreme variations of the same problems that occur among normal persons. The generalization that asocial, hostile, aggressive characteristics are associated with resistance to persuasion is drawn from research on such people. All of us temporarily vary our reactions and states of mind with the pressures we face (or think we face), the kind of issue involved, and our state of fatigue. People with heavy anxiety problems such as hypochondria, insomnia, or an obsession with an unreasonable idea tend to be more difficult to persuade.[13] Our tolerance levels vary from person to person, from issue to issue, and within ourselves from day to day. We all have sensitive areas where even minor intrusions may cause disruptive reactions.

Kelman extends our insights into attitude functions and required contrary behavior when he suggests *identification* and *internalization*, along with *compliance*, as processes of social influence.[14] **Identification** is also a form of compliance based on a keen desire to relate satisfactorily to a special person or group. For Kelman it is a role relationship that may form a part of a person's self-image. **Internalization** is simply acceptance of an attitude because it agrees with one's value system. **Compliance,** on the other hand, means accepting influence regardless of private beliefs because of favorable reactions, rewards, or avoiding punishments.

Many other social scientists have studied the idea of compliance or accepting influence. *Compliance* is getting the other individual to do what you want them to do, or to stop doing something you don't want to do. If you refuse to do something, your compliance level is low. If you are easily influenced to do something, your compliance level is high. You take part in **compliance-gaining strategies** when you are attempting to influence others to do what you want them to do. You take part in **compliance-resisting strategies** when you want to resist another's influence over you. What makes us compliant or not is rooted in social influence.[15]

Kelman suggests a distinct set of antecedents and consequents. The likelihood of a given process being involved is a function of the *importance* attached in terms of a person's goals, the *power* of the persuader (for example, control of the means to a goal), and the *prepotency* or predominance of the induced response.[14]

*Compliance* is distinguished by antecedent concern for the *social effect* of behavior. *Identification* is distinguished by concern for attractive *social* groups and *anchorages* in them. The motivational base for *internalization* is concerned with an agreement of value or *value congruence*. In terms of power of the influencing source or agent, *compliance* is dependent upon the control the agent has over the means to a desirable goal; *identification* is based upon the attractiveness of the agent's social role; *internalization* is based on the agent's credibility.

In the Kelman theory, influence in a strict compliance situation occurs through a limitation of behavioral choices toward a goal, in identification through a defining of role requirements, and in internalization through reorganization in the individual's conception of means-end relationships. The three processes of influence are then determined by the nature of these three antecedents.

There are three classes of consequences in the Kelman theory: (1) conditions under which the persuasion is expressed, (2) conditions under which attitude can be changed, and (3) the type of behavior system in which the persuasion is found. Behavior and attitude predispositions acquired under circumstances of compliance are best discharged under conditions of surveillance by the influencing agent. Responses adopted through identification circumstances are best discharged under conditions in which the agent's role is salient as it relates to the receiver. Behavior and attitude predispositions acquired under internalization circumstances will tend to be expressed when the relevance to certain values is perceived.

Compliance responses will cease when they are no longer perceived as the best way to reach social rewards. Identification responses will be abandoned when they no longer maintain satisfying, self-defining relationships. Internalization-acquired responses will cease when they are no longer perceived as the best way to maximize one's value system.

Finally, compliance responses and opinions exist in a behavior system of specific, external demands, identification responses and opinions exist in a behavior system of expectations defining a specific role, and internalization responses exist in a behavior system of human values. If an attitude or predisposition has certain antecedents, it has predictable consequents. A summary of the distinctions between compliance, identification, and internalization is charted in Table 7.1.

**TABLE 7.1**   SUMMARY OF THE DISTINCTIONS BETWEEN THE THREE PROCESSES

|  | COMPLIANCE | IDENTIFICATION | INTERNALIZATION |
|---|---|---|---|
| **Antecedents:** | | | |
| 1. Basis for the *importance of the induction* | Concern with social effect of behavior | Concern with social anchorage of behavior | Concern with value congruence of behavior |
| 2. Source of *power of the influencing agent* | Means control | Attractiveness | Credibility |
| 3. Manner of achieving *prepotency of the induced response* | Limitation of choice behavior | Delineation of role requirements | Reorganization of means-ends framework |
| **Consequents:** | | | |
| 1. Conditions of performance of induced response | Surveillance by influencing agent | Salience of relationship to agent | Relevance of values to issue |
| 2. Conditions of change and extinction of induced resonse | Changed perception of conditions for social rewards | Changed perception of conditions for satisfying self-defining relationships | Changed perception of conditions for value maximization |
| 3. Type of behavior system in which induced response is embedded | External demands of a specific setting | Expectations defining a specific role | Person's value system |

From Herbert C. Kelman, *"Processes of Opinion Change," Public Opinion Quarterly, 25 (1961) 67.*

## WE VALUE CONSISTENCY

April 5, 1761

On Feb. 8, 1761, London was rocked by an earthquake, and on Mar. 8 another severe tremor rumbled through the capital. Noting that exactly four weeks had elapsed between the two quakes, a soldier in the Life Guards named William Bell made dozens of speeches throughout the town predicting the complete destruction of the world 28 days later, on Apr. 5. So quickly did the panic spread that even original disbelievers began to prepare for the worst. As the awful day approached, Londoners left the capital in great herds, heading for the safety of outlying villages, where exorbitant prices were being charged by villagers eager to take advantage of the mass hysteria. Because many believed that the destruction of the world would be in the form of a flood, all the boats on the Thames were filled to capacity. Nothing happened. On the following day, Bell was seized and thrown into Bedlam, London's notorious madhouse.[16]

Inconsistency abounds in the above example. The Londoners might have simply *rejected* the whole matter: "This isn't really happening—I'm out fishing." This becomes a somewhat difficult thing to do when you are standing in a boat in the middle of the Thames. Another possibility would have been for the people to *change* their attitudes about the imminent end of the world and about the credibility of Mr. William Bell. The embarrassment that went along with the change in attitude was ventilated on Mr. Bell—he's "mad." With these changes the people of London could have brought their beliefs into consistency with their behavior.

Sometimes we *fragment* or modify the original attitude to better explain our bizarre behavior. This desperate search for consistency worked for some astrologers in 1524.

Feb. 1, 1524

During the first half of the 16th century, London swarmed with fortune-tellers and astrologers. As early as June, 1523, a group of them concurred that the end of the world would begin with the destruction of London by deluge on Feb. 1, 1524. Because so many astrologers agreed, the prophecy met with implicit belief, and hundreds of families moved out of London to the high ground of Kent and Essex. By the middle of January, at least 20,000 people had left their homes. The prior of St. Bartholomew's was so frightened that he built—at enormous expense—a fortress at Harrow on the Hill stocked with a two-month supply of food. It was predicted that the inundation would be gradual, so that even disbelievers would have a chance to escape. Nothing happened. Yet so convinced was the metropolis that nearly the whole of London stayed awake, fearing that the deluge would suddenly burst and "take them like a thief in the night." The following day the astrologers had to account for themselves. Hurriedly they examined their figures and discovered a tiny error in their calculations. London would be destroyed and it would mark the end of the world—but in 1624, not 1524.[17]

When our attitudes no longer adequately reference new and changing situations—when we find old attitudes in conflict with new information—we tend to feel out of phase, off balance, *inconsistent*. Consistency theory supplies us with many useful explanations and predictions. "Our thesis is right; we're just off 100 years because of a computational error." Consistency theory would predict that.

**Cognitive consistency** refers to mental agreement between a person's notions about some object or event and some *new* information about those same objects or events. *Cognition* refers to the mental process or faculty by which knowledge is both acquired and known, our thought process. However, it is more than a search for meaning. It denotes the attitudes and images we hold of the world. The assumption is that when the new information is contradictory or inconsistent with a person's attitudes, it will lead to some confusion and tension. This tension motivates a person to alter or adjust attitudes or behavior. We seek a harmonious, agreeable, balanced, *consistent* set of relationships between our notions of the world and our latest perception of it. In some respects these theories might better be called "inconsistency" theories, since it is the inconsistency that causes the tension, which causes the motivation, which may cause a change in attitude or behavior. When we know how to change attitude or behavior, we have persuasive power.

**COGNITIVE DISSONANCE THEORY**   Cognitive dissonance is a consistency theory. **Cognitive** means "… any knowledge, opinion, or belief about the environment, about oneself, or about one's behavior."[18] The word **dissonance** replaces the word *inconsistency* used previously; *consonance* refers to consistency. One can substitute *frustration* and *disequilibrium* for the word *dissonance*. Therefore, cognitive dissonance is an inconsistency in our thought process. The essential notion, as before, is that people have a strong need for agreement (consonance or consistency) among their beliefs and actions. The basic hypotheses according to Leon Festinger, chief architect of this highly regarded theory, are:

1.  The existence of dissonance, being psychologically uncomfortable, will motivate the person to try to reduce the dissonance and achieve consonance.

2.  When dissonance is present, in addition to trying to reduce it, the person will actively avoid situations and information which would likely increase the dissonance.[19]

Motivation springs from the existence of confuting relations among cognitions, a practically unavoidable condition in a wide variety of situations. Festinger suggests some typical sources of dissonance between two cognitions: logical consistency, cultural mores, past experience, and one specific opinion being included by definition in a more general opinion (for example, Democrats aren't supposed to favor a Republican candidate for office).[20]

The theory clearly postulates that behavior can cause influence. As we know, the ability to influence gives us power. Many very creative researchers support this point and provide implications for involvement and self-persuasion.[21]

Festinger's second hypothesis regarding active avoidance of information and situations, which might increase rather than reduce dissonance, also has much relevance interpersonally. How a message is organized and stated becomes very important. For persons already suffering dissonance, to begin or start a message with dissonant information or an argument may sound like a logical way to get their attention; but it may, in fact, be just the opposite if it causes the receiver to "tune out."

Still another astrologer, a German, had his end-of-the-world prediction fortuitously *fragmented* by a violent storm on the predicted day. It could, after all, be rationalized by the gullible as a close call. An identical prediction was made again, but this time the disaster would occur four years later. Festinger's *avoidance* then took place. When that day arrived, the people ignored the whole thing. Fear of dissonance is of interest interpersonally because it may very well make people reluctant to commit themselves either verbally or behaviorally. The dissonance avoidance theory, like most of the cognitive consistency theories, has wide support.[22] It seems quite clear that psychological inconsistency affects interpersonal influence.

A number of theorists have built upon the basic consistency model. Among them are Rosenberg and Abelson.[23] According to their theory attitudes consist of two elements, feelings (affective) and beliefs (cognitive), and people seek balance or consistency between them. Influence is thus possible by modifying *either* the affective or the cognitive. The model presumes an imbalanced or unstable state when a person's feelings and beliefs suddenly do not agree on an attitude object. If long-time Representative Jones is suddenly discovered getting kickbacks from his staff after their salaries have been padded, you may suffer considerable dissonance (or inconsistency) in terms of supporting him. Your new, observable, public belief information (he's dishonest) is inconsistent with your longtime affection for Jones, the man.

To achieve consistency in this dilemma a person can do one of three things: (1) *Reject* the data and communications that brought about the difficulty—"I simply don't believe it"; (2) *fragment* the original attitude by trying to isolate the affective and cognitive element—"Others do it. He just got caught," or "The good he's done outweighs the bad"; or (3) *change* your attitude by accommodating the dilemma in such a way that your feelings and beliefs are consistent—"I'll not vote for him. My feelings have changed. I don't believe in dishonesty."[24] One could also presumably escape by repressing or trying not to think about the inconsistency.

**BALANCE THEORY**   Heider developed this early cognitive consistency theory.[25] Heider's intrapersonal theory is also interpersonal in that he illustrates only the interaction between two people and an event or object of mutual concern. According to Heider, when two people interact in relation to an event or object of mutual concern, the intrapersonal and interpersonal situations are cognitively balanced or unbalanced. Unbalanced situations produce a tension that generates motivation to change attitudes (restore balance). It should be clear that persuasion can only operate after some "felt tension" (unbalanced situation). If the relationship is balanced, little motivation to change is present and persuasion is doubtful.

Suppose, for example, that two people, John and George, are talking about automobiles (Chevys). There are eight possible relationships that can exist. Four are considered balanced and four unbalanced. Figure 7.5 presents the balanced states. In any of these states little tension exists, hence the probability of attitude change is very low. Attitude change is possible, according to Heider, in unbalanced states. People are motivated to balance their cognitions. Figure 7.6 represents the four possible unbalanced states. In all of these situations the inherent tension allows for the possibility of interpersonal influence.

These are the classic models of Heider modified a little for clarity. The basic point is that unbalanced states exist if an odd number of the three relationships are negative. (One *hate* and two *likes* or three *hates* is unbalanced.) An unbalanced state produces tension in a person's life, which generates motivation to restore balance.

Despite adages to the contrary, Heider argues that comparable personalities attract, and that, other things being equal, familiarity breeds attraction, not contempt. "With similar attitudes proximity will increase the degree of positive

## FIGURE 7.5    BALANCED STATES

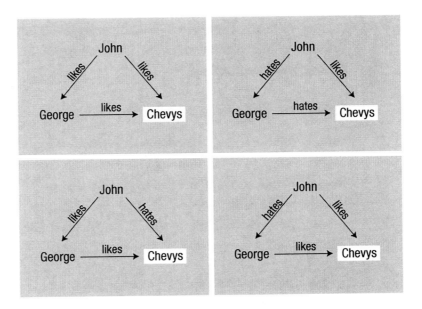

**FIGURE 7.6    UNBALANCED STATES**

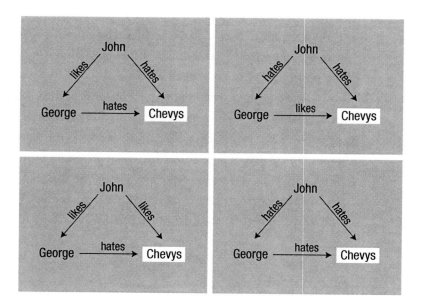

sentiment; with slight dissimilarity of attitudes a mutual assimilation might be produced, and with it an increase in friendliness; with strong dissimilarities the hostility will be increased."[26]

## Motives, Values, and Needs

Interpersonal influence is better understood, if not always affected, by an understanding of human motives and values. Seldom are we influenced by only one thing. Success and satisfaction foster motivation. So do failure and dissatisfaction. We are *motivated by need and by plenty*. We are often persuaded through social compliance and laws. We have avoidance needs as well as growth needs.

**DEFICIENCY AND ABUNDANCE MOTIVES**    Our human motives have been defined by Krech and Crutchfield as *survival, security, satisfaction,* and *stim-*

*ulation.*[27] These are grouped into *deficiency* motives (survival and security) and *abundance* motives (satisfaction and stimulation). **Deficiency motivation** is characterized by needs to avoid danger, threat, disruption, and discomfort. **Abundance motivation** is characterized by desires to grow, discover, create, enjoy, and achieve.

**VALUES AS MOTIVES**    According to Rokeach, values act as life guides. He identifies two kinds: **terminal**, the ultimate goals that motivate us and **instrumental**, the guidelines that motivate our everyday behavior. He has found that values vary and change somewhat according to a person's condition as well as sex, age, race, and education.

**AFFILIATION NEED**    Social scientists have long referred to humans as *social* animals. Social tendencies have been called *gregariousness, companionship,* and *succor*—that is, seeking *others* for help, encouragement, and sympathy. This urge to sociability appears to be stronger in some people than in others. It does, however, as we learned in Chapter 2, appear to affect us all, particularly in times of trouble or threat. When our beliefs are seriously threatened, we tend to seek out people of like mind as if to soften the hurt. It has also been theorized that some people socialize just for the sheer joy of it. Schachter said of affiliation, "Most of us have experienced occasional cravings to be with people, sometimes with good reason, frequently for no apparent reason: we seem simply to want to be in the physical presence of others."[28]

Schachter points out that anxious people seek out other anxious people. Misery not only loves company, it loves miserable company! Affiliation apparently provides much of its own communication. Just being with other people who have similar problems seemed to reduce tension, even when no verbal communication takes place. All of us like to hear our beliefs confirmed; we like to be reassured by others who share our opinions. This is an important insight. Our desires to hear what we want to hear, to think what we want to think, sometimes take over when feelings run high or when we are desperate to reassert a shaken belief or value. Many times people themselves, apart from the issues, become important to us because they provide approval and support. Affiliation can be a fairly strong basic motive.

## Hierarchy of Needs

> *Swiss Family Robinson*
> Chapter I
> The Wreck
>
> For many days we had been tempest-tossed. Six times had the darkness closed over a wild and terrific scene, and returning light as often brought but renewed distress, for the raging storm increased in fury until on the seventh day all hope was lost.
>
> We were driven completely out of our course; no conjecture could be formed as to our whereabouts. The crew had lost heart and were utterly exhausted by incessant labor. The riven masts had gone by the board, leaks had been sprung in every direction, and the water, which rushed in, gained upon us rapidly.
>
> My heart sank as I looked round upon my family in the midst of these horrors. Our four young sons were overpowered by terror. "Dear children," said I, "if the Lord will, He can save us even from this fearful peril; if not, let us calmly yield our lives into His hand, and think of the joy and blessedness of finding ourselves forever and ever united in that happy home above."[29]

> STORYLINE
>
> After a terrible hurricane crashes their ship on the rocks, the family rigs a raft and, after much travail, reaches the shore.

Obviously the Robinsons' motivation as a family group was heavily survival oriented, but still crisscrossed with individual motives of responsibility and self-respect.

Many scholars have worked at classifying human needs. They run the gamut from long lists to a single global need like libido or sex for Freud, happiness for Aristotle, self-importance for Adler, or self-actualization for Goldstein. While more theorists discuss the physiological or self-preservation needs, there is surprisingly little effort to suggest a systematic hierarchy in terms of importance. Kurt Goldstein did suggest a hierarchy of needs in which their importance changes with their relative state of satisfaction. He felt that all the needs were but special aspects of self-actualization.[30]

It was Abraham Maslow, an admirer of Goldstein, who gave us a general dynamic theory involving a hierarchy of needs called **Maslow's Hierarchy of Needs.**[31] Despite varying cultures, Maslow felt that the basic needs for all people are essentially the same. They are part of human nature and are of a psychological as well as a physiological order. In his writings he listed in order of importance five general categories of needs: physiological, safety, belongingness, esteem, and self-actualization. The rank order and practical importance of these dynamic needs are subject to the degree of satisfaction attendant upon each need. The degree of satisfaction is constantly changing as circumstances and conditions vary. At one time one's need for love may predominate; at another the need for esteem may be foremost, with one's motivation being altered accordingly. This hierarchy of needs has been diagrammed as steps, a ladder, or a triangle.

**FIGURE 7.7    MASLOW'S HIERARCHY OF NEEDS**

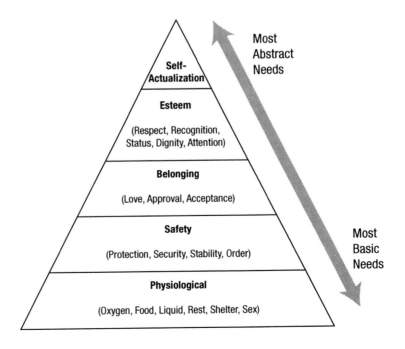

As our story opens, we find the Robinson family concerned mostly with the bottom two rungs of the ladder—physiological and safety needs.

**PHYSIOLOGICAL NEEDS**   **Physiological needs** are our biological needs. They are directly related to self-preservation. Although generally rated first in importance, their importance diminishes as they are satisfied. The primary physiological or self-preservation needs are oxygen, food, water, rest, exercise, avoidance of bodily damage, and shelter.

---

STORYLINE

All the crew being drowned, the castaways work diligently and before the ship is destroyed manage to salvage a great number of things. ...

---

Their grim survival needs surface again as they meet a thirty-foot boa constrictor that completely swallows a donkey that has survived the shipwreck.

---

The Serpent

The reptile advanced with writhing and undulatory movements, from time to time rearing its head to the height of fifteen or twenty feet, and slowly turning it about, as though on the lookout for prey.

As it crossed the bridge, with a slow, suspicious motion, I withdrew, and hastily rejoined my little party, which was preparing to garrison our fortress in warlike array, but with considerable trepidation, which my presence served in a measure to allay.

We placed ourselves at the upper openings, after strongly barricading everything below, and, ourselves unseen, awaited with beating hearts the further advance of the foe, which speedily became visible to us.[32]

---

**SAFETY NEEDS**   **Safety needs** reflect our desire for a sense of security and our dislike for personal violence, harm, or disease. Most often we prefer a safe, predictable environment to one plagued by unknown events. This protective desire may prompt us to be concerned with insurance and with jobs that offer security.

Like biological needs, our safety needs do not dominate our lives except in times of emergency or danger. Nevertheless, many people are seriously concerned with threats to their security. A change in a work routine, even when carefully explained, often causes visible anxiety. The change in environment experienced by college freshmen is often an extreme threat to their safety needs. They may be quite open to persuasion that promises more security in terms of campus organizations, housing, trips home, and friends. The first year of military service is a similarly threatening experience. All of us have a strong need for psychological safety.

---

STORYLINE

Anyone who has even heard of Disneyland or Disney World knows that the Robinson family built a marvelous tree house. The tools and parts salvaged from the shipwreck are ingeniously incorporated into the design.

---

The Tree House

Fritz and I then ascended the tree, and finished the preparations I had begun the night before. All useless boughs were lopped off, leaving a few about six feet from the floor, from which we might sling our hammocks, and others still higher, to support a temporary roof of sailcloth. My wife made fast the planks to a rope passed through the block I had fixed to the boughs above us, and by this means Fritz and I hauled them up. These we arranged side by side on the foundation of boughs, so as to form a smooth solid floor, and round this platform built a bulwark of planks, and then throwing the sailcloth over the higher branches, we drew it down and firmly nailed it. Our house was thus enclosed on three sides, for behind the great trunk protected us, while the front was left open to admit the fresh sea breeze which blew directly in.[33]

---

The family has achieved safety and no little comfort. They begin to cultivate the land and tame native animals to serve them. They have a loving family made stronger by the experience. They are proud of their house and their self-reliance.

Some of the higher needs are being met, and their motivations have gone from *deficiency* to *abundance,* from survival to self-fulfillment.

**BELONGING/LOVE NEEDS**    People must be loved and in turn must express their love. Sharing our life with others is important to us, and we often react quickly to even the possibility that this need of ours will be denied. We satisfy our love needs most often through our family and close friends, but the category extends beyond this. We desire the approval and acceptance of our classmates, our fellow workers, and the many groups of people with whom we associate and with whom we tend to identify ourselves. We alter our behavior and perhaps even our standards in order to be accepted, to belong, to be loved by our chosen friends and groups. To be well adjusted we must give as well as receive love. Our lonely-hearts clubs owe their existence to this powerful need to give and share love.

**ESTEEM NEEDS**    When our physiological, safety, and love needs are satisfied, our esteem needs become most important. These needs go beyond the more passive belonging or love needs into a more active desire for recognition and self-respect. Esteem needs involve pride and self-evaluation. According to Maslow, they are of two slightly different types, or sets.

> [One is] the desire for strength, for achievement, for adequacy, for confidence in the face of the world and for independence and freedom. Secondly, we have what we may call the desire for reputation or prestige (defining it as respect or esteem from other people), recognition, attention, importance, or appreciation.[34]

In most cultures esteem needs are very important. Americans are often accused of being self-centered. A threat to our ego or self-esteem, whether real or fancied, often prompts swift reaction. Our radio and television commercials appeal to our esteem needs by emphasizing the prestige attached to a certain expensive car or by suggesting that our status in a group is threatened if we don't buy a particular product.

The satisfaction of esteem needs leads to self-confidence and a feeling of personal worth. Esteem needs are often accompanied by many frustrations and personal conflicts, since people desire not only the recognition and attention of their chosen groups, but also the self-respect and status that their moral, social, and religious standards call for. When the chosen groups call for behavior that conflict with a person's standards, that person must often make heroic choices in order to remain well adjusted. People play many roles in order to satisfy some of the different groups to which they belong.

The esteem needs of some poorly adjusted individuals are so great that they will seek achievement (or what they consider achievement) at the great price of their own self-respect.

---

STORYLINE

Some marooned years later during an exploring trip one of the boys now grown to young manhood discovers a young English woman stranded even as they have been. He brings her back to the family tree house named "Falconhurst". …

---

In another moment, he emerged, leading by the hand a slight, handsome youth, by his dress apparently a young English naval officer. The pair advanced to meet us; and Fritz, with a countenance radiant with joy, briefly introduced his companion as Edward Montrose.

"And," he continued, looking at his mother and me, "will you not welcome him as a friend and a brother to our family circle?"

"That will we, indeed!" I exclaimed, advancing and holding out my hands to the fair young stranger. "Our wild life may have roughened our looks and manners, but it has not hardened our hearts, I trust."

From the expression made use of by Fritz I perceived that the girl wished her sex to remain unrevealed to the rest of the party until the mother could obtain for her a costume more suited to her real character. …

The mere fact of meeting with any human being after so many years of isolation was in itself sufficient to raise the boys to the greatest state of excitement; but that this being should be one so handsome, so gay, so perfectly charming, seemed completely to have turned their heads …[35]

We're well up the ladder now; perhaps even some self-actualization is going on here. With all those boys around, Jenny wanted out of her tattered sailor suit!

**SELF-ACTUALIZATION NEEDS** This term, first used by Kurt Goldstein, refers to what might be called self-fulfillment, or self-realization—our desire to reach the height of our personal abilities and talents. In Maslow's words, "What a man can be, he must be." This need becomes increasingly important as the previous four needs are satisfied, and in our culture it is a very important aspect of human behavior and motivation. The large number of retired or established people who return to college or take adult courses in art, writing, or drama in order to satisfy creative urges is one response to self-actualization needs.

Maslow talked of "trends to self-actualization."[36] He spoke of growth needs when referring to young people "growing well" on their way to self-actualization. Just before his death, Maslow suggested an extra or half step up the needs ladder between esteem and self-actualization. What Frank Goble diagrams as growth needs,[37] Maslow called being-values or meta-needs.

---

STORYLINE

Three more years pass and finally a ship comes to search for the young woman. The parents have discovered such happiness and self-fulfillment on their island that they decide to live there always with two of their sons. The other sons and Jenny return to their old home in Europe and take their places in a long forgotten world. Oh yes, Fritz marries Jenny and Franz goes to school.[38]

---

"A good school is exactly what I want," said Franz. "Among a number of students there is some emulation and enthusiasm, and I shall have a chance of rising in the world. Fritz will probably return here some day; but it might be well for one member of the family to go home with the intention of remaining there altogether, and as I am the youngest I could more easily than the rest adapt myself to a different life."[39]

STORYLINE

On the evening before our separation, I gave to Fritz the journal in which, ever since the shipwreck, I had chronicled the events of our life, desiring that the story might be printed and published.

"It was written, as you well know," said I, "for the instruction and amusement of my children, but it is very possible that it may be useful to other young people …"

Night has closed around me.

For the last time my united family slumbers beneath my care.

Tomorrow this closing chapter of my journal will pass into the hands of my eldest son.

From afar I greet thee, Europe!

I greet thee, dear old Switzerland!

Like thee, may New Switzerland flourish and prosper—good, happy, and free![40]

The End

## SUMMING UP

Interpersonal influence is most often a subtle change in one person's thinking, feelings, or behavior attributable to another person.

Sources of power for one who would influence include referent power, legitimate power, expert power, persuasive power, reward power and coercive power. In regard to ethical proof, Aristotle set forth the general rule that "there is no proof so effective as that of the character."[41] In modern times character power or source credibility has been discussed in terms of good intentions, trustworthiness, and competence or expertise. Position or status refers to power born of legitimate status and/or achievement. How well one wears legitimate power has a lot to do with how influential it is interpersonally. Common ground refers to attitude and experience similarity, which leads to an interpersonal identification - a kind of common, referent power. Information can be a strong source of power. Experts of whatever stripe are powerful people when the situation demands their special knowledge or information. Those with good communication skills, other things being equal, are perceived as more credible—no small source of power.

Interpersonal influence is interactive, and it works both ways. The sources of power do not stand alone, and they may change over time.

An attitude is a tendency to respond in a given way or "a predisposition of an individual to evaluate some symbol or object or aspect of his world in a favorable or unfavorable manner."[42] Attitudes are held with different intensity or ranges of acceptance referred to as latitudes of attitude. An attitude can be held about objects, products, and social issues. A large latitude or rejection toward an attitude object predicts difficult persuasion; the larger the latitude of acceptance or noncommitment, the less difficult. A large latitude of rejection also predicts ego-defensiveness.

Attitudes serve different functions for people. Among them are: (1) a referencing function, (2) a self-identification function, and (3) an ego-defensive function. Attitudes supply reference points for better comprehending an often complex world. We gain identity as well as satisfaction from the expression of some cherished attitudes and also from relating to a special person or group. Some attitudes protect us from conflict and frustration (ego-defensive). They help us reduce anxiety and help us adjust to threat. When such attitudes are totally unrealistic and persistent, they can hurt us by delaying objective solutions to problems and slowing our social adjustment to the real world.

Compliance motivation means accepting influence because of favorable reactions, rewards, or avoiding punishment regardless of private beliefs. Compliance is distinguished by antecedent concern for the social effect of our behavior and is dependent upon the control the influencing agent has over the means to a desirable goal.

The assumption of consistency theory is that when new information is contradictory or inconsistent with a person's attitudes, it will lead to some confusion and tension. This tension motivates a person to alter or adjust attitudes or behavior. We seek a harmonious, agreeable, balanced, consistent set of relationships between our notions of the world and our latest perception of it. Cognitive dissonance theory hypothesizes that inconsistency motivates us to try to reduce dissonance or to try to avoid it. Affective-cognitive dissonance theory postulates that people seek a consistency between their beliefs and their feelings about an attitude object. In some dilemma situations (your friend is accused of stealing), consistency theory predicts three options: (1) Reject the data—"I don't believe it," (2) fragment the original attitude—"Others do it," or (3) change your attitude.

Comparable personalities attract and familiarity breeds attraction. "With similar attitudes proximity will increase the degree of positive sentiment; with slight dissimilarity of attitudes a mutual assimilation might be produced and with it an increase in friendliness; with strong dissimilarities the hostility will be increased."[43]

Our motives have been defined as survival, security, satisfaction, and stimulation (Krech and Crutchfield). These are grouped into deficiency and abundancy motives. Deficiency motivation is characterized by needs to avoid danger, threat, disruption, and discomfort. Abundancy motivation is characterized by desires to grow, discover, create, enjoy, and achieve.

Values act as life guides. Rokeach identifies two kinds: terminal, the ultimate goals that motivate us; and instrumental, the guidelines that motivate our everyday behavior.

The affiliation need refers to our social tendencies. These have been called gregariousness, companionship, and succor—seeking others for help, encouragement, and sympathy. Anxiety heightens the affiliation need and is directional (misery loves company of like misery).

Maslow provides us with a classification of dynamic, interactive human needs. In the order of their baseline importance these are physiological, safety, love, esteem, and self-actualization. A satisfied need is no longer a motivator according to this theory. Physiological needs include self-preservation, oxygen, food, liquid, rest, and shelter. Safety needs include security, stability, and order. Love needs include belonging, approval, and acceptance. Esteem needs include self-respect, recognition, status, dignity, and attention. Self-actualization needs include self-fulfillment, competence, growth, and creativeness.

## NOTES

1 Dillard, J.P. (1990). Primary and secondary goals in interpersonal social influence. In M.J. Cody & McLaughlin (Eds.), *The psychology of tactical communication* (pp. 70-90). Clevedon, England: Multilingual Matters.

2  Raven, B.H., Schwarzwals, J., & Koslowsky, M. (1998). Conceptualizing and measuring a power/interaction model of interpersonal influence. *Journal of Applied Social Psychology* 28, 307 – 332.

3  See Dorwin Cartwright, ed., *Studies in Social Power* (Ann Arbor, Mich.: Institute for Social Research, University of Michigan, 1959). See also Bertram H. Raven and Jeffrey Z. Rubin, *Social Psychology: People in Groups* (New York: John Wiley & Sons, Inc., 1976), chap. 6, pp. 199–243.

4  Aristotle, Rhetoric, 1377b21–1378a19.

5  James J. Bradac, Catherine W. Konsky, and Robert A. Davies, "Two Studies of the Effects of Linguistic Diversity Upon the Judgments of Communicator Attributes and Message Effectiveness," *Communication Monographs,* 43 (March 1976), 70–79.

6  Eldon E. Baker, "The Immediate Effects of Perceived Speaker Disorganization on Speaker Credibility and Audience-attitude Change in Persuasive Speaking," *Western Speech,* XXIX (1965), 148–61. G. R. Miller and M. A. Hewgill, "The Effect of Variations in Nonfluency on Audience Ratings of Source Credibility," *Quarterly Journal of Speech,* L (1964), 36–44.

7  James D. Moe, "Listener Judgments of Status Cues in Speech: A Replication and Extension," *Speech Monographs,* 39 (1972), 144–47.

8  D. Katz, "The Functional Approach to the Study of Attitudes," *Public Opinion Quarterly,* 24 (1960), 163.

9  M. Fishbein and I. Ajzen, *Belief, Attitude, Intention, and Behavior: An Introduction to Theory and Research* (Reading, Mass.: Addison-Wesley Publishing Co., 1975), p. 399.

10  From assimilation-contrast theory. See M. Sherif and C. Hovland, *Social Judgment* (New Haven, Conn.: Yale University Press, 1961), pp. 150–57.

11  With apologies and appreciation to D. Katz who identified four functions: adjustment, ego-defensive, value-expressive, and knowledge; D. Katz, "The Functional Approach," pp. 163–204. See also M. B. Smith, J. S. Bruner, and R. W. White, *Opinions and Personality* (New York: John Wiley & Sons, Inc., 1956), pp.41–44.

12  Katz refers to this as the knowledge function.

13  I. L. Janis, "Personality Correlates of Susceptibility to Persuasion," *Journal of Personality,* 22 (1953–54), 504–18.

14  H. C. Kelman, "Process of Opinion Change," *Public Opinion Quarterly,* 25 (1961), 57–78; H. C. Kelman, "Attitudes Are Alive and Well and Gainfully Employed in the Sphere of Action," *American Psychologist,* 29 (1974), 310–24.

15  See James B. Stiff, *Persuasive Communication* (NewYork: Guilford, 1994), pp. 199-211; David R. Seibold, James G. Cantrill, and Renee A. Myers, "Comunication and Interpersonal Influence," in *Handbook of Interpersonal Communications,* 2nd ed., eds. Mark L. Knapp and Gerald R. Miller (Thousand Oaks, CA: Sage, 1994), pp. 542-588; O'Hair, M.J., Cody, M.J., & O'Hair, D. (1991). The impact of situational dimensions on compliance-resisting strategies: A comparison of methods. *Communication Quarterly* 7, 256-281; Marshall L.J. & Levey, V.M. (1998). The development of children's perceptions of obstacles in compliance-gaining interactions. *Communication Studies,* 49, 341-357.

16 Incidents April 5, 1761, (p. 636) in *The People's Almanac #2* by David Wallechinsky and Irving Wallace. Copyright © 1978 by David Wallechinsky and Irving Wallace.

17 Incidents Feb. 1, 1524, (p. 635) in *The People's Almanac #2* by David Wallechinsky and Irving Wallace. Copyright © 1978 by David Wallechinsky and Irving Wallace.

18 Leon Festinger, *A Theory of Cognitive Dissonance* (Stanford, Calif.: Stanford University Press, 1957), p.3.

19 Ibid.

20 Ibid. p. 14.

21 I. Janis and B. King, "The Influence of Role-playing on Opinion Change," *Journal of Abnormal Social Psychology,* 49 (1954), 211–18.

22 R. P. Abelson and others, eds., *Theories of Cognitive Consistency: A Sourcebook* (Skokie, Ill.: Rand McNally & Company, 1968).

23 M. Rosenberg and R. Abelson, "An Analysis of Cognitive Balancing," in *Attitude Organization and Change,* eds. C. Hovland and M. Rosenberg (New Haven: Yale University Press, 1960), pp. 112–63. See also M. Rosenberg, "An Analysis of Affective-cognitive Consistency," in *Attitude Organization and Change,* pp. l5–64.

24 M. Rosenberg, "A Structural Theory of Attitude Dynamics," *Public Opinion Quarterly,* 24 (1960), 322.

25 F. Heider, "Attitudinal and Cognitive Organization," *Journal of Psychology,* 21 (1946), 107–12. See also F. Heider, *Psychology of Interpersonal Relations* (New York: John Wiley & Sons, Inc., 1958).

26 Ibid. p. 190.

27 D. Krech and R. S. Crutchfield, *Elements of Psychology* (New York: Alfred A. Knopf, Inc., 1958), p.279.

28 Stanley Schachter, *The Psychology of Affiliation* (Stanford, Calif.: Stanford University Press, 1959), p.1.

29 Jean Rudolph Wyss, *The Swiss Family Robinson* (Akron, Ohio: The Saalfield Publishing Company), p.7.

30 K. Goldstein, *The Organism* (New York: American Book Company, 1939).

31 A. H. Maslow, "A Theory of Human Motivation," *Psychological Review,* L (1943), 370–96. See also A. H. Maslow, *Motivation and Personality,* 2nd ed. (New York: Harper & Row, Publishers, Inc., 1970).

32 Wyss, *The Swiss Family Robinson,* pp. 167–68.

33 Ibid. pp. 55–56.

34 Maslow, "A Theory of Human Motivation," p. 382.

35 Wyss, *The Swiss Family Robinson,* pp. 224–26.

36 A. H. Maslow, *Toward a Psychology of Being* (New York: Van Nostrand Reinhold Company, 1968), p.25.

37 For another attempt, see Frank Goble, *The Third Force* (New York: Grossman, 1970), p. 50.

38 Wyss, *The Swiss Family Robinson,* p. 248.

39 Ibid. p. 250.

40 Ibid.

41 Aristotle, *Rhetoric,* 1377b21–1378a19.

42 Katz, "The Functional Approach," p. 163.

43 Heider, "Attitudinal and Cognitive Organization," pp. 107–12.

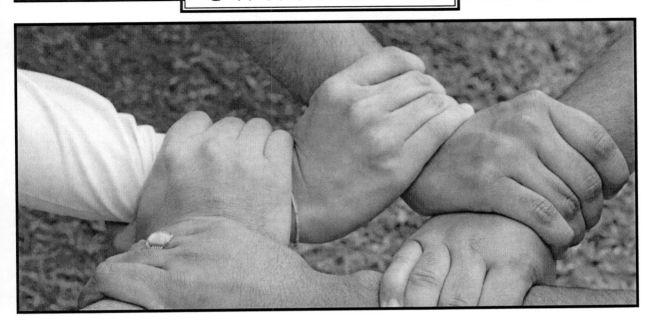

# INTERPERSONAL RELATIONSHIPS

# UNIVERSALS OF INTERPERSONAL RELATIONSHIPS

Communication is complicated yet clearly necessary. We couldn't survive if we didn't take part in communication. Relationships are also critical. Communication that creates, manages, and destroys relationships are conduits for many of life's greatest joys and deepest sorrows. The study of relationships and the interpersonal communication involved in them will help us be more successful communicators.

In this chapter we will explore the range of relationships from impersonal to interpersonal, how and why we start, maintain and end interpersonal relationships and the different contexts in our lives within which the majority of our interpersonal relationships take place.

## Definitions

A **relationship** is any connection that is established when two people communicate

*A relationship is established when two people communicate with each other.*

with each other. You will remember from Chapter 1, we define **human communication** as a process of sorting, selecting, and sending symbols in such a way as to help a receiver find in his or her own mind a meaning similar to that intended by the sender. Imagine this: You begin an interaction by placing a soda on the counter at your local party store. The clerk says, "Dollar ten"; you hand the clerk $1.10. The clerk says, "Thank you" and you reply with "Have a nice day." The clerk finished the interaction with "You, too". Based on our above definitions, you and the clerk have a relationship. In fact, you have a good relationship with the clerk. It is very simple and clear—you want to buy soda, and the clerk wants to sell it to you. You both get what you need out of the relationship. As you know, not all relationships are this impersonal and simple.

The majority of relationships that we need in our lives for our own well-being are much more complex and interpersonal. In Chapter 1 **interpersonal communication** is defined as a distinctive, on going, ever changing, transactional form of human communication that involves mutual influence usually for the purposes of relationship management. When communication becomes more interpersonal and that interpersonal communication becomes more frequent, we are most likely in an **interpersonal relationship.** An *interpersonal relationship* is an ongoing, interdependent, ever changing, intimate connection that is developed between two individuals as a result of the interpersonal communication between them. Our definition of *interpersonal relationships* shares several characteristics of our definition of *interpersonal communication.* This is because interpersonal relationships are grounded in interpersonal communication. You can't have the relationship without the communication. In fact, the definition of interpersonal communication includes the words interpersonal relationship and vice versa.

## Characteristics of Interpersonal Relationships

The definition of interpersonal relationships is based on four distinct characteristics: shared perception and interdependence, ongoing ever-changing connections, relational expectations, and a continuum of intimacy.

**Shared Perception and Interdependence**   At the root of the definitions of interpersonal communication and interpersonal relationships is the idea of interdependence. In Chapter 2 we define an **interdependent relationship** as one in which the individuals are dependent on each other. One person's actions affect the other person. In interpersonal relationships there is some exchange of influence. Individuals in these relationships affect each other simultaneously. This simultaneous affect is best explained through the *transactional communication model* discussed in Chapter 1. The golden rule here is that in order to have Person A affect Person B, Person B has to be at least aware of Person A. This idea revolves around the concept of **shared perception.** You can have an interpersonal relationship only if *both* individuals are aware of each other and perceive the continuous interactions as a relationship.

My favorite television show is <u>Ugly Betty</u>. No matter how many Thursdays I spend in my living room with the lead character Betty Suarez, or how much I can relate to her daily life, or how much it seems as though we are friends, we do not have a relationship. I have two hits against me. First, Betty Suarez is not a real person. Second, if she were, she would have no idea who I am and most certainly would not perceive our interactions via the television as a real relationship. The situation with Betty and me is called a **parasocial relationship.**[1] A parasocial relationship is a one-way tie with an individual in the media. Usually this media personality (real or fictional) reminds us of a real relationship we have, or long to have, in our lives.

Unfortunately, individuals can have a similar type of one-way relational tie with actual people they come into contact with. This can lead to the harmless school girl crush where a young woman scribbles her first name with the last name of the boy that sits in front of her even though he doesn't know she exists. It can also lead to dangerous situations like obsessive behavior or stalking.

Basically, both individuals involved in the relationship need to be on the same page in terms of the nature of the relationship. When we are in a true relationship, there is mutual influence and a mutual understanding of what the relationship is and where it is going.

**ONGOING EVER CHANGING CONNECTION**   Interpersonal relationships are ongoing connections that are constantly changing. We should think of them as a process that has a past, present and future. As we will discuss later in this chapter, relationships are moving constantly to new stages and are being redefined. Rather than visualizing the process of interpersonal relationships as a straight line with a finite beginning and end, we should think of a cycle through which relational partners move through a series of stages.[2] In relationships we may pass through the same stage several times; but each time we do, it is at a new level because we have new relational experiences between each visit to a particular stage.

For example when we are in a long term, close relationship, like with a spouse, we will go through the stage of "learning new information about each other" for the life of the relationship. I often find myself saying things like "I didn't know you hated rice pudding" to my husband even after several years of marriage. This "find-

*An interpersonal relationship, such as a marriage, is an ongoing process comprised of a series of stages that may be experienced several times throughout the relationship.*

ing out new information" stage is much different now that we have been together for several years than it would have been on our first date. If I found out he hated rice pudding on our first date, and I also hated rice pudding, I may have thought, "Wow! We both hate rice pudding this may lead to a serious relationship." Now, after several years together, I respond with "note to self, never make rice pudding." Same stage different level. One constant in the ongoing cycle of changing connections is the need for relational maintenance. Like most things in life relationships need regularly scheduled maintenance in order to have a smooth flowing process.

**RELATIONAL EXPECTATIONS**    As relationships develop, so do expectations about the relationship. The expectations we place on a particular relationship and relational partner come from external sources like social and cultural influence, as well as internal sources such as the personal predictions we make based on past experiences. On several different levels culture and society influence many expectations we have about relationships. Your ideas about things like at what age you should develop friendships and get married are greatly dependant on what sociocultural environment within which you were raised. For example, in the United States women can be well into their forties before they are first married and have children. In other cultures, if a woman is not married and does not have children by the time she is in her early twenties, there is a problem. Dependant upon our culture, we are expected to have a marital relationship at a certain age.

Relational expectations also come from within. Any time we interact with someone we bring to the interaction a set of expectations based on our past experiences. As our interactions become more interpersonal and interpersonal relationships form, we tailor our expectations to meet the uniqueness of an individual and our relationship with him or her. If you have a friendship with someone that is based on a long weekend run you share, you can basically expect that your interactions will involve running.

Expectations can backfire when, either internally or externally based, we feel they are violated. If our relational partner does not have the same expectations for relational stages as we do, we experience a conflict. When one relational partner is expecting "love, marriage and the baby carriage", and the other is just looking from some casual company, expectations are sure to be violated and feelings of both disappointment and fear are sure to arise.

**INTIMACY CONTINUUM**    All relationships fall on a continuum of intimacy from *impersonal*—buying a soda from your local party store clerk—to *interpersonal*, "love, marriage and the baby carriage". **Interpersonal intimacy** is closely linked to our sense of self and the degree to which individuals in a relationship can confirm and accept each other's sense of self. It is through open disclosure with our relational partners that we are able to gain information about our sense of self. These relationships help to strengthen our self confidence and self image.[3] We can measure the level of intimacy in a relationship by each partner's ability and willingness to share with the other the true self or inner most thoughts and feelings.

Intimacy also involves feelings of connection and closeness. We experience emotional bonding that leads to unconditional support, openness and honesty and affection and warmth. In most cases, we experience a high level of interpersonal intimacy with family members. This is where we first learn the concept of unconditional acceptance and support. As relationships grow more intimate, we begin to experience the phenomena of "unconditional" with individuals that are not family members. These experiences lead to strong friendships and life long relational partners.

We can better understand that the movement from impersonal to interpersonal relationships is greatly dependant on intimacy by examining five types of relationships: role relationships, acquaintances, friends, good friends and intimate relationships.[4]

**Role relationships** have to do with your interaction with others based on the roles you both play within the interaction. For example, if you are reading this book, you are most likely a student and you have a teacher. Therefore you have a student-teacher relationship. It is not necessarily interpersonal in nature and your behavior is dictated by your role in the interaction. The teacher assigns work, and you do it. This relationship is based on your roles of assigner and doer. **Acquaintances** are people with whom you share a common context or experience. This context or experience can be short term or long term. For example, you may sit near someone in class with whom you share notes, study tips, opinions and attitudes about the class, and from time to time dirty looks about the professor. You may not have any type of ongoing contact with this person outside of class and don't tend to share personal opinions and attitudes with them. You are simply acquainted through a mutual class. **Friends** are more than acquaintances because you have an ongoing relationship that may extend over several contexts. You share more personal information with friends than you do with an acquaintance and tend to discuss a greater range of topics. **Good friends** are more than friends because you know much more about each other than just a friend. We tend to be more open and honest with good friends because we know them well enough to be confident that their reactions to our disclosures will be comforting and accepting. The mutual acceptance of each other leads to more spontaneous behavior and mutual dependency. **Intimate relationships** are much like good friends but have some significant characteristics. Good friends may not care at all that you have other good friends. An intimate partner on the other hand may care a great deal if you have other similar intimate partners. Also, good friends don't mind discussions of past good friends, but intimate partners may not feel comfortable discussing past intimate partners. With an intimate relationship comes emotional, intellectual, and spiritual intimacy. In some cases intimate relationships may include sexual intimacy. Do not confuse an intimate relationship with a sexual encounter. An intimate relationship consists of greater commitment and longer duration than any other type of relationship. Neither commitment nor duration is involved in a one time sexual encounter.

As you have learned, we have several types of interpersonal relationships- on several different levels, with several different people. Local party store clerk or soul mate, each relationship we encounter also has a particular structure. Interpersonal communication relationships can be one of at least three structures: complementary, symmetrical,[5] or parallel.[6]

## Structures of Interpersonal Relationships

**COMPLEMENTARY STRUCTURE**   *Complementary* relationships are characterized by behaviors (verbal, nonverbal, or both) that complement each other. Complementary relationships tend to maximize relational differences. In a two-person (dyadic) complementary relationship, one person must occupy a "one-up" (↑) or dominant, position while the other occupies a submissive, or "one-down" (↓), position. The following set of utterances might be characteristic of a complementary relationship:

Boss: Don't leave that towel lying on the counter like that! (↑)

Employee: Sorry, my mistake. (↓)

Value judgments, like good-bad, desirable-undesirable, should not necessarily be placed on either the submissive or the dominant role in complementary interaction. Submission can sometimes even function as a relationship control strategy. Submissive roles can be more powerful than dominant roles in interpersonal relations.

**SYMMETRICAL STRUCTURE** *Symmetrical* relationships are characterized by behaviors (verbal, nonverbal, or both) that reflect each other. Symmetrical relationships are based on equality rather than difference.[7] In a two-person symmetrical relationship both persons engage in similar one-up ($\uparrow$), one-down ($\downarrow$), or equivocal ($\rightarrow$) communication behaviors. We must again stress that there is nothing inherently desirable or good in symmetrical relationships. Some are quite stable; others can be overly competitive. Consider the following symmetrical utterances:

Husband:    What do you want to do tonight, dear? ($\downarrow$)

Wife:          I want to do what you want, honey. ($\downarrow$)

Husband:    Whatever you feel like is fine with me. ($\downarrow$)

**PARALLEL STRUCTURE** *Parallel* relationships are characterized by communication behaviors (verbal, nonverbal, or both) that are different but not opposite.[8] For example, if one member of a dyad tends to engage in one-up (dominant) communication behaviors, and the other member is equivocal (neither one-up nor one-down), the relationship is probably a parallel relationship. Communication behaviors are different, but they are not opposite in this case. As is shown in the following utterances, it is equivocal or "one-across" behavior that allows for the possibility of the parallel relationship:[9]

Person A:    Go clean up the den, okay? ($\uparrow$)

Person B:    Gee, it sure is raining hard today. ($\rightarrow$)

## Relationships and Control

Relationships can be defined by the communication behaviors that seem to occur regularly. A communication behavior within a relationship is usually one of the three previously referred to types: one-up, one-down, or one-across. The three types of interpersonal communication relationships can be defined based on the interaction of the communication behaviors that make them up. Figure 8.1 illustrates

**FIGURE 8.1**    **A COMPARISON OF RELATIONSHIPS BASED ON THEIR RELATIONAL CONTROL CHARACTERISTICS**

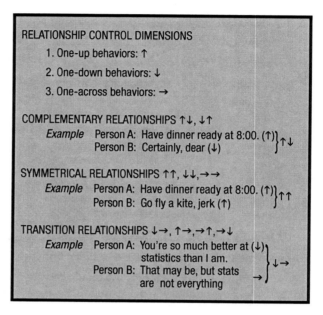

Adapted from Frank E. Millar and L. Edna Rogers, "A Relational Approach to Interpersonal Communication" in *Explorations in Interpersonal Communication*, ed. Gerald Miller (Beverly Hills, Calif.: Sage Publications, 1976).

these three relationships (symmetrical, complementary, and parallel) and their compositions.

A quick reminder: Relationships are also defined analogically. The words alone (digital communication) do not always define the relationship. We (the authors) are forced to operate in a medium (textbook) that is sometimes more digital than we would like. The point we are trying to stress is that very often an "analogic sensitivity" is as important to interpersonal communication competence as is rhetorical sensitivity.

## Rules of Interpersonal Relationships

**RULE SHARING**    Once upon a time a young man ran a truck over a neighbor's dirt pile, and it was quite a large dirt pile at that! Why? "Because it was there." In any event, it made quite a mess, and the neighbor was not happy, to say the least. In punishment, the neighbor took a toolbox from the back of the truck when it was parked in town one day. It was quite obvious to Jim who had taken it. They met several days later.

Jim:      Hello, Larry, how are you today? (just a touch of sarcasm)

Larry:    Don't get smart with me, boy… you're in enough trouble already. (in an irritated voice)

Jim:      Larry, how was I being smart? I just said hello and asked how you were today.

Larry:    I should've pulled out that front-end loader and buried you and your damn truck in that dirt pile! (getting more irritated)

Jim:      Oh, come off it.

Larry:    Come off it, hell; maybe we should just have a talk with the sheriff.

Jim:      Okay Larry, a good idea. You see, somebody stole my toolbox …

The interaction is a classic example of the negotiation of relationship-defining rules. Both wanted the "one-up" position. Larry's strategy was to maintain a consistency between the content and relationship dimensions of his language. The content (words) of his utterances was clearly dominant (one-up). His nonverbals (relationship) were also dominant. Jim's strategy in the interaction was to mix the relational control features of the content and relationship elements of his utterances. The content of "Hello, Larry, how are you today?" qualified it as a conventional greeting-hardly a "one-up" move. But the relational aspects (sarcastic tone) of the utterance made it clearly dominant.

Larry's problem was that he realized Jim's utterances were dominant, but he had no avenue to attack them. It's more difficult to counter the analogic (relationship) elements of an utterance than the digital (content). Jim did his best to focus only on the digital elements: How was Jim being smart? He just said hello and asked, "How are you today?" Larry was clearly frustrated.

Larry and Jim were functionally engaged in negotiating the rules for their interaction. Larry wanted to "fight" communicatively in a toe-to-toe fashion ("slug it out"), and Jim wanted to "dance." Jim was able to force his rules, to "play to his own corner" so to speak. Larry was not as conversant (competent) with these interactional rules as Jim; hence, he quickly became frustrated. Of course, Jim shouldn't have run over the dirt pile in the first place, and neither Jim nor Larry had read our chapter, "Coping with Conflict."

**RULES CONFLATION**   Not all interaction similar to the previous example involves conflict, but all interaction is governed by rules. We can't even talk to one another if we don't at least know how to employ some basic grammatical rules; we have to put a noun and a verb together to make a sentence. We have seen that there are also rules which govern relationships. Rules get more complex and tentative as we move up the levels of the meaning hierarchy. "I love you" means one thing to a "swinging single" and another to a person looking for a "long-term relationship." A conflation of rules is a combination or a sharing of rules between people. To the extent people share common interpretive rules, they are able to coordinate their meanings.

## INTERPERSONAL RELATIONSHIP STAGES

Think of one or your closest friends. You most likely have a "how we met" story. Some times this story can start with a common incident such as "we lived next door to each other when we were kids" or an extraordinary incident such as "we were sitting next to each other when we survived a plane crash". Whether your meeting story is common or extraordinary, if you still maintain a relationship with this person, your story most likely ends with "and we have been friends ever since".

Now think back and try to remember how you went from the first meeting to your current relationship of close friends. It is doubtful that you met each other for the first time and instantly agreed that you would be life long best friends. Most likely several experiences along the way culminated your close friendship. Once we have been in a relationship for several years it is difficult to go back and remember every little incident that caused us to take our relationships into different directions. For example, I can't remember at what point my husband and I went from casual dating to exclusively dating only each other. I don't remember any formal or informal agreement that we would have a monogamous relationship, but I know it somehow happened. The result of this event (even if I can't clearly remember it) was a positive forward movement in our relationship. The events or incidents that result in a change, whether positive or negative, in our relationships are called **turning points**.[10] Turning points are the moments when relationships tend to move from one phase to another.

Scholars such as Knapp and Vangelisti,[11] have developed the **model of relationship stages** to help explain these phases. This model breaks down the life cycle of relationships into ten stages: initiation, experimenting, intensifying, integrating, bonding, differentiating, circumscribing, stagnating, avoiding and terminating. Basically, this model describes the beginning, middle, and end of relationships. The beginning portion is referred to as the process of *coming together,* the middle portion is thought of as the process of *relational maintenance,* and the end portion is considered to be the process of *coming apart.*

It is not difficult to imagine what stages fit in each portion of the relationship. The *coming together* process involves the stages of initiating, experimenting and intensifying. **Relational maintenance**—the communication we have in an effort to keep relationships running smoothly—involves the stages of integrating, bonding, differentiating and circumscribing. The *coming apart* process involves the stages of stagnating, avoiding and terminating. It is important to keep in mind that the model of relationship stages is only a tool used to help us better understand relational development. All relationships are different, and this somewhat linear model of how they begin and end cannot neatly predict the messy situation of relational development. This model best describes romantic relationships, but is also very useful for viewing close non-romantic relationships as well. Nevertheless, a closer look at the stage model and the interpersonal communication theory that grounds it allows us to obtain a greater understanding of how and why we have the relationships we have.[12]

## Stage One: Initiation

This is the "making a connection stage" of relational development. At this stage our goal is to let an individual know that we are interested in making contact with

---

**FIGURE 8.2**    STAGE MODEL OF RELATIONSHIP DEVELOPMENT

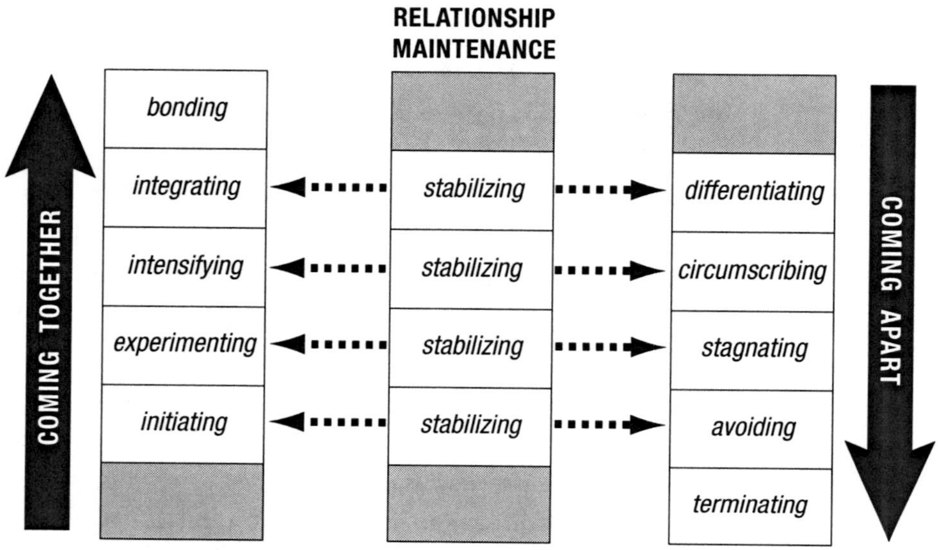

Adapted from Knapp and Vangelisti's Model of Relationship Stages.

them and that we are worthy of making that contact. Our communication is brief and impersonal at this point because our primary goal is to secure future contact, not necessarily to get to know each other well. We initiate contact based on our **short-term attraction**—deciding the individual has potential to be a relational partner. Short-term attraction may lead to **long-term attraction**—deciding the individual has the potential to be a close relational partner and is worthy of going through the next stages in relational development. Either way, the stage of initiation is very is deeply rooted in the interdependent nature of interpersonal attraction. According to the **Theory of Predicted Outcome Value**[13] we pursue attractions beyond initial stages and initiate relationships if we think they will yield a positive outcome. If we predict a negative outcome, we skip directly to termination. It is important to better understand some of the principals behind what sparks interpersonal attraction.

**INTERPERSONAL ATTRACTION**    Are you attracted by people who live or work near you? For the most part do you like people like yourself? How important is physical attractiveness? Is being seen with high status people important to you? Do extremely competent people attract you or make you nervous? Do you most often seek out well-adjusted people? Are you attracted to blunt talk?

Research into communication encounters suggests that attraction is not haphazard but rather is shaped and strengthened by five factors related to the above questions. These factors are: *nearness and exposure, similarity, physical attractiveness, status and competence, and social adjustment.*

The answers break down a bit when two or more factors overlap and conflict. For instance, forced exposure to someone of widely dissimilar attitudes does not typically lead to attraction; perhaps with luck it may lead to some better understanding. Another problem is that all people don't perceive these factors in the same way. Recall the earlier examples of people's perception.

Do we get better (more accurate) in our interpersonal perceptions as we get older? Following are some answers to this question and others like it.[14] Regarding *age,* we generally do get better as we get older. What of *intelligence?* Smarter people are usually more accurate. *Sex?* Are men more accurate than women? No, there is no good evidence; in fact, there is a tendency for women to be more accurate. Beyond these factors very few personality characteristics stand out. Good and bad interpersonal judges are found among a wide variety of personalities. That some people are better judges of people than others (most of the time) seems obvious.

*Nearness and Exposure*    After three years of eating Spam a young soldier was heard to say, "After a while it grows on ya, and I almost like it." Sheer exposure was getting to him. A man seeking advice about how to cut down on his alcohol intake at the social interactions which were part of his job was counseled, "Order the one drink you really can't stand and your glass will remain full." He ordered the hated martini and for six weeks his problem was solved. Then he related, "Guess what?

I've developed a real liking for martinis." The nearness or proximity finally got to him.

Is this also true of people who live near us, work with us, go to church with us, or are in some way physically near us? Other things being equal, that is. We do tend to develop ties to those who are near and to whom we are frequently exposed. After initial attraction has been established, separation or a lack of proximity will usually weaken the relationship unless other factors are strong and positive.

Unless the person is a real boor, this is not surprising. This finding does suggest that we form attractions more readily to those near us, providing other factors are not in gross conflict and providing there is opportunity for communication.[15]

***Similarity***    On-line dating services try to match people of similar traits and characteristics. Some users say that it has failed miserably. Yet the similarity-attraction notion is not all bad. It makes most sense in terms of beliefs, values, attitudes—in short, attributional agreement. We tend to like people who agree with us, that is, people who make similar attributions about any given event or attitude

*Similarity is one of the five factors that influence our attractedness to another. It is a primary focus of dating services, which attempt to match people of similar traits and characteristics.*

object. An on-line dating service programmed to seek out these agreements across factors such as educational values, social attitudes, political opinions, and religious beliefs may indeed find you an attractive date. This is not to say that other factors such as physical attractiveness or social status are ignored. These will be discussed shortly. What the computer dating service really does is reduce some of the *uncertainty* (also discussed shortly) about what you're getting into.[16] It saves the time of questioning and inferring one another's attributions about these important matters. In a study in which students checked off their attributions about various social and political issues, it was clearly demonstrated that they liked most those others who agreed with them.[17]

The heavier attitudes and agreements about social, political, and religious values are more important they become than the more superficial opinions or even physical characteristics. While there is some evidence that racial similarity leads to attraction (superficial for some), it is probably more accurate to say that the amount of perceived prejudice against one's race leads a person to like or dislike another.[18]

Momentary feelings of anxiety or insecurity that are perceived as similar, even among total strangers, often trigger a fellowship tendency.[19] We find it attractive to seek company, especially company of like mind or like situation. Misery not only likes company, it likes miserable company. Similar personalities as well as attitudes—despite exceptions and old sayings to the contrary—do attract; and familiarity, other things being equal, breeds attraction, not contempt.[20]

We tend to find others more attractive when we perceive them as making attributions about issues and events similar to our own. This presents an opportunity for deceit; unscrupulous persons may lead us to believe they hold attitudes similar to ours (when in fact they do not) for the purpose of selling an object or gaining a vote. This interesting fact of interpersonal attraction also suggests that each of us should be more open and objective when we listen to individuals who have attitudes that are different from our own. Such an occasion may be a good time for us to reexamine our own attributions and the reasons behind them.

The point is that if you have really strong opinions about controversial issues such as abortion, aid to parochial schools, and God, then the attitudes you perceive in others toward these issues will affect their attractiveness to you (and your attractiveness to them). Our personal attraction, even to an old friend, may be strained if the friend suddenly discovers an attitude we hold toward race, cheating, or drugs that is quite different from his or her own. This is often true of lighter topics as well. If you like sports trivia, movies, Chinese food, or skiing, you may be attracted to someone who has those same preferences.

In the face of all these similarity arguments there are some who sincerely believe that "opposites attract." After initial similarities bring two personalities together, they may find their relationship easier (if not more attractive) if there is a complementarity.[21] A dominant wife might find a submissive husband more attractive than an equally dominant one, and vice versa. These are normal role and situation adjustments for the most part.

***Physical Characteristics***    When we first see another person we are affected by what we see and how we make attributions even before we communicate orally. Large, fat, sloppy, handsome, beautiful, cool, or whatever, each characteristic will attract or repel us. Physical characteristics generate more attributions than just physical attractiveness, although in an initial or brief meeting, especially with an unusually striking face or body, we may start there.

In one "computer dance" study, individuals were randomly paired with one another. The participants were surveyed as to how much they liked their partners, how much they wanted to date their partners again, and how often they did, in fact, date their partners again. None of the personality and scholastic aptitude characteristics tested predicted couple compatibility; the largest determinant of a participant's liking for his or her date was physical attractiveness.[22] In an initial or short-term encounter in a predominantly similar group this factor must be worth something; in more serious, long-term relationships it is probably less important. I once met an extremely physically attractive person until that person talked and talked and talked.

Other things being equal, well-adjusted, smart young people are perceived as more attractive than those who do not possess these characteristics. There is some evidence that physical attractiveness is more important between the sexes than within each sex. That is, women tend to care more about what their men friends look like than what their women friends look like (and vice versa). The roles of clothing, cosmetics, calorie counting, surgery, and other possible means of improving our appearance become critical when added to what nature gave us.

***Status and Social Standing***    We usually are attracted to and enjoy being with people of high status and social standing because they offer us some reflected recognition. "Tiger Woods was seated at the next table," we report as if he were an old friend. "I shook hands with the President," we say with pride. However, when critical issues override, as may be the case with some high-ranking politicians, we may have some conflict.

Some status and position is earned through special skills such as those that athletes and actors possess; some through unusual achievement whether in sports, the arts, or business; some through superior competence, whatever the endeavor or situation. While we find people such as these attractive, in general, there are moments of ambivalence that sometimes cross our minds. This is especially true of the super-achiever and the extremely competent. If you perceive yourself in any kind of competition with such a person, your admiration may be tempered with some jealousy, envy, or even inferiority. If after great effort you've achieved a B average, your attractive roommate may lose some luster as he or she reports his or her usual A+ grades with only average effort.

In summary, we tend to enjoy being with people who provide us with real or reflected status, position, and recognition. Manipulators, be on guard; those who would play games with this factor of interpersonal attraction will fail miserably if their status is found to be unwarranted or phony.

***Social Adjustment***    There is good evidence that we find well-adjusted people, those with healthy self-concepts, more attractive than those who are poorly adjusted and have negative self-concepts.[23] Interestingly, people with super-positive self-concepts, people who exhibit an inconsistency in what they really are and what they *think* they are, are not perceived as attractive.

We all lose our tempers on occasion, but a really short-tempered person across all issues and situations is not perceived as very attractive and may even thought to be in need of counseling.

Behaviors thought to improve another's perceptions of a person's social adjustment, and therefore attraction, include establishing rapport easily and quickly, fairness, and showing anger rarely and usually only toward those who "should know better." People who exhibit these traits are sociable and interested individuals.

Behaviors or traits found to be blocks to perceptions of good social adjustment are the personality extremes: on the one hand superiority and egoism, as exhibited by aggression, overconfidence, sarcasm, boastfulness, and a domineering attitude; on the other hand excessive inferiority, as shown by dependence, depression, withdrawal, listlessness, and excessive timidity. Either extreme can lead to defensive communication behavior by the receiver. Social adjustment is a most significant factor in interpersonal attraction.

## Stage Two: Experimenting

In the experimenting stage we have moved from making a connection with an individual to whom we are attracted to investigating where that connection will lead us. A big part of this stage is reducing uncertainty about each other. The **Theory of Uncertainty Reduction** explores the process of monitoring social environments in an effort to gain greater knowledge about yourselves and others.[24] We gain knowledge by gaining more information. You will remember my example of returning to this stage with my husband when I found out he hates rice pudding. In this stage we take part in a bit more detailed *small talk* than we did in the initiating stage. We move from questions of "do you like music?" to "what is your favorite song?" While experimenting, we gain enough information to make decisions about the likelihood of a long-lasting, close relationship.

## Stage Three: Intensifying

If the experimenting stage leads to the decision to continue a relationship, the relationship begins to enter the intensifying stage. The intensifying stage is marked by much more personal, intimate and informal communication. It is in this stage that *Social Penetration Theory*, discussed in Chapter 2 most applies. **Social Penetration Theory** allows us to understand how much and what type of disclosure we share with others at different stages of relationships.[25] **Social Penetration** is the process of increasing disclosure as a relationship develops. At this stage relational partners begin to develop their "own language" by including terms, phrases or nonverbal behavior that only has meaning for the two of them.[26] We also begin to see commitment statements and talk about future activities involving both relational partners. This is often deemed the infatuation stage where we experience a sense of euphoria including sweaty palms and pounding hearts, when we fall in love. This stage is most often shown in television shows and in the movies because it is the most exciting time in a relationship. Often the movie ends at this stage leading us to believe it goes

*The intensifying stage is marked by much more personal, intimate and informal communication.*

on forever. However, as we all know, the complexities of life and relationships get in the way and end this stage. The passing of this stage does not mean the relationship is dead; it simply means that the now long-term commitment to each other has forced the relational partners to integrate necessary aspects of their lives.

## Stage Four: Integrating

Once the euphoria wears off, and people are still together, they have officially integrated or become a couple. This is the stage where the partners make their relationship public. You are seen as "friends" or "dating" rather than two individual people. At this stage the partners become one unit and are invited to events as one unit.

For example, my brother Heath has a best friend named Dave. They are chronically single. If Dave or Heath is invited to a party or a celebration, it is just assumed that the other will be there as well. Also, in this stage partners begin to share common property. We also become more obligated to our partners in this stage because we become more dependent on one another. We often no longer make overt statements about our needs and how our partners can satisfy them because we have become so familiar with one another.[27] At this point we almost form a new identity. We give up some of our distinct personal characteristics and gain shared identities.

## Stage Five: Bonding

The bonding stage of relational development usually results in a major turning point. This is the stage in which we take part in symbolic rituals to share with the world the level of our commitment to our relational partners. A very common form of bonding in romantic relationships is an engagement or marriage. We also take part in bonding in non-romantic relationships as well. Things like contractual agreements or shared financial investments between friends constitute bonding. Whether romantic or non-romantic, bonding is a major stage that is difficult to undo.

## Stage Six: Differentiating

Just as quickly as two individuals reach the peak of coming together, bonding, they begin the process of coming apart. Differentiating is the first stage of relational tension and can be the start of partners growing apart. This is when we remember that we are different from our relational partner and those differences, at times, make relational management difficult. At this stage we begin to feel uncomfortable with the shared identity and begin to miss our personal individual identities. Our language shifts from the bliss of the "we" language to the reality of the "I" language. Even individuals in extremely committed relationships have a need to reveal, and have respected, their individual identities.

The stage of differentiating is likely to begin when a relationship experiences its first true source of stress or tension. For example, we cannot be a part of a couple with a completely shared identity while simultaneously maintaining a total individual identity. This is what is known as a **dialectical tension** or two opposing forces that cannot be in existence simultaneously.[28]

**DIALECTICS THEORY**   *Dialectics Theory* focuses on the human condition as several sets of opposing forces or tensions that naturally exist in relationships.[29] These opposing forces result in a tension felt by relational partners as they desire both opposing ends. Communication theorists Baxter and Montgomery discuss three common dialectical tensions commonly experienced in interpersonal relationships; connectedness versus autonomy, certainty versus uncertainty, and openness versus closedness.[30]

**CONNECTEDNESS VERSUS AUTONOMY**   Like the example above of the impossibility of being a part of a couple with a completely shared identity while simultaneously maintaining a total individual identity, the tension of connectedness versus autonomy deals with our desire to be autonomous or independent (our own personal identity) while simultaneously desiring connection (a shared identity) with our relational partner.

**CERTAINTY VERSUS UNCERTAINTY**   This tension deals with our desire to have stability or the ability to predict our relational interactions while simultaneously longing for novelty and the unexpected. Humans are creatures of habit. We often choose safe and predictable situations. These situations make us feel comfortable. Though we are in comfortable and safe situations, we also feel the need to throw caution to the wind and do something dangerous and new. As you are well aware, you can't be both completely safe and completely dangerous at the same time.

**OPENNESS VERSUS CLOSED**   This tension balances the need to disclose fully to our relational partner in order to reach a higher level of intimacy, while simultaneously feeling the need to hold back on disclosure to be sure we are safe from our partner's disapproval. This is when we debate the contradictory ideas of "sharing everything with each other" and "some things are better left unsaid."

Regardless of the tension this stage may bring, differentiating is one in which good interpersonal communication and relational maintenance is most important. Committed relational partners can easily overcome differentiating with a dedication to maintaining a strong commitment to the relationship while purposefully creating opportunities for being individuals. As we have discussed before, strong relationships are those that go through and overcome things like differentiating. If relational partners decide that the effort needed to overcome differentiating is not worth the benefits provided by the relationship, they may choose to end the relationship.

## Stage Seven: Circumscribing

Thus far we have discussed the growth of relationships. Though several relationships may work through differentiating and go on to " 'til death to us part", others will begin to come apart and go through several stages of decline leading to dissolution. The stage of circumscribing represents a decrease in both the quality and quantity of communication that takes place between relational partners. We have learned that in order to make it as a long term relational couple communication is paramount. We reach circumscribing when we begin to restrict our talk about the relationship specifically and our communication in general. This does not mean we stop all communication. In this stage we will judge how much effort it would be to discuss something versus just dropping the topic. Most relationships that reach the circumscribing stage choose to just "drop it". When we begin to make decisions about withdrawal being easier than discussion, we most likely have begun to lose interest in, and commitment to, the relationship.

## Stage Eight: Stagnating

Stagnating is much like our idea of the "old married couple". It is a heightened extension of circumscribing. We tend to go through the motions with very little emotion or reward. The sense of novelty and excitement has taken a back seat to daily routines. At this point we feel that we already know what our relational partner will do or say, so we don't even bother to bring it up. Communication scholar, Honeycutt refers to this as an **imagined conversations**.[31] In an *imagined conversation* one partner will conjecture the conversational roles to be played by both partners. After the rehearsal in one partner's head it is decided that the conversation would not be worth the effort so the partner, having imagined this dialogue, doesn't even initiate the conversation. Like in the circumscribing stage, they simply "drop it".

## Stage Nine: Avoiding

If the stage of stagnating goes on for too long and becomes too unpleasant, relational partners usually try to stay out of the same place at the same time. This is known as the avoiding stage. Because it has become too painful to accept the idea that the relationship is no longer beneficial, partners will either directly or indirectly avoid each other. This is where we make excuses like "I had a hard day at work and need to stay in; you go out without me" or directly tell partners that we want time away from them. If physical separation is impossible, like two siblings who are forced to share a room, partners will simply ignore each other or contract an agreement to "stay out of each other's way." Either way, this is most likely the beginning of the end for the relationship.

## Stage Ten: Terminating

As we have mentioned, not all relationships end. There are several successful "we have been friends ever since", and "till death do us part" relationships. However, as we are well aware, not all last forever and they somehow, some way, come to an end. Terminating refers to the process of ending a relationship. This process is played out jointly by both relational partners or individually by one relational partner and leads to a permanent separation. Often relationships are terminated in the same day they are initiated. You see an individual across the room and find them attractive so you make your way over to them (initiated). You strike up a conversation and quickly find out the physically attractive individual is racist and unintelligent, so you make an excuse to go to the bathroom never planning on returning (terminated).

Other relationships go through the termination stage only to begin a different type of relationship. For example, individuals that are divorced with children have terminated their marriage relationship yet are forced to have a different type of relationship whether that be friends, joint decision makers, or those financially connected. Regardless of how the termination stage is started and ended, it is always difficult for all parties involved and will forever be on of those experiences you have had that will dictate the relational decisions you will make in the future.

## SUMMING UP

An interpersonal relationship is an ongoing, interdependent, ever changing, intimate connection that is developed between two individuals as a result of the interpersonal communication between them.

Based on this definition, interpersonal relationships are based on four distinct characteristics: (1) shared perception and interdependence; (2) ongoing, ever-changing connection; (3) relational expectations; and (4) a continuum of intimacy.

Interpersonal communication can be one of at least three structures: (1) complementary, (2) symmetrical, and (3) transition. Complementary relationships tend to maximize relational differences. Symmetrical relationships are characterized by verbals and nonverbals that reflect each other. They are based on equality rather than difference.

Transition relationships are based on behaviors, both verbal and nonverbal, that are different but not opposite. Very often an "analogic" sensitivity is as important to communication competence as rhetorical sensitivity.

The model of relationship stages puts forth ten stages of interpersonal relationships. As we enter a new stage, we usually experience a turning point in the relationship. Stage 1 is initiation where the idea of short and long-term attraction is particularly relevant. Attraction is shaped and strengthened by at least five factors: (1) nearness and exposure, (2) similarity, (3) physical attractiveness, (4) status and competence, and (5) social adjustment. Stage 2 is experimenting, and the theory of uncertainty reduction helps to explain our actions during this stage. Stage 3 is intensifying and is made clear through social penetration theory. Stage 4 is integrating. Stage 5 is bonding. Stage 6 is differentiating, and we begin to experience dialectical tension. Dialectics Theory discusses three common dialectical tensions commonly experienced in interpersonal relationships: connectedness versus autonomy, certainty versus uncertainty, and openness versus closed. Stage 7 is circumscribing. Stage 8 is stagnating. Stage 9 is avoiding. Stage 10 is termination.

## NOTES

1. Horton D., & Wohl R. (1956). Mass communication and parasocial interaction: Observation on intimacy at a distance. Psychiatry, 10, 215-229.

2. R.L. Conville (1991). *Relational Transitions: The evolution of Personal Relationships*. New York: Praeger

3. Mead (1934).

4. Berko

5 Watzlawick, Beavin, and Jackson, *Pragmatics,* pp. 67-70. See also Gregory Bateson, *Naven,* 2nd ed. (Stanford: Stanford University Press, 1958).

6 Frank E. Millar and L. Edna Rogers, "A Relational Approach to Interpersonal Communication," in *Explorations in Interpersonal Communication,* ed. Gerald Miller (Beverly Hills, Calif.: Sage Publications, 1976).

7 Watzlawick, Beavin, and Jackson, *Pragmatics,* pp. 68-69.

8 Millar and Rogers, "A Relational Approach," pp. 96-97.

9 Ibid. p. 97.

10 Ibid.

11 Knapp, M.L., and A.L. Vangelisti.(2005). *Interpersonal Communication in Human Relationships.* 5th ed. Boston: Allyn & Bacon

12 Knapp, M.L., and A.L. Vangelisti.(2000). *Interpersonal Communication in Human Relationships.* 4th ed. Boston: Allyn & Bacon

13 Sunnafrank, M. (1986). Predicted Outcome Value During Initial Interaction: A Reformulation of Uncertainty Reduction Theory. *Human Communication Research,* 13, 3-33. See also Sunnafrank, M. (1991). "Interpersonal attraction and attitude similiarity: A communication based assessment," in *Communication Yearbook,* 14, edited by J.A. Anderson, Newbury Park, CA: Sage.

14 See Mark Cook, *Interpersonal Perception* (Baltimore: Penguin Books, 1971).

15 See Mark Abrahamson, *Interpersonal Accommodation* (Princeton, N.J.: D. Van Nostrand Company, 1966).

16 See especially C. R. Berger, "Task Performance and Attributional Communication as Determinants of Interpersonal Attraction," *Speech Monographs,* 40, no. 4 (November 1973), 280-86.

17 See Donn Byrne, *The Attraction Paradigm* (New York: Academic Press, 1971).

18 G. Lindzey and E. Aronson, eds. *The Handbook of Social Psychology,* 2nd ed., vol. 2 (Reading, Mass,: Addison-Wesley Publishing Co. Inc., 1968), pp. 498-500.

19 See Stanley Schachter, *The Psychology of Affiliation* (Stanford, Calif.: Stanford University Press, 1959).

20 R. S. Ross, *Persuasion: Communication and Interpersonal Relations* 4th Ed. (Englewood Cliffs, N.J.: Prentice-Hall, Inc. 1994), p. 139.

21 George Levinger, David J. Senn, and Bruce W. Jorgensen, "Progress toward Permanence in Courtship: A Test of the Kerckhoff-Davis Hypothesis," *Sociometry,* 33 (1970), 427-43.

22 Elaine Walster and others, "Importance of Physical Attractiveness in Dating Behavior," *Journal of Personality and Social Psychology,* 4 (1966), 508-16.

23 J. McCroskey and others, "The Effects of Communication Apprehension on Interpersonal Attraction," *Human Communication Research,* 2, no. 1 (Fall 1975), 51-65.

24 C.R. Berger (1987). Communicating under Uncertainty." In M.E. Roloff & G.R. Miller (Eds.), *Interpersonal Processes: New Directions in Communication Research.* Newbury Park, CA: Sage

25 I. Altman and D. A. Taylor, *Social Penetration* (New York: Holt, Rinehart & Winston, Inc., 1973).

26 L.K. Knobloch and D.H. Solomon, (2002) "Information Seeking Beyond Initial Interaction: Negotiating Relational Uncertainty Within Close Relationships," *Human Communication Research,* 28 April, 243-257.

27 R. A. Bell & J. G. Healy (1992) "Idiomatic Communication and Interpersonal Solidarity in Friends' Relational Cultures." *Human Communication Research,* 18, 307-335

   M. Roloff, C.A. Janiszewski, M.A. McGrath, C.S. Burns, & L.A. Manri (1988). "Acquiring Resources from Intimates: When Obligation Substitutes for Persuasion" *Human Communication Research 14,* 364-369.

28 Baxter, L. & Montgomery, B. (1996). Relating. Dialogues & Dialectics. New York: Guilford Press.

29 ibid

30 ibid

31 Honeycutt, J.M. (2003). *Imagined interactions.* Cresskill, NJ: Hampton Press.

# Index

CPSIA information can be obtained at www.ICGtesting.com
Printed in the USA
LVOW110800030712

288679LV00001B/14/P